# You Didn't Grow In My Tummy-You Grew In My Heart

by

## Keri Swain

Bloomington, IN          Milton Keynes, UK

authorHOUSE®

*AuthorHouse™*
*1663 Liberty Drive, Suite 200*
*Bloomington, IN 47403*
*www.authorhouse.com*
*Phone: 1-800-839-8640*

*AuthorHouse™ UK Ltd.*
*500 Avebury Boulevard*
*Central Milton Keynes, MK9 2BE*
*www.authorhouse.co.uk*
*Phone: 08001974150*

*First published by AuthorHouse 10/5/2006*

*ISBN: 1-4259-6655-1 (sc)*

*Printed in the United States of America*
*Bloomington, Indiana*

*This book is printed on acid-free paper.*

FOR MY BEAUTIFUL DAUGHTER BETHAN LOUISE,
-MY BO

# *THANK YOU*

"MY STORY" would not have ever reached fruition without the love, support and confidence in me that I have received from those around me.

These "THANK YOU'S" are given with immense gratitude and the most heartfelt love for you all.

My Bo- Without you this story would have never happened. Thank you for blessing me with Hope, Morganna, Angharad and Rhiannon, and for everyday that you are still in my life. I love you so much Bo, you will always be my little girl.

To Hope and Morganna - for filling my life with so much joy, and my heart with so much love- oh yes and for drawing beautiful pictures on our walls!

To Angharad and Rhiannon - we had too short a time together, but every day I spent with you will carry me through the years that we are apart. Come home one day girls.

And to your new Mammy and Daddy, Thank you for loving my girls, care for and treasure them always. One day I hope we will meet.

Kevin - My rock, my crutch, my safe place and the great love in my life, without you I doubt I would ever have written this, and "my girls" may not have been given this legacy. We have travelled this journey together, at times it has pulled us in different directions but we have always managed to pull it back again. Thank you for being the gentle, courageous, loving and deeply supportive man you are. I know that I have not thanked you enough, Thank you for giving my children the best Step father they could have ever needed, Thank you from the bottom of my heart for accepting Bo's life choices readily and for uniting with me to fight for what I believed in. Thank you for being the most wonderful father to Oliver - our son. On behalf of Hope and Morganna, Thank you for being "our Daddy" they truly have the best in you, they are very lucky girls.

But most of all Thank you for being mine, and for putting the sunshine back into my life - I love you so much.

To my sons Stephen and James - For supporting me as I have travelled on this rollercoaster, and for not leaning on me when your own worlds were rocking. For continuing to love Bo. I am so proud of you both.

To Oliver - mine and Kevin's ray of sunshine, what a gem you are. Thank you for being you, I have expected so much from you over the past 5 years and you have given it all. Thank you for sharing Daddy and I with Hope and Morganna. It has not been easy on times but you have made even the hardest of situations easier to bear - I love you stixs x

To my family - Mam and Dad, what can I say, without you two there would have been no me! I think that between you, you have managed to create a woman who is determined if nothing else, and one I pray you are proud of. Thank you for all you tried to do for Bo. This year you celebrate 48 years of marriage-what an inspiration, For always being there over the past 5 years Thank you x

To my siblings and their spouses - David and Clare, Michael and Nita, Deb's and Geoff- For supporting me throughout this journey, None of us know what our future holds, none of us can predict what will befall our children. I pray that none of you will ever feel the pain that has shaken me to the core. Thank you for surrounding me with love and support.

Deb's - I can remember when Mam and Dad brought you home, from that day onwards I had someone special in my life, ours is a very special relationship, maybe this is why I have fought so hard to keep Hope and Morganna together, and why I feel so devastated that Angharad and Rhiannon are not with them.

Without the best friends that life has encircled me with I would have gone slightly mad over the past few years. Thank you all, I would like to pay a special Thank you to the following -

Heather and Raul - Thank you both for being by my side every painful step of the way, and for sharing my pain, tears, frustration and fears, and for the wonderful evenings the four of us have spent together talking and laughing which has brought me some kind of normality. Kevin and I have such true and much loved friends in the both of you. Heather - thank you for grounding me and for reminding me what is good in my life. Raul -Thank you for painting my world with vibrant colour, and encouraging me to pick up my music again.

David and Sandra - Good friends are hard to find, I have found two in you, Thank you both for always being there, and for the blissfully tranquil hours I have spent in your wonderful home.

Lynn - What fun we have had over the years that we have known each other, Thank you for supporting me when my world has fallen apart, and for being a brilliant Godmother to Hope and Morganna Thank you for the laughter and for drying my tears.

Gordon - for loaning Lynn to me without complaining and for being the gentle soul you are.

Sue and Colin - Thank you both for everything and for looking after Oliver for us when we needed to be in Pembrokeshire.

To Sally, our Solicitor - Sal we owe you such a depth of gratitude. Thank you for everything you did for us all, and for the friendship you have given us
And to Kamala our Barrister - Thank you

To all the agencies who were in some capacity involved in the lives of Hope, Morganna, Angharad and Rhiannon.

To Gwen, Darren and Sonia -Thank you for making what was sometimes an impossible situation easier to struggle with, Thank you both for supporting Bo and for all you tried to do for her.

Jackie - Thank you for everything.

Jo, Tracey and Ian, Steven and Paul - you know why I am thanking you, from the bottom of my heart "Thank you"

Wendy - You do the most important job of all in maintaining the letterbox contact between me and my girls, Thank you.

To all the staff on the Labour wards and Neonatal and SCABU units at Singleton and Withybush General Hospitals for all you have done for Hope and Morganna, Angharad and Rhiannon. And to SURESTART for their input with Bo and the girls for the short time they were together.

To Homestart - and especially to Margaret for those wonderful and much needed two hours of "me" time every week, and for being Godmother to the girls.

To the complete "AurthorHouse" team- especially Natalie my publishing assistant, -Thank you for everything Natalie, it has been an absolute joy to work with you. Thank you all for the part you have played in getting my book into print in the way that was so important to me, " my words, my voice" so that one day my girls can read it as if I were talking to them.

To anyone else who I have not mentioned Thank you all

# *"You Didn't Grow In My Tummy - You Grew In My Heart"*

It was a magnificent sunny afternoon in late may 2005. The air was still, the birds were singing away in the fields that surround our 16<sup>th</sup> century cottage in rural Oxfordshire. This beautiful late spring chorus was occasionally interrupted by the harsh tenor tones of the crows squawking as they squabbled amongst each other high up in the treetops of the trees in the woodland two fields away from our back garden. On the farm track that runs alongside our cottage the swallows were frantically visiting the few last remaining muddy patches, their impeccably timed visits expertly avoiding the thundering hooves of the farms dairy cows as they ran down the track from the milking parlour and out to the fresh green pasture they were to graze. My girls have always climbed onto the frame of their swings to watch the cows running past the beech hedge that forms a thick barrier and separates our garden from the farm track. The girls try everything they can think of to entice the cows close enough to the hedge for them to be able to touch and stroke their black and white heads, occasionally one of the cows will be brave enough to stretch her neck out far enough for her nose to investigate and sniff the outstretched little hand that is desperately trying to stroke it, and sometimes the cow will catch one of the girls off guard and lick her with her long rough tongue, much to the girls delight.

On this particular afternoon my twin girls, Hope and Morganna were far too engrossed to take any notice of their black and white four legged friends. They were lost in their fantasy world of fairies and princesses, whilst I was sat quietly my nose deep into a book which I was busy studying for my next exam. Excitedly the girls began running towards me from their little wooden house which they call *Lavender cottage*, and what a sight it was to behold. They were both dressed up in their pink and lilac fairy costumes, and they looked wonderful. The strands of their hair that had managed to escape from the glittering crowns I had placed on their heads earlier - and replaced for what seemed like a hundred times was now flying out behind them, the skirts of their dresses were cascading and billowing out around their little legs, the wings on their backs flapped furiously, and the bells around their ankles were jingling merrily, adding yet another sound to the birds summer chorus. Hope was holding onto Morganna's hand dragging her bigger twin sister behind her and shouting

"Come on Anna"she has always called Morganna, Anna.

My two little darlings had smiles on their faces that were as wide as their arms were spread, and whooping with laughter my two little fairies threw themselves into me with a crash. My books went flying; their crowns fell off their heads and rolled under the rose bushes, whilst all three of us ended up on the grass roaring with laughter.

This idyllic picture was what you may consider to be a normal part of our lives, but my idyllic picture has a sad and bitter story. It was Hope that broke into this wonderful picture with a question that was to be the first of many that were going to break my heart.

Hope has always been the inquisitive one of them both; she looked at me and said.

"Mammy you know Auntie Debbie has a baby in her tummy, well when we grew in your tummy did we grow in there together"?

*Oh my God, it's happened, and it's too soon, much too soon I'm not ready for this yet*

But I had no choice I had to be ready. This question was to become one of the first of a chain of innocent questions that were to tear me apart inside. There was no time to think and I certainly could not ignore her question. So I sat them down next to me on the grass and holding each of them in my arms I tenderly told them.

"Darlings, you did not grow in my tummy, you grew in my heart"

They both looked up at me, Morganna said nothing, but in her eyes I saw mirrored the immense and immeasurable love that I felt for the both of them. Hope looked at me and smiled her beautiful smile- the one that makes her whole face radiate warmth and can melt the hardest of hearts.

In that moment, that very sacred and special moment, I recognised the unconditional love that is there between a mother and her child. I had seen it before many times with my own children.

Hope picked up a book that they had brought to me earlier on that afternoon,

"Oh ok then, will you read us this story now please" she cheekily asked me.

And that was that, they just accepted what I had said as if it was normal. They were both happy that they had grown somewhere inside of me, and I had not lied to them. We sat there snuggled up together warm on the outside as the sun cast its rays down on us, and warm on the inside as we each understood in our own small way just how special that time had been. I read them the story and when it was finished they jumped up from the grass and danced around the garden just as they had before they had thrown themselves at me. It was no big deal, she had asked a question and I had given them an honest answer. They will one day understand just how honest an answer it was. They now will tell people in quite a matter of fact manner that they grew in my heart and not in my tummy.

I had made a conscious decision a long time ago that when the girls asked me why they were brought up by me that I would never tell them that they were special and that I had chosen them, after all what a statement to live up too, as every child is special. I grew up with someone that had been told just that by her adoptive parents and she strove all her life to make sure she stayed special.

I spent the rest of that day feeling relief and gratitude. Relief that from out of nowhere and completely unrehearsed I had been able to come up with such a beautiful answer. Somehow I don't think if I had been able to lock myself away for days agonising over what I would tell them if and when they had asked me such a question, that I would have been able to come up with a answer as perfect and as individual as the one I had given. It truly was a beautiful answer for my beautiful girls, and I had told them the truth for they did grow in my heart. From the very first moment that I saw them, lying so motionless in the incubators placed next to each other in the neonatal unit of the hospital where they were born, they had won a place in my heart.

I also felt gratitude that the girls had not pressed me further, I don't think I could have followed that answer. Today when I think about that day in May and what I had told the girls it makes the hairs stand up on the back of my neck. It truly is a beautiful thing to have been told, and I am sure that when they are old enough to fully understand "my story" they will come to understand just how true a thing they were told that day. Many of my friends have hid their tears when one or other of the girls have told them that they grew in my heart and not in my tummy.

As time goes on I know that I will have other questions from them, they have a right to be given truthful answers. One day I had to explain to the girls why their two younger sisters are not with them, and when you are bringing up twins you soon learn that some of the things we as singular children never give a thought to are common place with twins. They instinctively know what a brother or sister is as they have had one with them since the day they were conceived. They know that they are special that they are lucky to have a brother or sister whom they can share everything with. But at the same time they are also unfortunate because they are forced together 24 hours a day 7 days a week, they do everything together, and although we do try to give the girls individual time they inevitably spend the major part of their lives in each others company. So they find it more difficult to understand why their two younger sisters are not here with them sharing their lives, sharing everything with them, growing up together here with us, and it breaks my heart.

As the girls get older their questions are of a more inquisitive nature. When writing the birthday cards for their younger sisters in March this year, they asked if they are going to their party, and if we were going to go and buy new party dresses. Through tear stained eyes and a voice that was cracking under the emotions that their innocent question had stirred in me I tried to explain to them that I did not know where Angharad and Rhiannon were living now.

How in Gods name do I tell them gently and lovingly something that breaks my heart every day without also teaching them a pain so deep that it rips your heart out. I should never have had to try and explained something to my beautiful girls that was one day in the future as they begin to understand what had happened all those years before and robbed them all of a lifetime

4

of growing up together, going to break their hearts, pain like that should never touch anyone, but it does, and somewhere in our futures it will touch my girls hearts, and no matter how hard I try to pave the way and prepare them for such heartache, I know whatever I do it will not be enough to spare them that pain.

As tenderly as I could I told them that their little sisters Angharad and Rhiannon had gone to live with their new Mammy and Daddy and that they too would grow in their new Mammy and Daddy's heart, just as they had grown in mine. They understood this but Hope - always being the more questioning of the twins said "well Rhiannon lives with Bo, she is her mammy", I had to go on to explain something that I could not fully comprehend myself. Why is it that when a women becomes a mother, some will not for one reason or another bring up their children, some will for no apparent reason not bring up their children, whilst others - gladly the majority of mothers become good Mammy's to their children,. The girls looked at me with inquisitive eyes almost hanging on waiting for my answer, what I told them was simply that sometimes a woman will have a baby, and become a mother, but that a mammy was the person who is there for you everyday she is the one who cares for you, feeds you looks after you when you are ill, and does all the things for you that need doing and who also tells you off when you are not so good. The girls both looked at me a bit bewildered, so I went on to tell them in a more day to day way what I was trying to explain to them. I told them that almost everyday here on the farm a mother cow has her baby calf, oh they knew that only too well as looking out for new baby calves has become part of the girls morning routine as we drive together to take Oliver to meet his college bus. By the time I take the girls off to pre-school, the mother cow and her baby will have been taken from the field (or the nursery, as the girls call it). Now both the girls understand that a cow has to have a calf to give the farmer milk, they also know that once the cow has had her calf she returns to the milking herd, whilst her baby calf goes into the calf shed and is looked after by John. I went on to tell them that when a mother cow has her baby calf, she goes back into the milking herd to be milked, and she lives with all the other cows in the milking herd, and that her baby calf goes to live in the calf shed with all the other baby calves, and is looked after by John, which means that John becomes their mammy. Hope looked at me and said "Oh so Angharad and Rhiannon are being looked after by their mammy now, just as you look after us"

They had accepted that explanation as well. These lessons will continue to go on and be learnt as the years roll on, and I dare say that they are going to teach me just as much as I will teach them. I will endeavour to stay mammy for however long I am needed to be one.

Today is the 8th April 2006, Morganna came running into the house shouting "Mammy, Mammy, where are you" I ran to her thinking something awful had happened. There before me were my beautiful little girls. Gently cradled in Morganna's arms was the smallest of wild baby rabbits. We are so fortunate to live here, everyday in the fields that lie at the back of our garden; we are rewarded by some of natures beauty, or the sight of a wild animal, we often see rabbits, deer and all sorts of other wildlife. We also have hedgehogs that visit our garage every night to eat the cat's food, and Oliver regularly has to rescue a hedgehog that has fallen down between the bars of the cattle grid. The girls aren't at all surprised at what one of our two cats bring in to the back garden in the hope of finding a quiet corner somewhere to torment or to sit and eat its tasty catch.

"I took it off Peggy mammy" she told me excitedly.

Now Peggy (who is Morganna's tabby cat) must have been pretty miffed about loosing her prized catch. I told her that we would put it into a box and when Daddy came in for lunch they could go with him to put it back in the field as its mammy would be looking for it, she agreed to this. Oliver went off to fetch a box, and as I turned away Morganna said to this baby rabbit "Its Ok little sweet one your in my mammies house now and she looks after us all, she will look after you until daddy comes in and then we will take you back to the field so your mammy can find you" What is it they say about out of the mouths of babes? Maybe I have got at least that part of what I am striving to achieve here right, even if on times it has been very difficult for me, I have obviously got something good installed in the girls, as in her own way Morganna had also grasped what I had said to them on that sunny afternoon in May 2005.

It was Hopes untimely question that forced me to think about what I would tell the girls in the future, but what if I was not here to tell them. I had to have a contingency plan. This book started as a letter, and it grew into a book. It is the result of many shed tears; much heartache and months of agonising over how it could still be my words that would tell all four of my precious girls what happened if I was no longer here.

# LIFE EVENTS

As small children we begin to build our make believe world, declaring to all who will listen what it is we want to be when we are big girls and boy's. "When I grow up I want to be a Princess, a Fireman, a dancer, a nurse, a magician a ........."

We all have our dreams, our goals, our ambitions, and as we grow up we believe we will reach these dreams, but then why couldn't we, why shouldn't we, oh if only we were all blest with hindsight, I wonder how different a world we would all live in.

Then all too soon one day reality takes the place of our make-belief games, we are turned out of the safety of our make-believe world, and we are faced with making the choices that will mould our future, whatever those choices may be we will leave our safe world and enter the big bad world. We will think we know it all. We may even be so complacent that we still think there is time to make changes, and yes there is, it's never too late to make changes, but then time has a habit of creeping away and before we know it we are looking back on our life, and the way in which we chose to live it. How many times have we listened as someone has said "oh if only I had......", I for one can join the merry band of the "oh if only's"

The life choices we all make are different and unique to us alone. Some of us choose to further our education, then seek out a career, throwing ourselves directly towards success and strive to succeed no matter what the cost may be. There are those of us who will just slip into whatever path we choose and spend the rest of our lives ticking away nicely. There are those of us who will choose to have a family, we will leave school, marry and have children, dedicating our lives to bringing up the next generation, then there are the ones who choose as I did to try and juggle both, I chose to have a carer and have children, something that is definitely not for the faint-hearted.

Whatever our choices have been life, events will happen to all of us, some of these are inevitable, some are expected and part of our everyday life, some come out of the blue and shatter our world leaving us reeling. How we cope with these events will depend on many things but it is the person we ourselves have become that will eventually see us through these life events.

Some of the events that may affect our worlds we will have experienced as we travel along in life, we can all identify with many of these, the birth of a child, the loss of a job, lack of money, separation, divorce, illness, death and so the list goes on. However, sometimes life will throw something at you, something that leaves you not only reeling, but also in total despair it will make you question the life choices you have made, it even makes you question life itself. You ask yourself and those closest to you how the hell life could be so cruel - so damn soul destroying.

The event that I am sharing with you was to be one of those events that happen to other people, you know the kind of thing I mean we all read about them in magazines and newspapers, they just don't happen to people we know,

Not to you....... Not to me.

What happened to me was to test everything I had grown up believing in. It made me question everything about myself and everything I held most dear in my life, I felt singled out, alone and pretty damn desperate. I was placed on an emotional rollercoaster, one that no matter how hard I tried to apply the brakes it just took me further and further along and downwards to the depths of life I thought I would never in my life time see. And just as I thought it was all beginning to settle down at long last, it picked me up only to catapult me into my worst nightmare.

In fact, the truth is even if someone had been able to spell it out for me as something I was to encounter, firstly, I would have told them they were barking mad and secondly if I had been blest with hindsight, no amount of preparation could or would have in a million years prepared me for what was going to shatter my world. It ripped my heart out and juggled with it so many times that at one point I doubted I would ever be the same again. I put so much energy into trying to become all things to all people, that I forgot completely about my own needs, somehow I did not matter anymore, I was driven by a power that just seemed to be intent on destroying me. I endeavoured to hold my family together, whatever the cost may be.

This event will affect my world for the rest of my life; it has changed both me and my world. It is a bitter/sweet event, it was and remains to be the source of the most overwhelming and heartbreaking pain I could have ever imagined, reducing me to tears over and over again. But it has also brought me a continuing great joy that now makes me smile and to laugh, Please God may it always continue to do so because for a long time I did neither, I was so overwhelmed with grief and loss, that I simply forgot what it was like to experience either. I have learnt so much about not only myself, but about others too and the different worlds we live in.

I was told a long time ago by an elderly gentleman that I had met that "If you smile the world will smile with you and that if you cried, all too often you would cry alone" I have cried alone so many times over the past years, sometimes longing for the pain to go away, but it was relentless. In the early days I had someone who's shoulder I could cry on then the time came when I felt I had exhausted all those people who I could turn to, after all you can only keep on going on about something for so long before other people get fed up with the same old story. It was then that I turned inward; I also at this time began to feel a huge amount of shame. This shame was over my daughter, how could she do what she was doing. I questioned myself as to where I had gone wrong, and where I had failed, but I now know I did neither, I now listen to other grand parents as they ask the same question of themselves.

I still do have my private tears, they creep up on me when I least expect them too, I can be out shopping and see a grandparent holding their grandchild's hand, or watching something on television, or just sat quietly indulging in my great passion for music, I shall share these tears with you throughout this story.

I shall also share some of the smiles and the laughter.

What I have been through has also taught me to value all that I have in my life, and to live for today. I try to enjoy my today's for I have learnt that what comes along with tomorrow can so easily break my heart, but if I have laughed, smiled, enjoyed and done or seen something wonderful today the memory of it may just carry me through a rough tomorrow. It has also taught me to treasure all those in my life, whether they are with me sharing my life everyday, or if they are away from me, living in their own world surrounded I trust, by family that truly love them, and who will keep them safe until they come back home to us again. They will live safe in my heart forever, they are my waking and my sleeping thoughts, they continue to tip toe through my mind even on times when I don't expect them to, I can even smell them, it is a smell I shall never forget. They are here within me and I love them both so very dearly, so very deeply that it hurts, and for every day that I feel this pain, I know that although Angharad and Rhiannon may not be here with me in my earth world, they are most definitely still in my heart world - they are still here with me. One thing is for sure if you ask any Grandparent who is for what ever reason estranged from their grandchild, if they can remember them, the answer you will get is a resounding yes, along with a description of that most precious, much missed and longed foe Grandchild.

The event that I was to encounter has taught me such a lot, as well as teaching me the true values of life, it has also taught me a pain so deep that I thought I would never recover. It took me into a world I never imagined I would ever know, but even in taking me there it was to teach me much about how the people living in this strange world of theirs survived. It taught me how to fight for those I loved and when to recognise that no matter how hard I tried some battles I just could not win. And whilst this event has given me two little girls I love so much, it has also taken away another two little girls I love. It does not balance, it never will. People have been left hurting; I am just one of them.

No one else can or will ever understand this pain, this overwhelming sense of loss - not unless they too have been in this awful place I call my hell. It is a pain I would never wish anyone else to experience.

# TO ALWAYS BE A GRANDPARENT

In 2001, whilst waiting in the local Drs surgery to see my GP I was flicking my way through a magazine when I came across an article about Grandparents rights - or rather the lack of them. It was something I had never thought about before - indeed I wonder how many of us do think about it. We watch our daughters or our sons partners blossoming with a progressing pregnancy, waiting in anticipation for our precious grandchild to be born, we look forward to this wonderful event along the way making mental plans for all the wonderful things we are going to do with them, and of all the things we are going to teach them, after all I don't know about you but some of my most treasured memories are those of the times I spent with my paternal Grandfather, he died when I was only 6 years old, but boy did he leave me with some memories, to this day I cant smell bluebells without the memory of walking hand in hand with him in the woods which lay behind his house in Cardiff. I will also think of my grandfather if a spot a packet of liquorice allsorts as they were his favourite sweets, he always used to keep them in his bedside drawer, I can hear his voice now "Keri, be a good girl and go and fetch me a sweet from my drawer". I loved them then as I do now the coconut swirl ones, even the smell of them somehow makes me feel warm inside, transporting me back to my carefree childhood.

Never do we stop to contemplate the effect it may have on our relationship with our grandchild if their parents were to hit one of life's events. Spend a moment or two to think about this, for I wish someone had brought this to my attention and I had done so. What if our grandchild's parents were to encounter one of the following, separation, divorce, illness, mental illness, a prison sentence, drug or alcohol abuse, domestic violence, or the death of one of them? How would that affect us as grandparents? My daughter was to hit one of life's events and sadly I know all too well the devastating effect that this can have on this most precious of relationships I learnt this lesson hard and it cost me dear, it cost me the most precious gift we are ever given - my Grand children.

I was just 38 years old when I became a grandmother for the first time, and I loved it, I was so proud, but that also makes me think of something else we give little thought to and that is that we are living longer and that grandparents are getting younger and are more active. When I became a grandmother at the grand old age of 38 years! My parents were only in their early 60's when they became great grandparents, they are now nudging 70 years young, and as active as ever, it is quite probable that they will become great-great grandparents before they leave this world.

So it's not only us grandparents that loose out when things go pear shaped, it is also great-grandparents, and of course the rest of the family, aunties, uncles, nieces, etc-----not to mention siblings themselves. I have learnt from my Mam that no matter how many years you are separated from your siblings, you never stop thinking about them; she thought and longed for her siblings for over 55 years.

During the 1950's when my Mam was a young girl she and her disabled younger sister Eleanor were placed into the care of a children's home in the welsh valley's, Mam also had a younger sister and a younger brother, they were both adopted as babies, my Mam never met her baby sister, but she used to visit her baby brother in the children's home he had been placed into. Eleanor died whilst in care, she never saw her younger brother again until one day over 55 years later I set to and traced the sister she had never met, and the brother she has longed for everyday for 55 years, and I united the three of them last October. It breaks my heart to know that even today 55 years later social services are still separating siblings, Social services really do have a lot to answer for. They underestimate the capability and determination of Grandparents and they truly do not value them for what they are and for what they can offer to their oh so loved grandchildren. All too often social services neglect to look to a child's Grandparents to provide day to day care and place them instead with foster families.

Grandparents often become the victims - I should know as I am one of these, if only I had been stronger,

If only.........

Amongst this article I was reading was the telephone number of *THE GRANDPARENTS ASSOCIATION* , which I jotted down into my diary, don't ask me why, because I don't honestly know, maybe someone up there was watching over me and knew more than I did about the event that lay ahead me, you can find the details and a write up on the association in the back of this book, please jot it down and keep it safe- -for you never know one day you too may be glad you did. That said I hope and pray that no one reading this book will ever need to use the number for anything other than to become a member and in doing so help the association to continue in the wonderful work they do.

A few weeks later in shear desperation I rang the advice/helpline number, my call was answered by a friendly woman's voice, she just said

"Hello Grandparents Association, can I help you ".

Well now that was a very good question could she? I truly doubted that she could, I actually at that point thought no one could. At first I could not even bring myself to begin to talk, but my wall of silence was broken by this quiet voice,

"Are you a grandparent dear? I am"

Those words were like a key to me they told me I was not alone, I instinctively knew that here on the other end of the phone was a lady who understood I began to talk and as I did so my story unfolded, then came the sentence that hurt me so much that every part of me ached, "I'm sorry, but I have to tell you this as, Grandparents do not have automatic rights in law to their grandchildren"

What the heck was she talking about, she must be mad, after all had I not all my life been brought up believing that we looked after our own, but eventually it began to sink in, gone were the days in which grandparents took over when things fell apart. My world crumbled, I cried and cried and as I did began to accept that what she had said was correct. That wonderful lady also did something else for me apart from listen and that was to give me some really good solid advice, she told me to find a good solicitor who dealt in family law. I did not know it then but finding such a solicitor was to be the first positive step I took to reaching my goal.

For listening and understanding, for sharing my tears and helping me - Thank you Wendy. Although Wendy and I have never met I have never forgotten her name.

Now I bet you're all sat there thinking, well what was her goal, well it was simply this. "To be a grandmother. To watch my grandchildren grow up, to lead an active part of their lives and not to loose the most precious of life's gift's MY GRANDCHILDREN.

Little did I know then that I was to become a major part of my grand daughter's lives.

I now give some of my time to the Grandparents Association, helping to man its busy advice/helpline, I am the one that can give time to other distraught grandparents as they painfully, and often through tears tell of their own situation, sometimes I finish my slot on the advice line and come away from that session thinking how lucky I am for two of my grand daughters are with me everyday.

But I also know and feel everyday the most devastating pain of not seeing your grandchildren as I have had to say goodbye to two of mine as they have been adopted, another family is watching them grow up, another grandmother is doing all the things with my girls that I so desperately want to do, but I cant.

At first I was going to write this just for my girls, but the more I thought about it the more I felt that it was right to share this with everyone. After all there are no big secret here; we do not hide away the reasons why the girls are here with us for that has never what it was all about. It would have been so much easier for us to have taken the easier option and moved away to somewhere where no one knew us, we could have lived a life of pretence until one day we could no longer avoid the awkward questions from the girls. We would have got away with it as both Kevin and I are only in our 40's and look young enough to actually be the girl's Mammy and Daddy. But that would all have been so wrong, and why should we run away. I may be ashamed of the way my daughter has chosen to live her life, but at no time have I ever been anything other than extremely proud of the girls and of us. I have nothing to fear in sharing this story with you all.

So I decided that the sharing of this book has to be a good thing. For if it makes a grand parent consider the relationship they hope to have with

14

their future grandchildren. Or if it serves in some small way to give another grandparent comfort and hope as they to find themselves estranged from their grandchildren, or they struggle without any support to bring their grandchildren up, it will have been more than worth it. But even more than that I hope that "My story" finds its way into the hands, minds and hearts of someone who is influential and well placed in life, and that it will make them think, hopefully they can then pass what they have read onto other influentially placed people, and the whole thing will start a snowball effect, and that together we can all go on to make a difference, turning us back into a nation that truly value grandparents for what they are and for what they can impart to our future generations.

But for the most heartfelt of reasons I am writing this for "My Girls" Hope, Morganna, Angharad and Rhiannon. It is important to me that I be the one to tell them our story, especially as if left to my family as they will receive a one sided retelling not just of how it was but also of how my family felt and still feel about watching me going through this most devastating event. They will tell how it tore me apart, and of how they could do nothing but stand by me helplessly, unable to do or say anything to make it all better. It is true that in the main my family understandably have no time for my daughter whilst I still feel that my girls have a right to know her, and I want them to know her, to grow up loving her as they do now. If I am not still around to be the one who is there to nurture the relationship between my girls and my daughter, who else will do this for me, my girls and my daughter. My family will be unable to do so as they stand steadfast in their decision over my daughter. It is true it did and has had a profound effect on my life, but that is just it, it was and is my life, I do not want the girls to feel quilt for what I went through or to feel that they were the reasons that I experienced what I did. If left to social services and to a social worker that knows nothing at all about the case they will be told in a matter of fact way of this events happenings, I feel strongly about them not hearing it from a social worker as I know all too well that not all social workers are good ones, there is good and bad in everything in life, and whilst they might have the best of intentions at heart, they have absolutely no idea what it feels like to live through this, they have no idea how it tears a grand mother or grand father apart to have to say goodbye to their most dearly loved and wanted grand child, or of how that pain stays with you each and every day for the rest of your life.

Over the past year I have watched as 2 of my friends have died early in life, I always imagined that I would be around forever - well at least until my girls were all grown up and ready to listen and understand as I told them this story myself. But I realize that God may not grant me my one wish to still be here to sit with them and take them protectively into my arms and gently tell them this story. Writing this was another way that I could still tell them the whys and how's of this events happenings, and why what occurred changed not just my life but theirs forever. I wanted to continue to give them the truth without hurting them, which to me is so very important. I also wished to be the one who was there to dry their tears as they begun to understand the true impact of what we have all lived through, I have dried their tears so many times since they came to live with us, and I know that there will be many more to come along the way.

So if you are listening God. If you are watching over me as I write this "My story" please be kind to me and to my girls and let it be me that is here for them always.

There is only one way in which I can write this and that is through my eyes and from the heart. This is how it affected me and my girls. It is our story, our life, our event. Long after I have finished writing this the lives of me and my girl's will I hope continue. I have on many occasions during the past years wanted to write this, but for one reason or another the time just did not seem right, and the words just wouldn't come to me. I now believe that the main reason this book eluded me was because I first had to reach a time and place in my life where I was at peace with myself, I did not want to write a re-telling of our story that was tinged with anger or blame, I have over the past year found this peace, I have moved on, I have grown. But more than that I have begun to heal I am not controlled anymore by the anger and frustration that used to be in the forefront of everything I did. I have seen that although bad things have happened, good things have too, and I hold onto these good things, I see the positive now and not the negative that was there each day I awoke, I live in a world that is sunny even on gloomy days, and although I so dearly wish that things were different, I have accepted that they are not and the reasons why. I still have regrets I still feel loss, I miss my daughter, but I had to let her go, you will understand why as you read this book. I also live everyday with the pain of missing my two grand daughters Angharad and Rhiannon. Having Hope and Morganna here with us is better than fantastic, but each day it also serves as a constant reminder of my loss, as they reach their milestones in life I find myself wandering if Angharad and Rhiannon are reaching theirs, and it tears my heart out.

However, there are a couple of things I wish to point out to you; I have changed Hope and Morganna's younger sibling's names. The names I have given to them in this story have been chosen especially for them and with much love. They are both welsh names, Angharad, means greatly loved one, Rhiannon means divine queen,. I have changed the girls names as it is very important to me that I protect their identity, writing this story is not about causing them or their family any pain, it must not intrude on their lives and they must be left in peace. As my story unfolds you will understand why this is so important to me.

Also I have not mentioned my daughters partner by name, believe me I would have liked nothing more than to name and shame him, but my feelings on this are irrelevant, it would serve no purpose and it would be unfair of me as he to has a family, he is someone's son, and I wish his family no further heartache, for heartache is something we have all had too much of.

In the early days as this story began to write itself, the only emotion I felt was fear, Tears were my new laughter and protectiveness my shield, I had to re- learn how to laugh and how to smile, there was nobody there to tell me it was alright to laugh at the humorous things that happened, albeit they were few and far between. I was so absorbed in a world where laughter just didn't happen and smiles all too often were left unseen, that I had forgotten how to feel these two wonderful emotions.
Well today I can smile again and yes I can laugh, but I still cry.

My grandmother was a lovely old soul; she told me one the birth of my son, who is now 27 years old,

"When they are babies they will break your backs, when they are adults they will break your heart"

How right she was ……………………………….............................

I know that writing this will be difficult for me as it will mean revisiting some of my bleakest of days. It will be cathartic. And as I relive this event and write it I know I will cry, it will make you cry as well. But I shall endeavour to make you smile as well, most of all I trust it will make you think. My aim is to tell of our story without apportioning blame, without unduly hurting anyone. I worry that my daughter may hurt, but then at some point she will have to be told how it has affected me, because up until this very moment in time I have never at any point told her how I feel, or how it has been for me. At the time I was not strong enough to let her see what it had all done to me, I had seen so much of her pain and the effect it had on her. I also felt that Bo had enough pain in her world that sharing mine with her would have been cruel. It may also have been the straw that broke the camels back, and I so feared that, I did not want to loose my daughter forever, I did not want to become a grieving mother who had buried her child.

For a long time Bo saw me as part of this evil plan to take her children away from her, which was completely untrue all I ever wanted to do was to protect all of them and that included her. Eventually the time came when I had to decide who I was trying to protect and who it was more important for me to protect. It had to be Hope and Morganna. They were so small, they were just babies, unable to care for themselves, and they became the focus of my world.

I still continue to support Bo emotionally, when she needs me.

# *THE FORTUNE TELLER*

In 1997 I was at the Royal Welsh Show in Buith Wells, promoting an album that I had recorded for a charity. Whilst there I did something I had never done before, I went to a fortune teller to have my fortune told. Now as a complete sceptic, I held a firm belief that our future was destined by fate and that none of us could predict what would befall us, which was probably just as well, as most of us would give up at the first hurdle if we could see into our future and of what it held.

I stood in line with the other people awaiting my turn; oddly, I noticed that all of the people stood there were women. As I waited I could overhear the others chatting, sharing their past experiences of what had been told to them in previous readings, most of which was seemingly accurate, in some cases it appeared to be extremely accurate. That was a bit unnerving and I began to feel a little uneasy, was I really going to go in and listen to what this fortune teller had to say. I must admit I began to fear what she would tell me, as some of the things that have happened to me I have never shared with a living soul, I have kept them to myself, my intention was and still is to take them with me to the grave, they were things that only I needed to know about and the sharing of them would only bring pain and distress to others.

I entered the fortune teller's caravan which was surprisingly cosy - I don't know what I expected it to be like, but there was a definite air of peace inside. I walked in and as I did so the fortune teller said quietly "come forward Keri, you have nothing to fear from me" now how on earth did she know my name? I concluded that someone who had been in before me must have recognised me from one of the newspaper articles that were being sold on the showground, and told her, after all most of the people there would have seen my face at the launching of the album.

I took my seat in front of her and looked at her studying her face as she studied mine. She looked like a true Romany gypsy, complete with a black lacy shawl around her shoulders; her face was lined and told of a hard life. She returned my look and acknowledged I was there, she said "cross my palm with silver dear" here goes I thought another loss of hard earned cash. I put the coins into her hand and as I did so she caught hold of my hand and into it she placed a glass ball which she had until that point kept wrapped in a cloth on her lap, she startled me," don't be frightened as there is nothing in me to fear, just hold that ball in your hand and pass your other hand to me" I did as I was bode and she took my hand in hers she studied the back of my hand and my fingers feeling each of them in turn then she turned my hand over so that it was palm side up and began to talk to me.

"You are here to promote something, it involves music, but whatever it is music will not bring you your fortune, this is because you will not allow it too, you do not appreciate the talent you hold, you are going to keep it private, something only the chosen few will know you for, you have sung to your children, but they have not inherited you musical gift, I see strings, do you play a stringed instrument?"

Oh very clever I thought, she had obviously read the local papers, all that she had told me up till now she could have read about me in any of them. "Umm" I replied at the same time wandering just what my Christian mother would make of her eldest daughter dabbling in such foolishness. My Mam bless her was terrified of the Romany gypsy that used to call at our home when we were children, she would actually hide from her! So goodness only knew what she would say to me if I was to tell her later what I had been up too.

By now she must have picked up on my sceptical vibes and worked out that she had her work cut out with me, she went on to tell me about my children.

She told me that I had 3 sons and a daughter she went on to tell me that my eldest son was working with water, and that it would try to claim his life, but it wouldn't succeed, she said this would happen twice, she was right, my eldest son is a fisherman, when I got home the following day I was to discover that he had got his leg tangled in the ropes of a string of lobster pots, and as he has shot the line of lobster pots back into the sea, the sea had dragged him overboard, but fortunately he had a knife and was able to cut himself free, then in 2001, he was fishing off the Cardigan coast when his boat was hit from underneath and was sunk, thank god my son was yet again saved, his boat was lost, but he and his crew were to survive, today he is still a fisherman. She went on to tell me that one of my remaining sons would work in the building trade and would one day have his own business, well son number 2 is a welder, he works for someone else, but who knows where he may be in a few years time. As to son number three, I had always expected him to one day take over the dairy farm my husbands family had, she told me this was not to be, she also said that we would leave the farm and go on to something else, something that would see us do well, this was unimaginable, and when I told my husband despite the accuracy of some of the things she had told me, we both laughed at this and dismissed it as being way off the mark. However, once again she was right as only a short time later we did leave the family dairy farm and went on to other things, still in farming, but we have gained so much. This move was going to prove very important later on. She told me that son number 3 would not work in the farming industry, she saw him as a musician and also surrounded by animals but not farm animals, well Oliver is a keen drummer, something he is proving to have a natural talent for, he also has a love of animals, and it would not surprise me in the slightest if Oliver together with his friend Jack were to become the next crocodile hunters as they are always off in search of some poor old creature.

The fortune teller went on to tell me that my daughter was going to break my heart, that she was already travelling along a road that was to take her into a lonely world, she told me that I was going to bring up three girls, but that I would also have to say goodbye to another 2 little girls, she told me that she could see me standing alone with my arms reaching far into the distance until they almost disappeared, I was crying, I was heartbroken, as a child was being carried away from me. She had already picked up on the fact that I had lost a little girl around mid pregnancy, and that this little girl if she had survived would have had a short and suffering life. She went on to say that Oliver had been one of twins and that I had miscarried the other twin, which she told me was also a boy early in the pregnancy, Until she had told me this I had remained sceptical and, I had not responded to anything she had told me, but now I did. I told her it was true that I had lost a baby in the middle stages of pregnancy, she was also correct that Oliver had been one of twins as I had bled during the early stages of the pregnancy and the Doctor had thought I had miscarried. It was only when 2 weeks later I was still suffering from morning sickness that I was to go and have a scan, and there he was all safe and sound. I told her it was impossible for me to have any further children as upon medical advice for my safety my husband had had a vasectomy after I had miscarried again 9 months after Oliver had been born, so she couldn't possibly be right about the other 2 girls I was to bring up or the 2 that I was to say goodbye to. But now I look back on her words and think she actually saw a lot more that I realised and a lot more than I believed.

How could she have seen into my future. I could never have seen what lay ahead of me, could I?

She also told me that I was to meet a tall dark man, one who would hold me in his heart from the very first time he met me until the day he died, he would look out for me and protect me,

"Ah" I said "that must be my husband as he is tall and dark"

She replied that my husband and I were to share a long tested life together, but that there would be immense happiness between us, she also told me that I would be with him for the rest of my life. The man she saw was not my husband and she said I would not feel the same way about this man as he did for me, I was not to return he love. He was to become very special to me, he would adore my singing voice and hold the uppermost of respect for my feelings, this she said was to become a very special platonic soulful friendship, she told me I had not met this man as yet, which of course ruled out many of my friends, but that when I did meet him I would know instantly that he was the one, well the jury is still out on that one as to this day he has not come into my life.

I left the fortune tellers caravan feeling somewhat strange, this woman had told me quite a lot about myself, some of it which was so true that I could not help myself in believing the rest. I was concerned about my eldest son and had this sick feeling churning away in the pit of my stomach. I felt the urgent need to speak to him, just to hear his voice and know he was OK, but I knew I couldn't as he would have been at sea, he would be out on THE SMALLS lifting his lobster pots. That sick churning feeling stayed with me for the rest of the day.

There was a lot that she told me that I had shut away, a long time ago I had chosen to lock it away, and after all it served no purpose to tell of. How did she know, I had given absolutely nothing away, I had said very little in fact, was I that open and easy to read.

Later as I mulled over what she had told me I knew that she had seen into my soul, she had read my thoughts and told me of them, she had walked inside my soul and learnt of my secrets, but she had also told me they were safe with her. I gave myself a good talking to, telling myself that I had to be more guarded next time - that is if there was to be a next time, as I had decided that there never would be, but then they do say never say never. Nine years have passed since I met that fortune teller and although I have been tempted to go and have my palm read in that time I have yet to go. I am too afraid of what I might be told the next time, maybe I would be too open to what I heard and interpret my future more easily, I would be scared to death of that, especially as I still believe that our future is already there waiting for us to arrive at the point in time we are to live through, now what purpose would be served as I couldn't change it anyway.

Most of her predictions on my future I can interpret as coming true in my life. Some have been undeniably correct, and I have found myself over and over again looking back on what she had said to me.

I truly believe now that she had foreseen the event that I was to encounter, she may not have seen its happenings - but then maybe she had and thought it best not to tell me. If she had I wonder what I would have done. I think I would probably have locked my daughter up and never let her out of my sight again.

The one thing she did not say was how it would all end; she said nothing that I could today interpret as the ending of my events story.

She did however tell me that I was going to have a very long and healthy life; she told me that I would survive to be a grand old age, let's hope she was right. She also told me I was one of life's givers and this would always show on my face, she said that although I had already been through some heartache and pain I would go on to live through heartache many times in my life, she told how this heartache would not show on my face, that I would remain young looking and not challenged. In saying this she may have been right as I still look younger than my 47 years on this earth, but that may be have more to do with genes as my Mam has always looked more youthful than her years, and as I age I see much more of my Mam in me. She told me that I had a big heart, she said I had an empathy that was seen in only a few, and that I was unaware of the spirituality I possessed, but that one day it would all fall into place, and after a struggle, I would emerge at peace. Once again time was to prove her right.

# THIS IS ME

   This story is not about just me, but I got thinking, the reason why writing this is so important to me is so that I can be the one to tell the My Girls what happened, therefore it seems only natural that I include a bit about where I came from, who I was and who I went on to become, as I may not be here to tell them about who I was either. After all it is part of their family history too, Hope and Morganna will grow up knowing their maternal family, even though they have lost a complete generation in it's make up, as Grandma became Mummy, Grand Dad became Daddy and their great grandparents fell into the place of grandparents and not "GG" and "GD" as my parents have become known by their other great grandchildren. It saddens me that this has happened, but we did try hard not to let it happen in the beginning. The girls obviously in the early days had a social worker, and they tried hard to install in us the importance of not allowing the girls to call us Mammy and Daddy as it would lead to confusion later on. Time went on and they learnt from our son Oliver that we were Mammy and Daddy; they would hear him calling us this all the time. It reached the stage where I was exasperated with keeping on trying to correct them all the time. One day I became aware that I was actually the nearest thing to a Mammy they may have, so I stopped correcting them and just let it happen. Now I do know and understand that some of you reading this will not agree with what I have quite naturally allowed to happen, but we do not hide anything away from the girls, they are hopefully going to grow up, just naturally accepting it all.

   I know the time will come when we have to sit the girls down and explain everything to them, but this is far away yet, and as our daughter (their birth mother) has played a very absent part in their lives, if they grow up in a "normal" family, goodness knowing what that is these days, but hopefully it means someone who can be a Mammy, Daddy etc, then the rest can wait until the time is right. For me it far more important to bring them up to feel secure and to know without any doubt that they are loved.

It is their two younger siblings that will grow up not knowing their maternal or paternal family. They will not grow up knowing and feeling everyday the immense love that I carry in my heart for them as well as for Hope and Morganna, they will not have learnt over the years who I am or what drives me. They will not understand any of this until they come back home to me.

This is me…………………………………...........................................................

I'm welsh, I was born in the welsh capital, The City of Cardiff I am the daughter of welsh parents my Dad a working man and my Mam a valley's girl, I was their first born, I was born with blonde hair and huge blue eyes. I was very bright so my parents tell me They often tell me of the time they took me on a bus ride through Cardiff, the bus was full as we travelled through the city we passed a wedding party as they came out of the church, apparently I asked my Mam and dad on the top of my voice when were they going to get married, which brought frowns of disapproval from the other passengers as at the time my Mam was heavily pregnant with my brother David. I have one other brother Michael, and a baby sister Deborah - all of whom I shall cherish forever.

I was a busy child and got into all sorts of mischief, the story goes that whilst my Mam was having David my Dad was busy white washing the front wall, I had asked for some milk, and not being one to wait for Dad to get one promptly helped myself to a drink of the white wash, I was very unwell and had to be rushed off to hospital. But I was later well enough to go home again, to this day I cant stand drinking milk, which is really funny as I married a dairy farmer.

When I was just 3 yrs old and David 18months my Dad and Mam moved us away from the city where we were born and took us to a small rural village in Pembrokeshire, here my Dad had secured work on a farm. I have fond memories of those days, I can still remember the smell of the farm and the freedom we were fortunate to enjoy. Sometimes we would go down onto the farm whist dad was working, we would play with the farmers children, there were quite a few if them, and we would play away the afternoon climbing trees and riding on the farm horse, who was never very amused at having such demands placed on him and more often than not would throw us off. The cottage we lived in was a nice little place in the summer, but was awful in the winter, it was freezing and if it rained David and I would be lying in bed at night listening to the persistent drip, drip, drip, drip as the rain came in through the roof and dropped into the numerous buckets placed beneath the leaky roof, believe me sometimes there was more buckets than floor!!

I went to a very small school, it was great as we all knew each other, we all played together and there was a true sense of belonging in that school, we did not have bullying, we just got on with things and helped each other. We were not a well off family, but we were surrounded by love. I can remember my Christmas's, there was always presents, but not as the children of today know Christmas. My Mam would have made me a new dress, I can remember one year she made me a green floral dress which I loved so much I wore until it was tread bare, and then there would be books which had been around once before as someone else's name would be scribbled out, its funny really as today I think nothing of going into a charity shop to search the selves for the next good book I was to read, and I have read loads, especially over the past 5 years as I was to spend most of that time caring for demanding babies, and reading allowed me to escape my pain.

Dad lost his job on the farm when the farmer emigrated to Australia and we had to leave our tied cottage, we moved into a brand new council house in a very small avenue just a couple of miles down the road. By this time my brother Michael had arrived and just like I had been he too was blessed with blonde hair and blue eyes, I can remember him winning a local baby show, and Mam coming home proudly carrying the small silver trophy he had won which was placed in the china ornament cupboard where we could all see it! I had also for the first time in my life experienced death as my much loved Grandfather passed away. I can remember visiting him in hospital when he was ill, one day I asked my Mam if he had bought me some new shoes, as I had a distinct memory that he had, she went on to tell me that my Grandparents had taken me out shopping one day and had bought me some new shoe. My Grandfather had fought for his country along with so many other brave men and women. He had served with THE WELSH REGIMENT, and had served in many countries worldwide, he had been stationed in Punjab in India, Shanghai in China and in Egypt, he was decorated with medals for his active service, these medals are now in my fathers care, and will be left to my brother David after my Dad's days. My Grandfather was one of the brave men that fought so hard for his country and to give us the kind of world we so freely live in, but he was to loose his battle with the cancer that took his life, taking away from me my darling grandfather.

I was fortunate as I can remember my Grandfather, I think David can as well, although his memories will not be as strong as mine as he is a little younger than me, my younger brother and sister never even met him. He was the only Grand father I knew as my Mam's father had died when she was just eight years old.

Dad had difficulty in finding work, so he returned to sea as a merchant seaman. How I hated those trips of his, they seemed endless the only thing that broke up the time that he spent away from us was the postcards and letters he would send back home. I can remember my Mam ushering us all into the lounge and we would sit on the floor in front of the fire, the four of us spread out around her feet and she would read to us the letters that Dad had sent back home, she used to try so hard to hide her tears, but I saw them, and I cried too, how I missed my Dad when he was away. The other thing he would send us was post cards, they would be of the ship he was sailing on, or the countries far around the world that he had landed on, and sometimes the postcards would have magnificent photographs of flying fish or exotic birds and animals on the front of them Dad would come back ashore for a while and then be off again, I have the greatest respect for my Mam and how she managed us children whilst dad was away. She had never learnt to drive so shopping meant taking all of us with her on the train and into the local town which was just a short train ride away. We would all traipse into the town with her and go shopping in WOOLWORTHS where if we were lucky Mam would buy a pound of broken biscuits, then we would go on to buy the groceries that we needed and the bags would be shared out for each of us to carry on the return journey home again on the train. When we got home I would go through the bag of broken biscuits fishing out all the coffee iced ones which I loved so much.

One day Dad returned home and all too soon he was announcing that he was going back to sea again. I remember crying my heart out, as he walked out of the front door. About half an hour later he returned, fed up with the tear ridden goodbyes, he had contacted his ship from the telephone box in the village as we didn't have a phone at home; he had informed them that he would not be sailing again, and my Dad was home to stay. On one of his trips away I can remember him returning with the most fantastic doll for me, she was wonderful, she stood almost as tall as me and if I held her hand she would walk beside me, I treasured that doll and was the envy of my friends, one day we were all out playing and Dolly was with us, my friend was walking with her and to this day I do not know exactly what happened but the result was that Dolly's head became broken, Dad and I tried to repair the damage to her head but she couldn't be fixed, so she was destined to spend the rest of her time stored away in the loft of my parents house.

Work began to create a new reservoir in the small village of Llysafran which was just a few miles away form our home, Dad got a job there and as children we watched that reservoir growing, today it is a lovely place to go and walk and spend time, there are some fantastic spots to picnic at. During his time at the reservoir Dad acquired an old van, he spent hours working on it, in a farm shed in Llysafran until one day he had finished and drove it home. What he had rebuilt this old van into was to provide us all with the perfect camper van to go off for weekends in, which was something we had not been able to do until then, we had not had family holidays, apart from the time we stayed in a caravan in Broad Haven, when it just poured with rain. Often the weekend would come and we would pack up the old camper van and off we would go. One of the places we spent a lot of time at was Aberieddy. When I was young this beautiful little cove was undiscovered, its shingle beach was a haven for us, and many weekends we would be the only people there, Aberieddy also had its own resident group of geese, they belonged to a man who lived in one of the beach cottages, and believe me they were the most ferocious things you could encounter, I was absolutely terrified of them, they used to chase us all the time and if we were unlucky they would catch us as well. But by far the most exciting place for me was Aberieddy's most amazing blue lagoon, which is just a short walk along the coastal path, I loved that place, it used to have small fishing boats moored upon her very still waters. Little did I know all those years ago that I was to marry a fisherman who lived on top of the steep hill that takes you down into the cove of Aberieddy. He had been born there, as was his father before him, and he came from a strong family line of traditional shell fishermen. So it was that one of the childhood places I treasured was many years later to become my home as a married woman. Today Aberieddy is packed with tourists who like I did as a child discovered this beautiful unspoilt natural, peaceful place.

Another place we used to go and camp at n the old camper van when I was young was The Rhos, which is a small riverside hamlet that lies on the banks of the River Cleddau, when we used to go there it was very quiet, even today you can be fortunate enough to spend the afternoon there and have the place all to yourself. Picton Castle is just up the road from the Rhos. We spent hours there as a family, Dad would indulge in his past time love of fishing, which often fed us all and eventually as we got older we would join in and fish alongside Mam and Dad, both my brothers still enjoy fishing. Dad even got himself a small boat and we would go out in that too. To a small child the Rhos was also very scary as it is surrounded by dense woods, and at night they have there own unique sounds, but what used to scare me the most was the slurping sound the lugworm would make as they went back under the mud, this mud was also dangerous as it could become like quicksand and suck you down, the more I think about it, the more I remember it as a scary place to be. That river bank fed us many, many times, as did the lovely beach of Sandy Haven, which was also undiscovered in those early days.

The estate that I grew up on was very small and everyone knew everyone else and their business too, there wasn't much that went on that everyone didn't know about. I had a lot of friends who lived on the estate or within the village. The village was a busy one it boasted its own Post office, a general stores, its own petrol station, a newspaper shop, a co-op, a butcher's, two pubs-one of which was run by the same gentleman who drove the village school bus, and also allowed us kids to knock on his back door and buy sweets from the pub, there was a thriving butter works, a agricultural merchants, a vet's practise, a haberdashery shop, a railway station, and not forgetting a small village sweetshop, which had shelf upon shelf of glass jars which were crammed full of every kind of sweet you can remember, I loved that shop! I got my first ever kiss on a walk back from that sweet shop, I can remember the boy as if it was yesterday, he was staying with a friend of my Mam's who was his foster carer, I often wonder what happened to him and where he is in life. The village also boasted a small chapel - Pennual, I became a member there and attended Sunday school. The village also had a small village hall, it was constructed from corrugated metal, and was nothing more than a broken down tin shake, but it was there that I was to make my Mam and Dad so proud as they watched their little girl sing for the first time, to this day I know my Dad is saddened that I did not go on to have a career in music, but for me it was always something that was special, I loved singing and playing my guitar, but somehow it was something that remained mine I did not want to share it, looking back I think it had more to do with the fact that I never considered myself to have a special talent, that was something I was not going to appreciate until I was in my 40's. Over the years I have sung to all my children, I have sung my grandchildren to sleep; the girls and I are always singing nursery rhymes, only these days they are trying to teach me the latest "BARBIE" songs! I joined in the local pantomime shows, always taking the role of lead or principle boy, I later joined the amateur dramatic society.

Singing was to become an important part of my life it became my solace, it was something that allowed me to dream it was and still is  my soul, it was my outlet for my emotions. My talent followed me through school and when I failed my 11+ and went on to the local comprehensive school, it was the one thing that saved me from being bullied in this big imposing place.

I was to experience some rough times in this school, I was unfortunate to have very badly protruding teeth, and at the tender age of 12 years I was fitted with the most hideous of contraptions. I was the first person to ever have this type of brace, it involved having silver rings on each of my teeth, through which thin wires were threaded and then a metal brace was not only attached to my teeth, but also protruded outside my mouth and was attached to what I can only describe as the inside of a crash helmet - it was a remarkable piece of engineering, that is the only way I can describe it really, and it worked, it straightened out my teeth fantastically, but oh my goodness what a bullies delight. Eventually I became known as the girl who could sing like an angel, it was when I became involved with a local band that the bullies for some odd reason began to leave me alone, it was almost as if there was a respect for me as soon as I was involved with the band.

I had to persevere with this blessed contraption on my teeth for 23 hours in every 24, I was allowed to remove the outer brace for one hour a day which was never long enough, and more often or not I just didn't bother to take it off as it was more trouble than it was worth. It did little to discourage the local boys, and I was never short of a boyfriend, in fact I tended to get on much better with the boys in my year at school then I did the girls. In the village where I lived a new hall was built and the old tin one eventually disappeared, along with the new hall came the dances it held, once a month I used to go to the dance there with my friend Helen, sometimes Mam would come with us. We would take to the dance floor wearing the latest fashion, which in those days was the maxi skirt and dance around to the sounds of "SLADE" and "SWEET" blaring out over the village, much to the annoyance of the local people who lived close to the hall, who I feel sure did not understand our taste in music, much like today when my son is playing his music at top volume and I declare that I do not understand how he can possibly listen to such rubbish, or laugh when he sings along to a track that I used to listen to when I was young and someone has copied it again. I was always given a curfew and always ran it to its time, always being one to get all I could get out of something. I can remember one night I was late going home, I had met this handsome creature, (I thought he was handsome, my parents thought he was a creature!) he was a biker, he had long greasy hair, he was clad in leathers with a crash helmet in one hand - which had somehow found its way around my waist and a cigarette in the other- every parents worse nightmare, he walked me home and to my horror we met my Dad coming the other way and he was not happy, he stopped me from going for a while, It was at one of these dances that I was to meet my first husband, I was just 14 years old, he was 19 years old, my parents were horrified, I took home my first boyfriend, and he asked Mam and Dad if he could take me to the local May fair, they reluctantly agreed, they were always saying he was too old for me, but I was hooked, he had everything, his own car, business, home and he lived by the sea, As time went on the more my parents said that I was to stop seeing him the more stubborn I became. I got a summer job in a bakery in the small welsh city of ST David's and spent the summer of 75, away from home living with my boyfriends parents in a tiny coastal hamlet near St David's, my beautiful childhood place of ABERIEDDY. This was also about the same time as my parents moved my paternal Grandmother in to live with us, she was a lovely old soul, she was ill and needed to be cared for, so she moved in and shared a bedroom with my little sister and I. it was difficult to say the least, just at the time when I was about to sit my CSE'S I found I had no peace to study. Nights were a nightmare in themselves as Nan would come up to bed hours after Deb's and I had gone and we would be woken up by her asking if we were asleep! Being away from home that summer was fantastic, I missed my little sister terribly, but I was working and I was beginning to enjoy my first steps of independence. The bakery owner offered me full time employment, which I accepted and I left home refusing despite pleas from my parents and my head teachers to go back and sit them fused to sit my CSE'S I left school, looking back on this my parents must have been devastated as I threw away my opportunities, I was a very bright pupil and would have gained passes in all my CSE'S, but of course I was young and thought I knew better. At the age of 28years I was to re-enter the educational system and attended college full time as a mature student, I was in a group of 18 year olds sitting my GCSE's, I passed all of the subjects I sat. Many years later I went on to study further and gain Diploma's which have now qualified me as Counsellor and "Woman's Stress Practitioner" - despite my qualifications I still do not understand my daughter.

I married my first husband in December 1976; I was just 17 years old. The day we got married there was snow on the ground and we didn't know whether we would be able to get from the registry office in Haverfordwest to The Salutation Inn in Felindre where we were to have our wedding reception. I gave birth to my first son when I was 19 years old; he was born in the old ST Thomas's Hospital in Haverfordwest. In 1981 I gave birth to my daughter

Bo. My first husband and I divorced in 1983; we had been together for nearly eight years. I met my second husband in 1984, and we moved in together and in February 1985 after I had suffered from a very bad stomach bug I found myself expecting my third child, he was born in December 1985 just five days before Christmas, I married my second husband in March 1986. It was not long before the cracks began to appear in our marriage. It was more to do with me than with him, I felt that I wanted more, I needed to grow, and I did not know how. It was in the spring months of 1987 that I saw an advertisement for students to enrol on courses at The Pembrokeshire College, it was then that I began to become aware that what I needed to do was to prove to myself that I was not the thick person I had been told I was for years, so I found a course that I thought I would like to do, applied and was invited to the college for an interview, which I passed. I had been accepted as a mature student. I then had to make childcare arrangements for my son who was not then one year old. I had no option other than to place him in a full time nursery, it cost me a fortune, but it was worth it. In 1988, It was whilst I was at college that I had begun to discover myself, suddenly I was made aware that I was a person in my own right, I wasn't just someone's wife or someone's mum, I was me and people actually found me interesting. This started a doubt inside of me over my relationship and I knew I wanted more than I had at that moment. Leaving college in the July I went to work for the summer in a local nursing home, I loved it, I enjoyed being around the old folk there, the tales they told were on times so funny that I would be in stitches laughing, but it was also a very rewarding job to do, that job also gave me something else I had not had since I was in school, for the first time in years I had my own group of friends

My husband accepted a job offer away from us and spent his working week away whilst I stayed behind with the children, when the children were at school I went to work. The last thing I was looking for was another relationship, I wanted to be alone for a while, to give myself room to grow but in the spring of 1990, I met Kevin, there was something very special about this shy and reserved man and he swept me off my feet, we spent hours just talking, nothing more, and then one day I realised I had in fact fallen in love with him. I said nothing to him, and he in turn said nothing to me, we were just friends, one day it went further and he admitted to me that he felt the same way as me. I told my husband that I had fallen in love with someone else. I think he had guessed anyway, but I had told him before anyone else. I was not proud of what I had done, but it had happened.

When my second husband and I separated it had a devastating effect on us all, I had not told anyone how I had been feeling, and the news shook my family especially when they found out about Kevin then instead of supporting me my family all sided with my estranged husband, there were arguments between me and my parents, as well as with my siblings, it was an awful time for me, at the very time I needed support I found myself without any. It was eighteen month before I was to speak to my parents again; those were the hardest months of my life. When Kevin and I got married my Mam and Dad came to the wedding at the last minute, they did not come to the reception. I was given away by Ken one of my oldest and dearest friends. I had asked my Dad to give me away, but he refused. Perhaps one of the reasons that I try to always be there for my children is because of what I went through back then.

To see Kevin with my family now it is hard to believe that they took such a disliking to this wonderful man, but then none of them knew him, so it may well have been the situation rather than the person that they were opposed to. I knew right from the beginning that Kevin was something special; I knew that I wanted to spend the rest of my life with him. I made the right decision; I have never regretted what happened. I regret causing so many people pain, and for that I am sorry.

When I was married to Bo's father I fell in love with a place called ST JUSTINIAN'S, This is where the St David's lifeboat is housed, it was also where we sometimes moored our fishing boat and where Bo's father and I used to set out to sea in the boat to lift the strings of lobster pots we had left on the SMALL'S - in its hay day THE SMALLS was a fantastic place to catch lobster, crayfish and crab. I used to go out with him and lift pots, in fact I worked pretty damn hard, I also became an expert on dressing crab, and when I wasn't dressing crab I would be delivering it to the hotels and restaurants around Pembrokeshire. The day came when the fishing industry was once again struggling to survive when someone discovered scallops in Cardigan Bay, again I put on my oilskins and in the bitter cold, wet and stormy weather, along with other hungry local fishing boats I would go out to sea, often in weather that truly should have seen us leaving the boat moored up safely in the harbour, and instead of being battered by gale force winds, we should all have been in our local pub, THE SHIP INN in LOWER TOWN FISHGUARD, which was where all the fishermen used to while away the hours alongside the old retired local fishermen who were all too willing to sit and spend their hours telling the younger fishermen how they used to catch fish. I have sat and listened to countless stories unfold of the biggest lobsters or the biggest catch that had ever been landed, as well hear as the old fishermen would sadly retell the tales of the many local fishing disasters and the loss of their family and friends who had perished out at sea, and there were many of them that had lost their family or friends this way.

I would leave my eldest son then just a small boy to be cared for by my husband's parents whilst I crewed the boat alongside my husband. There is no escaping someone when you are 30 miles out to sea and sharing a 36 foot fishing vessel. On nearly all the trips out there I was the only woman. I would return home to my son wet cold, fed up and totally exhausted. They were rich days, but they did not last long enough, Fishing is like farming, it's a hard life, and by God you really do earn every penny it brings you.

From the cliff tops of St Justinian's you can look straight out across Ramsey Sound and onto the Island of Ramsey, it is a magical, mystical place, even on the wind is blowing a howling gale and the sound is whipped up into a frenzy it is still magical, for me it became my thinking place, whenever I was in turmoil I would flee to the cliff tops of St Justinian's and sit and mull over whatever was bothering me.

I have worked in many professions since I left school I have been a school dinner lady, I have nursed the elderly, I have worked in an estate agents, to mention just a few. I have never been one to sit quietly. I held the chair and vice-chair positions on the friends committee in my children's school for years and along with other dedicated parents raised thousands of pounds to purchase equipment the school required. Along with a friend of mine the two of us set too and formed a welsh pre-school in my children's junior school, they were busy days, but oh so much fun.

Over the past 5 years my family have become my rock, they have in the main been there for me even if they have not fully understood or supported the event I was living through. They have on times become my crutch and held me up, as I have in turn been have able to do for them. We are a tactile bunch, my family; we find it easy to show each other the affection we hold for each, and on times the displeasure. As this is a normal family we have over the years fallen out, argued, disagreed with each other, but we always have been able to fix it again. My Mam instilled in us from an early age the importance of kissing and hugging each other goodbye, she told me once it was because we never knew when that time might be our last. Her lesson has throughout my life stayed with me, and is something to this day I can easily do to my own siblings and also to their partners in life and their children, I adore my nieces and nephews, they are such a joy to be around.

My Mam was brought up in the welsh mining valley of Fleur-de-Lis; this valley was to become a focal point of my life over the past 10 years. My Mam was brought up in a children's home from the time she was 12 years old, her younger sister and brother, were both adopted. Driven by the events in my life over the past 5 years I was determined to try and trace Mam's younger siblings, so once again I picked up the treads where I had left them a few years ago and started to and dig away at family records. My Mam had no records of her family at all, I became a woman on a mission and I kept on persistently going over and over old records until I eventually traced both her sister and her brother and united the three of them. In October 2005 at my home I threw a late birthday party for myself and my Mam, both of us have our birthday's in October, I invited all my family and some very close friends, On the morning of my birthday party I went out under the guise of doing some last minute shopping, my Mam had no idea that I was meeting her brother. I brought him and his wife back to my home where my Mam was getting ready for the party, I knocked on the front door and she came to help me carry in the shopping, as she came to the door I held her in my arms and turned her towards her brother, wishing her a happy birthday as I did so, the look on her face was one I shall treasure for always, it was a look of pure joy and of pain. Some of you will be reading this and thinking "what a remarkable thing to do" and yes it was. It was and still is for me the most wonderful and truly magical experience, but as my own story unfolds you will understand why for me it was such an important thing to do and why I feel so incredibly honoured to have been able to do such an amazing thing, my reward for those long hours of searching has been to watch the shear delight on their faces as they have got to know each other after almost a lifetime apart. I am writing this and at the same time wondering how my four girls will look when they meet up for the first time, I say when they meet up because I know deep down in my heart that they will, I am doing everything possible to make it easier for them to find each other again. I put my Mam and her siblings together for the very first time in their lives, they had been apart for over 55 years, and I pray my girls will not be apart for that long.

The woman I am today has been many years in the making, through my lifetime there have been things I have experienced and lived through and like all of us there is at least one story in my life waiting to be told. I have broken and repaired myself over the years, I have been hurt and I have hurt others, if you are reading this and I have in the past hurt you then I am sorry. I have laughed, cried, succeeded and failed, been happy and sad, I have been rich and I have been poor, I have been healthy and I have suffered illness. I have worked and I have been out of work. I have been married, separated and divorced I have had children and I have felt the pain of miscarriage, I have been a young mum, a single mum, and now I find myself a older mum- which I think I am so much better at, probably because I am so chilled out, I have done most of the things that I wanted to do, and although I have a nice cosy home which is now full of wall to wall toys, I do not crave a show home house anymore.

I have always been surrounded by people I love and who love me, but I have on times been lonely, I have loved and been loved. Throughout my adult life there have been special people in my life, and there have been those who have touched my life for maybe only the briefest of moments, but who have touched me deeply and left me feeling a richer person for having shared with them those special times. I have held people in my arms as they have left this world and gone on to the next, I feel honoured that I have been able to do that, it is so very special to know that you have been there for someone who would otherwise have died alone. I have been angry and frustrated. I have been so stressed out that on times I have questioned life itself. I have fought for what I believe in, and although as I grew up my Mam insured that I had a good Christian upbringing I am not a deeply religious woman, any beliefs I have had have been so deeply tested and retested over the past 5 years that I have to admit on times I have questioned all that was ever taught to me in Sunday school and church, I have lost count of how many times I have prayed over the past years and my prayers have not been answered, and of how many times I have asked why these terrible things have happened to me. My Mam has always told me that God only places difficulties on those who are strong enough to cope with them, well all I can say to that is that if he created me he created one hell of a strong woman, I do believe that when we die we leave this world for a better place and that some of us come back again, if I am fortunate enough to come back I would love to complete my musical goals, as that is my one regret, that I have had to put it on the back burner for a while, who knows maybe the next twelve months will see me complete a new CD.

The other thing that has battered my inner thoughts for years is that old question we as parents all ask ourselves when our children go wayward. If I had been given a pound for each time I have asked myself and others, where I went wrong, or what did I do wrong in bringing up my daughter I would be a very wealthy woman. In truth I now know that I did nothing wrong and that I always did the things I did with her best interests at heart., but it was not enough to protect her, I could not keep her safe, I felt as if I had failed as a mother, but I know I did not fail, I did everything I could to keep her safe. I had gone that extra mile.

I believe that the woman I am today is at last at peace with herself, that I feel comfortable with whom I am and that after many years of not accepting my size, I have stopped fighting with it and now accept the things I have. I have been so blessed with beautiful skin and genes that don't seem to age as fast as some so being larger than most is not so bad, anyway perhaps I need this body of mine to balance the personality with. I have tried every diet known to man, and made up a few of my own over the years, I have reached my goal weight once and liked the old me so much I got some of her back again! I have given up on it now and concentrate instead on wellbeing and not on how I look on the outside. Its ironic really that at the age of 47 years I have finally realised that people like me for me and not for what I look like.

I am an incredibly proud woman, and I believe this pride together with my welsh roots and beliefs have over the years made it difficult for me to admit defeat or to ask for help. In Wales we are taught from a very early age that family stay together, that we pull together. I am also the wife of a farmer, another breed that find it difficult to talk about their difficulties, farmers fall into the category of those at highest risk of committing suicide, little wonder then that I should find the past 5 years not only difficult to live through but difficult to talk about.

There is one person to whom I and my girls will remain always indebted, my husband Kevin, his unfaltering strength, his ability to give and show unconditional love to not just me, our own son Oliver, my older two sons, and our girls but also to my daughter Bo, who on times would have and did try the patience of all those who love her. All those who know Kevin are so fortunate for they will know someone who is such a beautiful person. A person who if you are lucky touches your life for the most fleeting of moments, but will stay in your heart forever. One of my very best friends always reminds me of his values- Thank you for doing that Heather, as there have been times over he past 5 years when I needed to be reminded of them as I could so easily have taken for granted this wonderful man who walks beside me everyday and protects us all.

Kevin has been more than my rock, he has been the one and only person who has always been there to hold me through my darkest of nights and my bleakest of days He has been my friend, my fortress, my crutch, he has never once complained, he is my everything. I love and treasure him and all that he stands for; he truly is a man in a billion. It is a testament to our relationship that we have remained together, I think there are many that would out of the stress of what we have lived through gone their own separate ways.

Kevin has not only been an outstanding stepfather to Bo, he has become an amazing father to Hope and Morganna, I watch them together sometimes and I have to remind myself that they are actually our Grand daughters not our daughters, the relationship they have with him is tremendous, the bond unbreakable, they worship him, they could not wish for a more decent and protective a father figure than the one they are so lucky to have in him.

There is one other person that has made this almost impossible situation easier to live through and that is mine and Kevin's son Oliver, he has inherited a mixture of both Kevin and I he has so readily and easily shared his Mummy and Daddy with the girls, never complaining once. He has been a constant help to me in the day to day practical caring of the girls despite him being only 9 years old when they came into our lives, he is a credit to us I am so very proud of him. Thank you Oliver you have behaved with a passion and knowledge far beyond your years, the girls love you to bits, they admire you, you will always be so very special to them, and to them you are a perfect "big brother". I know that you have watched me cry so many times over the past 5 years, you have never once said anything other than that you love Bo, continue to do so cariad.

# My Bo

I would have loved to have written a fairy tale story with the happiest of beginnings the completeness of a full life and a very happy ending, but just like so many of us I can't. The ending has yet to be written, and the life story so far has been dogged with overwhelming sadness. In the early days my Bo was just like any other little girl I held such high hopes for her future, I was the proudest mum in the world until Bo's life began to fall apart. Bo was beautiful, bright, very articulate and not afraid to express herself, she could hold her own with the toughest of them. Oh she was not perfect and she could and did challenge me whenever she could. As well as having a nice side she also had a difficult side, this difficult side would emerge when you would least want it to and it made life hell, but it was a part of her, all those who knew her accepted it as part of who she was, we all thought that one day she would settle down and reach all the goals she wanted to reach. Bo wanted to become a vet or a solicitor when she grew up, she never strayed from this decision and she could have easily achieved it with some hard work, but then one day it all went pear shaped, and as time went on I watched as she slowly slipped further and further away from me. I knew that because of the life choices she had made the two of us were going to loose that precious relationship which a mother has with her daughter, I was not going to do the nice normal things with her that so many other mum's did, I was not going to have the joy of even the simplest of things like a girlie day out shopping.

On the 6th October 1981, after a long and difficult labour I gave birth to my daughter Bethan, she was the most beautiful little thing I had ever seen, she had big blue eyes and the little dusting of hair she had was a lovely shade of strawberry blonde.

Bo eventually got her pet name from her older brother, he could not say Bethan, so opted for Bo instead, it stuck and we all call her Bo now.

Bo started school after the Christmas term that followed her 4th birthday and developed into quite a scholar, she also had a love for music, but could not sing, she learnt to play the flute, something she was good at, she was also good at sport she enjoyed swimming and loved sports day's. Whilst Bo was still a small child her father and I separated, I went to bits for a short time, but true to my old determined self from somewhere inside of me I found the strength to go on, I found myself a part time job that provided us with the money for our everyday needs, we struggled, but we got by, Bo was a busy child, always climbing, her moods would swing from that of being a delight to being an absolute horror, she was a challenge even as a youngster, and could run rings around her piers. When I met Kevin, she took to him straight away; he became an excellent stepfather and was incredibly supportive of her, together we encouraged her to achieve her best. One day not long after we had moved in together Kevin and I took the children to the local farmers mart, we were taking calves in to be sold. My children had not had much to do with farming at all until I met Kevin, we were walking along when Bo along with her younger brother James asked us what a table bird was, we went on to explain that they were poultry that would be reared for eating, they were not amused and went off again only to return to us asking if we would come and take a look with them, we did and there all alone in a cage was a turkey chick, well this blasted bird came home with us, the children called it Lurch and Kevin and I had to swear that it would not be for our table. As Christmas approached that year the turkey was huge, it was beginning to look very much like the tasty bird that we would buy for our Christmas dinner, and I began to imagine what it would look like minus its feathers and covered in melted butter and streaky bacon, but we had both promised the children, and so Lurch was most definitely off the menu, he sure would have been a tasty dinner. I was making mince pies one afternoon and had them cooling in front of an open window in my farmhouse kitchen, every now and then one of these pies would disappear, I thought it was Kevin and kept watch for him to tell him off, only to be confronted by a white neck and a beak, it was Lurch the turkey that was doing the pinching! How Bo laughed when I told her. When she was 11 years old Bo became ill, so ill that she was admitted into hospital, the Doctors and the Consultants could not discover what was wrong, but they knew it was serious, after a lumber puncture it was eventually diagnosed that

Bo had excess pressure within the fluid surrounding her brain, they did not know why, and thought it was hormonal, sure enough as puberty arrived Bo had a massive growth spurt, and almost as quickly as she had become ill she became well again. Everything seemed to go back to normal.

In June of 1993, I gave birth to mine and Kevin's son Oliver, Bo worshipped him and he loved her. It was just before Oliver's 1st birthday that we began to notice some changes in Bo, her behaviour became unpredictable and she began mixing with some unsavoury characters at school. Until then she was an exceptional pupil, achieving good grades and with a promising future ahead of her, she began to express her desires to become a vet and we were confident that if she kept on producing school results of the same standard she would be able to reach her goal.

Bo attended a local grammar school and was again pulling some good results. We saw the potential in her to go on to reach her goals, we enthused with her over her plans for her future and encouraged her to excel. Attending parent evenings was a pleasure as we sat and listened to the good reports her teachers were giving, none of her teachers had any concerns about her. Then one day Bo came home from school and asked me if she could stay with her friend for the weekend. Now we had always encouraged all the children to have a good social life, they have all gone through various after school clubs, such as Beavers and Young Farmers Clubs, and very often either they stayed at their friends homes for overnight stays on a weekend or their friends stayed with us. Our home was always full of children and I loved it. I asked her which friend she was referring to and she said a name which I had not heard before, I asked her who this friend was and how long she had known her.

"Oh" she replied, "she has only been at the school for a couple of weeks, she is new and lives with her foster carer".

"Do you now why she is with foster parents Bo"

She answered that she did not. I was pleased that Bo had befriended this girl as I felt sure she would be grateful of a friend in this new school so, I told Bo that as long as the girl's foster parents were to ring me and we made the arrangements then it would be alright. As the weekend approached no phone call came so on the Friday morning I told Bo that she could not go as I was not happy about it, she went mad and called me for everything.

Later that morning the farm accountant was visiting the farm, and as I prepared lunch for all of us my phone rang,

"Hello Mrs Swain, this is school secretary here, I'm afraid there has been an incident at school, can you and Mr Swain come in please"

I asked what the problem was and the she went on to tell me that Bo had made certain allegations and the school had called in social services. We were to attend the school and meet with social services. My blood ran cold, what the hell was she up to now, I called my husband in from his meeting and we decided it best to contact our solicitor as we had no idea what was going on. I rang our solicitors office only to be told that she was in fact on her way back from court in Swansea and would not be back until late afternoon, I rang her on her mobile, explaining the situation, she said there was no way she could be back in time to attend this meeting with us, she advised us that if social services were already involved should they say that they wished Bo to go into voluntary foster care for the weekend that we should agree with the request as otherwise they may go and obtain an emergency care order, which would make it very difficult to get Bo home, she went on to explain that if we allowed Bo to go voluntarily then if at any time over the weekend she wished to return home to us we could go and get her. On the way to the school Kevin and I discussed what we thought may have been the reason this was happening, and the only thing we could think of was that the week before this Bo had bunked off school and on asking her why, she had told me that she had been in court supporting her friend, when I asked what friend she mentioned someone I had never heard her speak of before, I asked why he was in court and she told me quite blasé way that this friend was in court for stabbing one of his mates. To say I was horrified doesn't touch how I felt. Later that night after the boys had gone to bed I challenged her about this boy and what he had done and also why she felt it was alright to do what she had done. Bo erupted into a frenzied rage and attacked me. I went to my room terrified. I was afraid of my own daughter, she had scared me half to death, it was the first time I had ever witnessed her violent behaviour and it was totally out of character for her. I remained in my room and later when Kevin came home he found me still sobbing. I told him what had happened and he was furious, he went across to Bo's room and shouted at her, asking her if she knew or cared what she had done to me.

The following morning she behaved as if nothing had happened.

On arriving at the school we were shown into the headmaster's office and in that room were not only social services, but also an officer from the child protection unit of the local police force. Kevin and I were both obviously shaken and after some time it transpired that Bo had alleged that she was afraid to come home, we asked why, but the social worker did not respond to our question, they did however ask for us to agree to her going into foster care for the weekend, and that on Monday they would call a meeting to discuss a way forward. I was besides myself I was crying and begging the social worker to let me see Bo, she refused saying that she didn't think it would be right and that Bo had expressed her wishes not to see either Kevin or I. I was furious, how dare this woman who knew nothing of my challenging daughter think she knew what was best. On talking to the child protection officer who told us quite plainly that he felt Bo was fabricating everything we reached the conclusion that this was all about me saying no to her requests to stay with the foster girl that I had said she could not spend the weekend with. The two of them had been talking concocting a plan that if she was to go into care she would be placed with the same family that had this young girl, well she was wrong as the child protection officer had realised that when Bo had mentioned her, and he had moved the other girl. They refused to let me see my daughter I was totally distraught. We had to go home and pack a weekend bag for her. Two social workers turned up at my home to collect this bag, to this day I wish I could meet up with them, they were awful, they treated Kevin and I like criminals, and even after it was all over and there was no case to answer, social services did not apologise for the heartache they had caused us that day. My father tried to talk to them, but they were rude, offensive and tactless. I could not wait for them to leave my home.

That weekend was our son Oliver's 1st birthday, we had planned a big party and I wanted to cancel it.

"No we are not, she is not going to spoil it for every one else" Kevin said.

Bo had the ability to spoil every thing that we had planned. So we went ahead with the party.

During the morning of the party the phone rang and it was Bo I had spoken to her a lot over that weekend as she had rung me several times, she had said she was missing me, this time she told me that she wanted to come home, we had guests arriving any minute and couldn't possibly go and fetch her, so I rang my parents and they agreed to go and fetch her on their way

43

over to the party. She acted like nothing had happened, I was so glad to have her home, yet at the same time I was hopping mad with her, but it was left unsaid. Monday morning came and we had a call from the child protection officer, it seemed that Bo had told the foster parents that she had lied, the case was immediately dropped, there was no case to answer. I was relieved, but I was also furious with Bo for what she had put us all through.

Things settled down and Bo went back at school, she behaved for a while and she went on a student exchange to France with the school, one of the last photographs I have of Bo looking happy was taken when she was on the French exchange. Then the French students came over to stay with pupils from her school, so we played host family to a French student, the student that stayed with us was a funny girl, we actually ended up with two of them, they stayed in the annexe of our farmhouse, for the whole of the time that they were with us they spoke hardly any English apart from "Please and Thank you" then on the day they leaving, she turned around to me and in good English said "Thank you very much I have enjoyed staying with you, I love your farm, it is a fun place to be" the little madam she could speak very good English all the time and just chose not to. We even held a barn party for all the students involved in the hosting of these French students what a night that was.

Again Bo started missing school, she would leave home and get on the school bus, but she did not arrive for registration at school. She began to lie to us about her whereabouts. We were to discover that our beautiful Bo was mixing with known drug and alcohol abusers, she had also begun a relationship with a young lad who was involved with this group of young people, he was drug and alcohol dependant, he also self harmed. He was often around our house spending time with Bo, our theory was that if they were in our home then at least we had some idea where Bo was, and we were trying to be responsible, trying to protect her. We had tried to put an end to her seeing him, but we couldn't as she just bunked off school and met up with him.

One night we were sitting watching television when Bo started screaming that this young man was choking, Kevin and I rushed to our upstairs bathroom to discover him frantically trusting his hand into his mouth and trying to pull something out, he was vomiting blood. My first reaction was that he must accidentally swallowed something, the truth was much more gruesome he had in fact deliberately swallowed a nail, and was now trying to pull it back up from where it had lodged in his throat. We got him into the car and rushed him to the A & E dept of the local hospital. This was the first of many other occasions that I was to witness someone self harming themselves and it is a terrifying thing to witness, I honestly thought he was going to die.

We tried everything to prevent Bo from continuing along this path, we would have her boyfriends over just so that we could keep an eye on them both, she then started disappearing at night. It was my dog barking that eventually alerted us that all was not as it should have been, Bo was slipping out at night and meeting up with her friends, who would drive out to the farm after dark and wait for her just down the road from our farm gate. We tried everything possible to try and protect her, we even at one point tried locking her in her room at nights. She admitted to me a while ago that she just used to wait until we were asleep and then would climb out of her bedroom window, her friends would wait in their car just down the road a little from the farm and she would get into the car and go off with them, she was so lucky not to have been killed as all those friends would have been drinking or taking drugs, possibly both - she was determined if nothing else.

We tried absolutely everything to help her, from counselling to covering up for her, nothing worked, she had hit the destruct button, she was slipping away from me and it broke my heart.

By the time Bo was 16 we had bought a guest house. One afternoon my parents were over for tea, we were all sat down when Bo came breezing in looking like something out of a horror movie, all dressed in black with a thick layer of black makeup on eyes and lips her hair resembled rats tails. This was the new "Goth" look that she had taken to wearing.

"I will be 16 next week, I shall be moving out" she said, without even saying hello to her Grand parents, who were shocked by her latest fashion trend, and they began to tell her off.

"Its Ok" I told my parents, I can handle this.

Turning towards Bo I calmly said to her,

"I'm glad you have told me as I have been racking my brains as to what Dad and I should buy you for your birthday, so if it's Ok with you we will buy you some big suitcases, you know the ones I mean the ones that have the wheels on, as that way you can take all your things out in one go, save you the trouble of coming back again to pick up the remainder of your things"

My parents were horrified, but I did later explain to them that I was in fact calling her bluff, as I knew she wouldn't leave yet.

Bo didn't leave, she stayed, but eventually her treats to leave began again and I knew that it was only a matter of time before she would leave. I hated the thought of her being away from us, so Kevin offered her our granny annex she agreed and we spent ages redecorating it so that she could move in there, having her there meant that she had a bit more independence and as it was connected to the guest house we could also keep a watchful eye on her, she enjoyed her new found independence but eventually her lifestyle began to have an effect on both James and Oliver. Home life was beginning to be a real struggle and none of us ever knew where we stood with her, Bo and I were like a flame to gunpowder, she could ignite so quickly and change from a pleasant girl to that of the most difficult of young adults.

Nothing I did was ever good enough and she would challenge me constantly, if we had visitors she seemed unable to cope with a crowd and would appear sullen, life was getting impossible and I was fast running out of ideas. Bo decided to leave home at first she moved into a bed sit in the local town, she was mixing with a rough crowd and I suspected that she was drug and alcohol abusing. I could not reach her, every time I tried to help her she would accuse me of interfering and then she would not contact us for a while, life was so strangely quiet without her at home, and I missed even the constant temper tantrums she would have - I missed her.

Bo's lifestyle was having a knock on effect on us all. The summer of 1998 was to see me leaving my beloved Pembrokeshire, leaving behind what I fondly call "MY THREE F'S" family, friends and familiarity. I knew it was going to be tough I hated the very idea of being away from my family and friends, but we had made our decision and there was no going back. Looking back on our decision Kevin and I actually agree that it was the best move we have ever made, apart from missing family and friends our lives are much the richer for making that decision.

Kevin had taken on a contract to run a dairy farm in East Sussex and we relocated. We were hoping that Bo would come too and that this move would also prove good for her, it would have given her the perfect opportunity to break free from the crowd that she was mixing with they were having such a bad effect on her. Bo became someone we did not know anymore, she was aggressive and secretive, she did not worry about how she looked and her attitude to others was appalling, she was also beginning to fall onto the wrong side of the law. I was horrified, now of course we understand that it is impossible to be a drug and alcohol abuser and not get into trouble. It was nothing for me to go into the local town where I myself had spent my youth to be told by friends that they had seen or heard that my daughter had been fighting in the streets with her boyfriend, Oh God the times I just wanted to have the ground open up and swallow me, as I listened to the stories of these awful incidents, they made me feel so very ashamed.

Bo refused to come, I had hoped she would change her mind and come too as this would have meant she would have broken the link between her and her undesirable friends, but she did not, she stayed behind. I did not realise at the time that when you mix with these kinds of people wherever you may be, wherever you may run too, they still somehow manage to find you.

This move did however provide me with a temporary peaceful place to be, although everyday I was so desperately worried about Bo, at least it was not in the forefront all the time, I could walk into the town in Tunbridge Wells and no one knew me, I became invisible and for a short time that was bliss. For a while I concentrated on work and being me. I even began to make plans for the future, something I had not dared to do for a long time.

I would ring Bo daily, if I did not get an answer each day I would begin to worry, usually though I would receive news from one friend or another during the periods that Bo went to ground, and these were frequent. I did not understand the world she lived in, I still don't, but I do understand some of the way she lives.

I soon learnt that on giro day she would be really cheerful and of course at this time of the week her life was full of her so called good friends, they would all go out and spend their weekly giro on booze, not giving a thought as to what they would eat over the coming days, then they would get together in one or another of their flats or bed sits, and end up completely out of it and no doubt in trouble again with the local police. Then the phone calls would begin as the week rolled on she would ring me saying that she had no money for food or electric, in the beginning I used to send her some money as I couldn't stand the thought of her not having anything to eat or being cold.

I knew only a portion of what hell she was living through, I used to dread my telephone ringing late at night in case it was more bad news as it often was.

This was to be a challenging time for my family too as they struggled to try and understand what was going on, there is much even to this day that they don't know and they never will. It has never been my intention to sit and relay it all, it used to overwhelm me so goodness only knows what it would have done to them, I do know and understand one thing and that is that they would have stopped being supportive towards her much sooner that they did.

It was later that year that I had a telephone call from a friend in Pembrokeshire who told me that if I did not come home to Pembrokeshire and rescue Bo, I would be burying her before Christmas. I needed to hear no more, Kevin and I returned to Pembrokeshire and after persuading her that we would do everything we could to help her Bo agreed to come back with us, I was elated I had my baby back. She was ill, she looked awful and she had problems, but I knew that I could help her; at least there was a chance. The few possessions she had left we had bungled into the car and off we set. That car journey from Pembrokeshire back to Sussex was awful as Bo slipped in and out of sleep, and when she was awake she was being violently sick, she was very tearful and fretful, her speech swayed from being slow and slurred to that of being so fast that her words would run into each other and were all jumbled up. I reached behind the passenger seat and caught hold of her hand, I spoke to her as if she was a little girl again, and tenderly trying to soothe her with the same soft melodic voice that I had spoken to her in when she was a small girl. Closing my eyes I willed my words to reach inside of her troubled soul and to bring her some peace. Oliver was only just 5 years old and he sat next to his much loved sister and cuddled up to her, he held tightly onto her arm and they both fell asleep.

There was no getting away from the unmistakable smell of vomit and an unwashed body that filled our car. I sat in there in silence, unable to rid my thoughts of what torment her troubled soul had been through. It scared me and I was afraid for her.

When we arrived back at our Sussex home late that night, Kevin carried Oliver into his bedroom and settled him down, and I helped my weak and broken daughter into the house leading her into the bathroom, where as we waited for the bath to fill I slowly peeled the sweat and vomit soaked clothes from her battered weary body and helped her to lower herself into the clear warm water of the bath. Gently and lovingly I washed my Bo with a touch so gentle, too afraid that if I rubbed her any harder I would hurt her already bruised and battered body. She sat curled up in the bath crying, whilst all the time I washed her silent tears fell from my eyes and mingled with the bath water. How I prayed that night for someone to help my daughter, how hard I asked God to spare her any more pain, but this was just the beginning, it was to be the first time of many that I would see my daughters body bear the scars of life's battles that she was yet to face.

In those early days with the help of our family GP we somehow got through the months that followed, they were not easy, neither Kevin nor I had any idea what we were dealing with at times it seemed bigger than either of us, and we did not talk about it to our friends and family, we just struggled on.

Then in the spring we reached a major milestone Bo began to show interest in going back to college and studying for her A levels, we went along with her to a local college that we had chosen quite deliberately as it held a positive approach to drug and alcohol abuse and had active groups within the college that met up and helped the youngsters who were having difficulties, she was to go on to actually help in these groups and was supporting others with problems she had found an outlet. We were so very proud of her.

In the October of that same year Bo and I reached milestones in our lives I became 40 years old and 3 days after Bo reached her 18th birthday- something on times over the past few years we doubted she would see, we threw joint birthday party, it was not a reward for her but rather a recognition from us that she was doing so well. I was at the time working full time for BUPA and along with our family and friends as well s Bo's friends we had a ball. The weather for October was unusually kind and as the band played we all had a great time, Later that night Bo and I took to the dance floor, we danced together and laughed so much I was crying tears of pure joy, I had my baby back and she was well, I was elated, my family and friends were also happy they could see that she was trying, they too fell in behind Kevin and I and supported Bo. Little could any of us have known but that night was to be the last time that any of us would see the little girl we all loved so much again, not one of us had any idea that over the next few months we were going to once again loose my beautiful Bo, as the hell that we had rescued her from all those months ago was to find her once again and taking her by the hand and lead her straight back to the devil she had been fighting so hard to escape.

Once again the devil was dancing with my Bo.

I was cleaning out her bedroom one day when I found a lump of what I thought was discoloured dry glue, I showed it to a friend who was a policeman he asked where I had found it, I told him and he said

"Well you know what it is don't you"

I looked at him dumbly and he said well it was cannabis resin, Bo's behaviour had got a little unpredictable  but we had missed the signs, my lovely daughter was once again using, when she came in that night Kev and I asked her about it, she went mad accusing us of allsorts, she then declared she was moving out. The following day she left home again and I was in pieces, we did not hear from her for weeks and despite all our efforts to find her we failed Bo had gone, once again leaving the safety of her family home. This time she went to live in Hastings and attended college there for a short time, but it was not to last and soon she was back mixing with the unsavoury characters that were having a detrimental effect on her; again she dropped out of college, and met up with a man we took an instant disliking to. We were to be right in our instant disliking of him and for the reasons we feared, not only was this man a drug and alcohol abuser, he would also attack my Bo attacking her.

One day we received a phone call from Bo  she was in a bad way, I picked her up and she was in an awful state, she was painfully thin her body was battered and bruised and her face was covered in spots, she looked unkempt. I was so angry, how could any man do this to my Bo, but then I did not understand her world or the people she shared it with. Today I understand that in her world violence towards one another is quite normal. It did not stop me from hating this man, I hated everything about him, on the occasions where I had seen what he had done to my daughter, and I actually wished him dead. I would have done time for him had he been stood in front of me at any of the times I have nursed my Bo's broken body, cleaning it and sticking butterfly stitches onto her wounds to hold them together as she would refuse to let us take her to hospital. Bo stayed a few days but then as always off she went, back to him again this pattern continued for a long time, and became something we got used to, although I have never got used to seeing my daughters bruised and battered body. We would bail her out of trouble, we would support her any was we could, and I would beg her to come home but she refused saying that she would only make our lives hell, we would tell her it did not matter, all that mattered was that she was home and safe, she always left again after we had put her back together.

By now her constant pattern of coming and going was having an effect on Oliver, and Kev and I made the decision that we could not keep on taking her back into the family home without her being committed to it all. We sat down with her and talked about what she wanted, her answer was the same as always, and that was "to be better". Later that evening she disappeared, I did not hear from her again. Christmas came and went as did the New Year and I was beside myself with worry, then one day my phone rang it was Bo. Her voice was frail

"Mammy please come and get me"

I jumped in the car with Kevin and we shot down to HASTINGS to the address she had given us, she was not there, I frantically rang her mobile and she answered it telling me where she was and that she had a friend with her. It turned out that her and this friend were running away from someone and they had had to flee from their bed sit as these people had found out where Bo was and they were coming after her, it was like something out of a television programme and as they both jumped into the back seat of our car, they were shouting at Kevin to drive away.

I was later to discover that my daughter had spent Christmas and the New Year in hospital she had tried to end her life of misery by swallowing a mixture of pills and alcohol. I also discovered that my beautiful Bo had been self mutilating she was cutting her arms with a razor, sometimes so deeply she needed hospital treatment, when I first found out about her self mutilating I was so desperate to try and understand why she could and would do such a thing, she was such a beautiful girl, she could not give me a reason, but one day after she had self mutilated I had taken her to the local accident and emergency department to be treated, and I asked her why she had done this to herself, she replied that she was bad inside and it was the only was she could feel good again, this was something that I have never quite understood.

My Bo and her partner had been living on the streets of Hastings along with many other of their so called friends. I discovered that Bo was going into a homeless shelter to have a bath and a hot meal whenever she could afford it, I also suspected she was begging for money from people in the streets, it makes me shudder to even think about those days as anything could have happened to her, she was apathetic to her situation. We used to go into Hastings and meet up with her, she would look a mess, totally unkempt and she often had a friend with her, we would take them for lunch somewhere, and then buy her some groceries, gone were the days when I would give her money as she would have spent that on alcohol, so instead we bought her things she needed, these things would inevitably turn out to be everyday things like tampons which we take for granted as just being in the cupboard at home, but she had no home, she had nothing. I can remember one winter we bought her a coat as she did not have one, I only saw it on her once, I asked her about it one day and she admitted that her boyfriend had sold it, to this day I suspect that many of the things we gave her ended up being sold, with the proceeds being used to feed their habits.

Bo and her partner decided to go back to Pembrokeshire; I think this decision was made due to the drug pushers that were chasing them for the money they owed them. The first I knew of them returning to Pembrokeshire was a phone call I received late on evening from the transport police in Peterborough, they had picked Bo and her partner up as they were trying to jump trains, they had got all the way from Hastings to Peterborough, they made the rest of that journey back to Pembrokeshire in the back of a police squad car.

Once again they got help and found a bed sit they moved in and we gave her some of the basics she needed to get by. The phone calls from her telling me about the abuse she was suffering became a regular thing I begged her to leave but she would not. I have lost count of how many flats and bed sits I have had to clean up or pay for after she had left them in bits, only to flee onto the next one, each time begging us for the deposit. As hard as it was for me I had to say no to her as I knew from our past experiences that if we continued to give to her she would never learn, many times we fell of this band wagon and give in to try and help her each time promising that it would be the last, but she was my child, she was my beautiful little girl and I constantly clung to one thing and that was hope.

We tried to be civil to her partner for her sake but he did not help himself and he certainly didn't make liking him easy. By now the two of them had quite a collection of court appearances between them, mostly for petty crime, but eventually it stepped up a gear and more serious charges were becoming part and parcel of their lives, both had a criminal record and as a mother I was so ashamed of this part of my daughters life, even amongst my family and friends this part of Bo's life has remained difficult for me to share or talk about with them. We were relieved when she told us that her partner was on remand as it meant that she was no longer under his influence, at this stage I was still blaming him for the bad things in my daughters life. They separated and I have to admit I was so pleased I once again clung to hope that she might just find someone half decent, after all she was a nice girl underneath it all, and I prayed that someone special might walk into her life and see beyond the young troubled woman she had become, realising that beneath it all was a beautiful person, he would have to be someone remarkable and I knew that too, after all I could still see the beautiful young girl who had made me smile and laugh when she was small, I could still see the little gem that made my days worth getting up for when her father and I separated, in those days it was all about us and nobody else. She was not alone for long, and had soon found another partner and it was not long before they were living together. Soon the old pattern we thought had long passed began to return and the strains of a  volatile relationships began to show, the physical signs showed easily, she was often black and blue, she self mutilated once again and her arms became a battle field of scars and fresh wounds, she made no attempt to hid these marks on her arms and I would have to ask her to cover them up if we were out together as other people used to look at them and it made me feel sick, she was a real mess once again. It was many months later that I was to discover that Bo was also violent, something we had not considered, she had a foul temper that was for sure, but I had never thought that a child of mine would be violent towards another person. In the early days I would justify her violence towards her partner by thinking that she hit out in self defence, here I was still protecting my child, or was I just protecting myself from the truth?

To say I was concerned for her safety would be an understatement I actually feared for her life, each day I lived in fear that she may self mutilate and go too far, cutting herself deeply and bleeding to death or that in a moment of desperation she might take her own life.

I also feared that she and her partner might do each other some real harm, the most frustrating thing I had to do was to stand back and witness the ability they both had for forgiving each other and then after a short time apart which was usually hours not days they would be back together declaring undying devotion for each other until the next time they had a fight, which was never far behind the incident they had just put behind them. I have never understood what it is that holds them together, as they hold each other responsible for the events that have happened to them as a couple. Somehow they seem to need each other, they live off each other, but honestly I can't see what there is in their relationship that it good.

I know as a qualified counsellor that I should not judge, and I do try not to, My friends and family have told me on many occasions that they could not do what I have done and they do not understand where I get the patience or the determination to go on from, they find it difficult that I can still emotionally support my Bo. But none of us actually know how we will respond and cope with an event until we actually find ourselves faced with it and then trying to live through it, we will all act in different ways. When a life event involves our own children, as parents we will stand by them, usually no matter what the event may be, we will support our son or daughter in whatever way we can. Sometimes though it gets to the stage where as a parent you have to face the reality that supporting your child is not making it any easier for them to cope on their own, you may have to decide as I did who it is you are trying to protect, and once you have reached a conclusion on that you have to let your own child go in order to continue to protect someone else.

When I became a mother, I became one for life, but then one day I had to let my Bo go in order to continue to protect my girls.

Bo chose her path in life. I know she would not have chosen to become the person she is today, it was not what she wanted, but she did decide to have her first drink, to take her first drug, no one else made her do these "first" things, for her they just have not stopped at the "tried that and didn't like it "stage, they continued. When she was a little girl I had watched and listened to her as she had played safely in her fantasy world, one day she was a Princess, the next day she would try out being a Doctor, I was so unaware all the way back then that my daughter would spend a lot of time in her adult life not being a Doctor, but actually being put back together again by one after she had self harmed, or felt so desperate that she tried to end her life, which would have robbed me, and the world of a beautiful person.

My beautiful, slim, vivacious, courageous and intelligent teenage daughter with a smile that could melt the hardest of hearts, who used to walk as tall as her height had everything going for her in life, she could have accomplished anything she chose to do, she could have made anyone fall in love with her and feel as if they wanted to spend the rest of their lives with her. She had it all. She could have lived in a sunny world forever, but for now she has gone.

I have lost her to a dark and strange world, where the people who live in it seem hell bent on destroying themselves and each other, they hurt each other and have a total lack of respect for any one who does not inhabit this strange world of theirs. They give priority to their habits needs and ignore the basic things they need to survive, the kind of things that you and I worry about having, security, love, food, warmth, the everyday things we all need to survive she somehow survives without.

Back in 1994, when my Bo was just a carefree thirteen year old teenager, I was looking forward to a future where my lovely daughter would achieve her dreams. I was looking forward to watching my only daughter experience the same wonderful events in her life that I had experienced, falling in love for the first time, choosing a wedding dress and getting married, having children, and then me one day becoming a Grandma, but it was not to be, I doubt I will ever experience any of these things with Bo. One day the devil got his claws into my beautiful girl and began to dance with her soul, with her very being. He has danced with her soul now for over twelve years, destroying my beautiful daughter along the way. Today Bo is a shadow of that beautiful teenager. She is painfully thin, her eyes are sunken and her skin flawed. She no longer walks tall, and her dreams are a million miles away from her.

Here we are in 2006, and the Devil is still dancing with my beautiful Bo.

But I still hold on to the one word that has given me the strength and courage to watch her go through this awful life of hers. It's only a small word, but for me it has such a big meaning.

HOPE...................

## "Mum I'm pregnant"

I can remember as if it were yesterday the first time Bo told me she loved me, we were in the park on the seafront in FISHGUARD. I was pushing her on the swings we were having a great time, just her and I, her hair was blowing behind her. It was winter time and she was all trussed up in a red all in one suit to keep out the cold wind blowing in from the sea. On top of her voice ringing clear over the crashing of the waves as they crashed heavily onto the stone seafront she shouted out "Mum I love you" I believed that those words were the most joyous of words a daughter can say to her mother, but there is one sentence that I know is just as magical and that is "mum I am pregnant" oh joy of joy's your daughter is going to become a mother too. Is it not something all us mothers wait for? When Bo told me she was expecting a baby I should have been overjoyed, oh god I so wanted to be but inside I was dying, inside my world was falling apart, I was frightened for her and her baby, I was also afraid for me. So much was going to depended on Bo being strong enough to cope with the demands that were going to be placed not only on her but also on her body as the pregnancy developed, I worried too about the effect her life choices would have already had on the baby.

Things had been pretty quiet for a few days I had not heard from Bo at all then one afternoon in August my phone rang,

"Hi" said my daughters unusually cheerful voice, she was on a high, "Guess what Mum, you will never guess" her excited voice was chatting away as if she was on an express train, she could not get all her words out quickly enough.

56

She was right of course I would never have guessed, but I suppose I should have been expecting it sometime, indeed looking back I am amazed it did not happen sooner.

"Well come on mum guess"

I replied "sorry darling you had better tell me"

"I'M PREGNANT, YOU ARE GOING TO BE A GRANDMA AGAIN"

Nothing could have prepared me for that, I tried so hard to share her joy, I so wanted to be happy for her, there was a part of me inside screaming to tell her I was happy, and I did, after all at any other time I would have been jumping through hoops, is it not every mothers wish to see her own daughter go through the wonderful experience of carrying and giving birth to her own child, but there was a big part of me that felt total fear, not just for her but also for her baby, I feared that this baby was in danger right from the start.

Kevin came in that evening after milking to find me in floods of tears, he knew all too well by now that this usually meant that something had happened to Bo

"Come on them let's have it, what has she done this time"

He listened patiently as I poured out the latest news, and he too shared my concerns. During the next few days I managed to convince myself that this pregnancy could be a good thing, that it might actually be the one thing that forced her to sort herself out, and turn her life around. After all she would not want to put her unborn child in danger, would she? And I knew that somewhere inside of my daughter there lay the ability to be a good mother; I had watched her with Oliver when he was a baby.

Over the next few months Bo kept on telling me that she had stopped drinking, I was once again proud of her, at last she was displaying a positive attitude towards herself and her baby, she was still however living with her partner and their relationship remained volatile and violent. We were still concerned about how she would cope but we began to relax a little and look forward, we began to see that she was capable of bringing up a baby with lots of support from her family, and if she continued to show her family that she was back on track they were all prepared to support her.

My birthday arrived and the postman delivered my cards from back home, amongst them was a card form Bo. I opened it pleased that she had made the effort, what was inside made me feel so much fear for her, she had enclosed a copy of her 12 week scan photo, and there amongst the black and white picture was not one little blob, but two, the reality hit me so hard I felt ill, she was carrying twins, oh my God, I knew that she was up against it with one baby, but with support I thought she would get by but two, how on earth was she going to manage. At one of her later scans Bo was told that she was carrying a boy and a girl, she was elated and quickly chose names for them both, the girl she had decided to call Morgan.

As the weeks passed by, I threw myself into my job. We had relocated again and were now living in Oxfordshire. I had made some good friends and Oliver had settled well into his new school, he was also going to the local youth club.

Bo continued to tell us she was not drinking and was quite rightly proud of herself, I could neither prove or disprove her as I was not around her every day, but it was looking promising. The relationship with her partner seemed to have also settled down and there was a lack of reports of violence, I knew this meant one of two things, either they had both settled down, or she had stopped telling me, I think even then instinct was telling me that she had just stopped telling me. Every time I had gone home to Pembrokeshire all seemed relatively quiet, I even went home to Pembrokeshire to attend one of her hospital appointments with her.

We were on a visit to Pembrokeshire I had a phone call from her, she had been attacked by her partner, Kevin and I rushed to her and tried to persuade her to come back to Oxfordshire with us, she refused and went back to her partner again. Once again the old fears came flooding back, we lived on a knife edge and we treaded on eggshells with Bo, afraid that if we did not support her and began to point the finger or show our displeasure and concerns about her relationship that she would stop contacting us and in doing so she would cut herself off from the one lifeline she had when she was in trouble. Then one day she rang crying she told me that her partner had pulled a knife out on her and made threats to kill her and the unborn babies. I was unable to get to her I was 4 hours down the motorway, so I rang my parents and asked my dad to go to her, her partner had as usual run off so there was no fear of them finding him there, I would not have put them in any danger. My parents took Bo to the local police station where she made a statement, and then they retuned to her bed sit and collected some clothes for her and took her back to their home and to safety. It did not last long within days despite my parents begging her to reconsider and think of the unborn babies, Bo returned to her partner, she also retracted the statement she had made, and helplessly we had no choice other than to watch. It was Over the Christmas period of 2001 Bo had after an awful fight with her partner come to Oxfordshire with us to "live" she began to make plans, look for a home for her and the babies, register with our local GP and we thought great she is really going to do this and with support from us she will cope ok, it was not to last she was constantly in contact with her partner and arguments between them over the telephone were a regular occurrence, she returned to him, I was totally devastated, I have never understood the hold he has over her, and I struggle to understand that she has put him and his needs above that of her children.

The violence between them continued and became a more regular part of her life, or was it that she was once again telling me of these outbursts in her life, whichever, my concern for both her and her unborn babies safety was almost unbearable. I could not afford that to happen she was and is my daughter and I love her today as I have always loved her, with the unconditional love a mother holds for her child.

I had to be there- no that's wrong I wanted to be there for her and her babies

In January 2002 Bo rang me saying that she was having pains in her stomach, she admitted that her partner had in fact hit her in the stomach and had now run off, I told her to go to hospital, she replied that she was in too much pain to get there, so I rang for an ambulance to take her. I also rang the antenatal ward and expressed my concerns to the duty midwife telling her what Bo had told me.

Later I had a phone call from the hospital saying that Bo had discharged herself against their advise and that they were informing social services as they were concerned about Bo self harming and the risk of domestic violence between Bo and her partner and the effect this may have on the unborn babies.

I also contacted social services. Now some of you will be thinking what an awful thing for a mother to do to her own child, but believe me the alternative was even more difficult to contemplate. If I did nothing, I was in fact leaving them all open to god knows what. I was trying to protect my daughter and my unborn grand children. I was terrified that harm may come to Bo and the twins. It was awful having to speak to a social worker about my own child it tore at my insides, it was a very tearful emotional conversation, and I cried through most of it, I have to say that the social worker I spoke to was brilliant.

I held preconceived feelings about social services and social workers for what they had put me and my family through when Bo was a teenager, I have never forgiven them for the way they treated my husband and I, but as fearful as I was I knew that Bo was going to need all the help we could find and I knew that social services would have become involved at some stage, better this way than when it may be too late.

Social services told me that they had already been called and that an initial assessment was scheduled to take place on February 14th 2001, Valentines Day. At least now I felt that someone closer to Bo and the unborn twins was may be able to do something to help her, and I didn't feel quite so alone with it all.

On February 21st 2002 I was at work when the telephone rang, it was Bo,

"Mammy" she said

Bo has always even to this day easily slipped back to her childhood name for me, when she is in trouble

"Help me, something is wrong and I keep wetting myself"

Panic set in as alarm bells began to ring inside my head, I realised that her waters may have broken, but they cant not yet she was only 28 weeks pregnant.

Trying to hold myself together so I did not alarm her I replied "Alright sweetheart, try not to panic, are you having any pains"?

She replied that she was and that her stomach was hurting.

"Bo has your partner attacked you again?"

As always she denied it, protecting him, but I had a gut feeling and it was making me feel physically sick. I told her to phone for an ambulance but she told me she couldn't as she had no more credit on her phone. I told her it was alright I would ring for an ambulance to pick her up. Hanging up that phone was terrible as I was worried that she may not be able to answer it when I rang her back

I rang her local hospital and spoke to one of the midwives on the antenatal ward, she shared my concerns and they sent an ambulance to fetch Bo, promising to ring me back once Bo had been admitted and they had checked her over, at this point I shared with her my concerns for Bo and the unborn babies, I told her that I feared she may have been attacked by her partner. I rang Bo back and held my breath counting the times in my head that the phone rang before she answered it and with each ring panic tightened its hold on me. Thank God, I thought as she answered the phone, I talked to her until the ambulance got to her and I knew she was safe.

I was back at home when the midwife called me back, she told me that Bo was in fact in the early stages of labour, that they had given her drugs to try and delay the labour, and some other drugs to help mature the babies lungs she added that every day they could buy the babies would benefit them, she was concerned for the babies as if born now their lungs would be too underdeveloped for them to survive, later that day I had another call from the hospital, they were preparing Bo to transfer her to Singleton Hospital in Swansea as they had the necessary equipment to help such young babies, Bo was in fact just 28 weeks into the pregnancy. I was worried for Bo and the babies and I couldn't settle. I rang work and told them I would be off until things had settled down. I can remember ringing my parents in absolute despair, I felt so totally helpless, what could I do. In truth there was nothing I could do apart from fret and to be there in case Bo needed me

Bo had been transferred to Singleton hospital and I had spoken to her, she was understandably frightened, she was worried about the twins and what was going to happen, she also had an intense hatred of hospitals, her partner was with her. Later I received a call from a midwife at the hospital, "Bo is in labour, we can't stop the labour this time we have to let nature take its course, Bo is asking for you"

I rushed around getting things together for Bo and had earlier been shopping to buy her some bits and pieces. By the time we left Oxfordshire it was nearing 11pm I had spoken to the hospital, its ok they said call in on your way through. I explained that Oliver would in fact be with us as we were taking him to my parents in Pembrokeshire, I was told not to worry that he could come in to see his sister on the way through, I was pleased about that as Oliver loves his sister and was worried about her, I hoped that seeing her may at least ease his mind a little. We arrived at the hospital at 2am in the morning. The staff at the hospital were great they let us spend time with Bo and when it was time to leave they said that her partner had to leave too, she was furious declaring that she would not stay without him. After much coaxing I managed to persuade her that we would take him home to Pembrokeshire with us and then pick him up again in the morning and he could come back up to the hospital with us in our car, eventually she agreed, and we left the hospital.

## February 22nd 2002

We had arrived at my parent's house in the morning in time for breakfast, we were shattered, after a cup of tea and some TLC from my Mam, she ushered us off to bed with the promise to wake us at 9am which she did. Leaving Oliver with my Mam Kevin and I set off to the hospital again, picking Bo's partner up on the way. I was impressed as he was not only ready, but had in his arms the most beautiful bouquet of flowers; I knew Bo would love that. The journey up was difficult her partner had been drinking and the smell was nauseating, you couldn't get away from it and the weather wasn't good enough to drive with the windows open, the air conditioning in the car didn't help much either, I was pleased when we eventually arrived at the hospital.

On arriving we were shown to Bo's bedside, she was sleeping. The staff nurse explained that nothing much had happened since we left and that they were pleased that she was resting during this lull as this meant that the babies were given a little more time. We spent the day with Bo and as nothing was progressing, on the advice of the midwife we left the hospital and returned to my parent's home in Pembrokeshire, leaving Bo's partner at the hospital with her. The midwife felt that it would be the following day before anything else happened, so we returned to Pembrokeshire which is 2 hour drive away. We had only been in my parents home long enough to have a cup of tea when I said to Kevin that I had to ring the hospital, I didn't know why- probably mothers intuition, the staff nurse informed me that Bo was now in full labour and asking for me, that was it I kissed and hugged our poor old son goodbye again and made a dash for the car, Kevin in hot pursuit. We got to the hospital in record time and ran to the delivery suite. Bo was screaming in agony, the midwife declared she was pleased to see me as she was finding Bo difficult to work with. We asked where her partner was, wasn't he helping her? The midwife pointed to a heap that was on the floor, he was tired she said, he has been asleep most of the day. I was furious and kicked the bundle gently on the floor in an attempt to wake him up, he grunted, but stayed asleep on the floor. The midwife said to leave him there as he had been of little use.

I stood at Bo's side throughout that day and night, holding her whilst she laboured, whispering comforting words as only a mother does when her child is in pain, I wiped her brow and encouraged her to push when the time was right. All this time Kevin stood by my side helping to hold me up comforting not just my daughter but also me, he was fantastic, he showed me a side of him that day that I had not seen before, and if it was possible I loved him all the more for it. Her partner had woken a couple of times and after telling her to keep the noise down fallen back into his world of sleep, which was probably the safest place for him to be, as if he had been in our world he would have been in deep water as Kevin was furious with him.

The midwife went off duty and another one came to take her place, the paediatric team were on stand by, and it all looked as if it was coming to an end, when all of a sudden things changed, I knew something was wrong, the midwife asked Kevin to push the bell at the side of the bed, I was told to tell Bo to stop pushing, which was difficult as by now Bo was screaming and shouting, at all of us and getting very week.. Another midwife came in and explained that the presenting twin was stuck and in difficulty, the consultant had been called in and the room was then full of all sorts of people. The consultant arrived examined Bo and said "come on quick get her into theatre"; he quickly explained to me that the presenting twin had a cord around its neck and that the other twin was descending forcing the presenting twin to struggle. Bo was wheeled out of the room by the midwife and a porter and the consultant rushed out after them, I followed begging him to save all three of them, he turned to me and said he would do his best.

By now her partner was awake and needing a cigarette, there was nothing we could do apart from pace the ward, we went downstairs and outside for a few minutes. Neither Kevin or I had given any thought to the fact that we had not eaten since the day before, we had not slept, we were on autopilot. We returned to the room where Bo had been and eventually the consultant reappeared, he told us that the girls were fine, I started crying and said "you lost the little boy, he died" No the consultant replied there was no boy your daughter has had two girls, they are small but they are fighting. The relief must have shown on my face, and Kevin held me as I cried, at least they were here now alive and fighting.

I asked the midwife if we could see the girls, "I'm sorry" she said "But I'm afraid that no one is allowed to see the babies until the mother has seen them, that is apart from the father". I knew that it had pained her to say that to me as she had been there most of the time with us and had seen how Bo's partner had been, later as we were gathering Bo's things up for her, so that they could be taken over to the other ward the consultant appeared again. We talked to him for a while and told him that we would be returning to Oxford the next day as Kevin had to go to work; I was tearful when I told him that I would not see the girls before I returned to Oxford.

"Come with me" he said in a gentle voice, "We'll see about that shall we"

Obediently we followed him over to the neonatal ward and he asked to be let in,

"Come on Grandma, you too Granddad"

I met my two beautiful little girls before my daughter, until now she has no idea that I did, I have never told her. I stood between their incubators crying my eyes out, whispering to both of them that I would be there no matter what, that I would do anything I could to protect them. A hand gently lay on my shoulder and the consultant's voice said" somehow I think they are going to need you". I fell in love there and then with these two precious tiny babies, they had tubes and wires everywhere and machines bleeped giving out readings and telling the specialised staff on that neonatal unit that things were ok or alerting them when they were  not. They did not have blankets covering them, they had bubble wrap, which of course is an excellent way to keep premature babies warm. It makes me laugh to think about that now especially as both the girls love popping the bubbles on bubble wrap, they would have loved it!!!

The staff on the delivery suite and the Neonatal ward at SINGLETON HOSPITAL in SWANSEA were amazing. I can not even begin to express the immense gratitude I feel towards them for their dedication to Bo, Hope and Morganna. If they have ever found themselves wondering what happened to the two beautiful brave little girls that were born that day, well now they will know.

Before leaving the hospital we went to see Bo, she was heavily sedated and not really with it at all, her partner was already there. The staff nurse on the ward said that Bo needed to sleep and get some rest, and that it was probably be best if we left and got some sleep as well aware that we had been with Bo all the time.

I can clearly remember leaving that hospital, it was pouring with rain, but I did not notice. I needed to phone my Mam and tell her the news so that she could let everyone else know. Kevin forever practical said that it would be a good idea to go and get something to eat and drink before we set out on our journey back to Pembrokeshire. Not wanting to go into Swansea and not really knowing the area too well we opted for the local "Tesco's" as it had a café. When we got there I decided to ring Mam, she answered the phone "Mam it's me" I got no further I started to cry hearing my mothers voice had made me give way I virtually collapsed, I was tired, emotional, and hungry, for the first time in a long time I wanted my Mam to hold me, to stoke my hair the way she does and to tell me it was all going to be OK. Kevin took my mobile from me and gave her the news, she was crying too.

We did go into Tesco's and have coffee and something to eat, I must have looked an awful mess, all tear stained, clothes crumpled and so tired I was falling asleep..

When we arrived at Mam's she was waiting, she took me in her arms and rocked me until I stopped crying, I had no tears left, I was emotionally drained.

Writing this has evoked such feelings in me that I am crying, Its as if time has taken me all the way back there right now and yet it all seems like such a long time ago now, I could do with a cuddle from my Mam right now, but she is 4 hours away. I love you Mam.

We returned to Oxford and over the next couple of days Bo rang me several times asking me to ring her partner as he had gone home after we had to fetch some clothes for her and was supposed to return to the hospital, he did not. I did eventually get hold of him, I had tried many times but he was not picking up his mobile, when he did he was drunk, I told him to pull himself together and go to the hospital to Bo, that she needed him. She did not see him again until she was transferred back to her local hospital on 27th February 2002.

"Today 7% of all babies are born prematurely - but nine out of ten of them will go on to lead normal and healthy lives."

# DELIGHTED AND PROUD TO ANNOUNCE

We the proud Grandparents are pleased to announce the premature, but safe arrival of

Hope Elizabeth Rose. 2lb 15ozs. Time 10.24am
And
Morgan Eleanor Grace. 3lb 5ozs. Time 10.25am

On 23$^{rd}$ February 2002 at Singleton Hospital Swansea. With endless gratitude to the wonderful staff on the antenatal and neonatal wards.

What Grandparent wouldn't be proud, I felt like standing on the highest mountain and shouting to the whole world that my beautiful Granddaughters had arrived, and that they were safe. The girls were born 10 weeks early, they put up such a strong fight right from the beginning and they continued to fight, and to win. I wondered at their determination, and at how quickly they progressed. One thing was for sure they had inherited the Stowell determination, they were fighters.

On 27$^{th}$ February the neonatal team at Singleton Hospital assessed the twins and made the decision that Hope and Morganna (Morgan) were stable enough to transfer back to their local hospital in Pembrokeshire, which was Withybush General. Bo had been discharged as she was now on the mend. It must have been hard for her to make that journey, knowing that she would have to leave the girls at the local hospital ,but at least they were close to her and visiting them each day would be easy as she lived in the town. My precious Grand daughters made that 2 hour journey back to Pembrokeshire in an ambulance.

Kevin and I were both back at work. I found this difficult as I wanted to be back home in Pembrokeshire, but we had a life here in Oxfordshire, Oliver was in school and one thing was sure, both Kevin and I knew that we would need to work as we could see that the twins were going to need a lot of basic equipment and clothes over the coming months, even years, we were only too pleased to be able to do this for them all seeing it as one of those things that as Grandparents you just get on and do, after all you just want to help and to give them a good start in life. The girls were so tiny that getting clothes to fit them was at first difficult I had no idea where to find them, but eventually I found shops that did stock clothes for premature babies, but even the smallest of these would have swamped the girls in the beginning as they were so tiny. The palms of Hope's hands were the size of my small finger nail, her head the size of a tennis ball. Morganna was slightly bigger, she had the smallest cutest ears I had ever seen, and they were so tiny.

That first weekend after the girls were born couldn't come fast enough for me, for I was returning home to Pembrokeshire to see Bo and the girls. I had to make this journey alone as Kevin was working that weekend. I packed my bag, and one for Oliver, dropped him off with his friend for the weekend, kissing and hugging him goodbye, promising that I would say Hi to the babies he hadn't seen yet, and off I went.

I met Bo at the hospital the following day it was the 3rd of March 2002, it was to become one of those dates that stay with you forever, a special day, a magical day. It was the first time I was ever going to hold a baby so small in my arms, I cried as the nurse on SCABU, placed Hope into my arms, she was absolutely beautiful, apart from being so tiny she did not look like a premature baby at all, her skin was perfect, her face was perfect, she was perfect.

I did not get to hold Morganna as she slept through my whole visit, babies grow when they are sleeping, but I stood by her incubator and was able to touch her tiny body, as she slept so peacefully. Hope and Morganna needed all the sleep they could get. This most special of days is etched on my heart; it is yet another one of those memories that will always evoke tears in me.

My Mam also came to the hospital with me that day, she to held for the first time her tiny baby great grand daughter, we both cried that day.

Bo's partner was also there that day, and I watched him with these tiny babies and for a short time I allowed myself to believe that this man also had a loving side, he appeared to be both gentle and caring towards the girls. I can never doubt that he did anything but love the girls, all four of them as each one arrived, but he was not able to be devoted to them, he could never see further than his own life, which is a shame because I think if things had been different he could have made a great father, but things weren't different, I was living in the real world, he was not and it scared me to death. I did not trust him with my daughter or my grand daughters, I still don't, I will not allow him anywhere near them.

I returned once more to my home in Oxfordshire, back to work and back to the familiar routine that was my home life. I was working for Age Concern, my work colleague Lynn had become a good friend, she is still one of my most treasured friends, she is also Hope and Morganna's Godmother, Lynn along with all the volunteers at that branch of Age Concern somehow managed to get me through the days in between my visits to Pembrokeshire, which were happening every weekend, one weekend I would go alone, with Kevin and Oliver accompanying me on the alternate ones.

On March 8th 2002 once again our car headed down the M4 and across the Severn Bridge towards Pembrokeshire, there was a very excited young man in our car for that journey, Oliver sat in the back seat, chatting away excitedly, he was looking forward to meeting his little nieces for the first time. The following day Kevin, Oliver and I went along to meet Bo at SCABU. This was day 15 of Hope and Morganna's life; they had come a long way already. When we got there both of them were wide awake, Oliver was thrilled, once again I held Hope in my arms, Bo had Morganna in hers, and the nurse said "Come on then Oliver stand in the middle, let's have a photo of you with the girls" He was made up, his face said it all, he looked like the cat that had got the cream. I held both the girls on this visit. It was the first time I had held Morganna and as I held her I welcomed her to my world.

The girls were getting really fat now! Hope weighed 3lb and 6ozs and Morganna weighed 3lb 12ozs!

I would ring Bo everyday that I was not with her; I would also ring the SCABU ward to find out how the girls were doing. At first they didn't tell me much just that things were alright and that the girls were gaining, it was left to Bo to give me any further information. But it soon became evident that Bo was not visiting everyday, or that when she did her visits were short, I became increasingly concerned. Social services then arranged for a meeting to take place on March 19th 2002.This had been scheduled as a Planning meeting, during which all the people and agency's involved with the care of the girls, could get together with Bo, and her partner and set up a support network that would give them both support in the caring of the twins, the ultimate plan was to get Hope and Morganna home to Bo and her partner, whilst giving them some much needed support. I think any mother of twins even where there are no difficulties to cope with would agree that it is a daunting and frightening thought to suddenly find yourself caring all day and everyday with the tiniest and dependant of babies, let alone two at the same time, Bo was going to need all the support she could get.

I was invited to this meeting as I had expressed my desire to be involved in Hope and Morganna's care to Social services, and that I would do all in my power to support both Bo and her partner in the care of the girls, I was willing to have them for weekend's and to do anything else needed from me, I was willing and able. Thank God for a brilliant social worker.

I attended this meeting alone as Kevin was working and Oliver was at school. I was not worried at all, it was just a planning meeting, and the social worker had told me there was nothing to worry about. I picked Bo and her partner up and we went to the meeting together. I was nervous when I walked into the room in the local council offices where the meeting was taking place; I had not imagined so many other people being there. During this meeting it was decided that because of the seriousness of the case the meeting should be changed to that of a Child Protection Meeting, now I was completely out of my depth, alarm bells were ringing in my head and Bo was besides herself, getting agitated and uncooperative, but then I think I would have been as well if I had been in her position.

Hope and Morganna's names were entered onto the Child Protection Register. I was in a dreadful state, I was alone, I felt numb and if I am honest I really did not fully understand the implications of what was happening that day. I did however know that this was as serious as it gets.

A plan of support was put together over the following few weeks, involving the girls Health visitor, the social worker and Sure Start, it meant that someone would call on Bo and the girls everyday, I felt reassured that this had been done as I knew that it would quickly be picked up if things were going wrong, but I still worried that Bo would in the main be on her own caring for the girls and for her partner who also depended on her. I worried about the difficult times like night feeds, and disturbed sleep, Bo was never very good at having her sleep disrupted.

On 19<sup>th</sup> march the girls had turned the corner they had both crossed the magic 4lb mark, Hope weighing  4lb 3ozs and Morganna 4lb 6ozs Hooray!!!!!!!!!!!!!!

There was still along way to go, the girls were not ready to leave the hospital yet, but they were heading in the right direction.

I continued to ring SCABU to check on the girls progress, things had changed a little now and the staff on SCABU were more accommodating of me, by now they realised that I was fully involved in the girls lives, that I was a continuing support to Bo, they also saw me every weekend, and Bo had given them her permission to talk to me about the girls, at last I felt a part of it all, and not left on the outside and from somewhere looking in.

During April 2002, Bo and her partner were allocated a two bedroom flat, it was not ideal as it was a first floor flat which was going to make it difficult to get a double buggy in and out of, but at least it was a home, until now they had been in a Bed sit. Bo and her partner got the flat ready for the girls coming home. We done what we could and bought baby essentials, I had been collecting baby things such as talc and baby wipes for months.

On the 8<sup>th</sup> April 2002 Bo and her partner stayed overnight to care for the twins at the flat in SCABU, Bo reported to me weeks later that during that overnight stay her partner had attacked her as she nursed one of the girls, it came to light later that this incident had been heard by the nurses on SCABU, but nothing was done about it. Kevin Oliver and I arrived in Pembrokeshire, Bo had asked us to be there and to take all four of them home, and the girls were being discharged.

April 9<sup>th</sup> 2002 we arrived at the hospital to take Bo, her partner and the girl's home. It was an extremely emotional time, we all cried. The nurses that had given Hope and Morganna so much care were also crying. It must be so rewarding to watch as the tiniest of babies thrive to be well enough to go home; they did a fantastic job on that SCABU unit.

Hope weighed 5lb 5ozs Morganna weighed 5lb 8ozs.

Over the next 6 weeks I continued to try and get home to Pembrokeshire every weekend. During the week days someone was calling on Bo and the girls everyday, but from the Friday visit until the Monday visit Bo was alone, she had no support and it was probably needed more on weekends than at any other time, so it felt crucial that I go to see her every weekend if I could. I felt it was especially important as Bo had during this time also told me of incidents of her partner drinking. On May 5th 2002 we travelled to Pembrokeshire again, this time we had agreed to have the girls overnight so that Bo and her partner could spend some time together, we picked the girls up from their home and went to stay at my sisters for the night. Bo rang us to say that her partner was drunk and that he had spoilt the whole evening for her, she was so hurt as she was really looking forward to that evening. About a week later Bo rang me and I as always rang her back -we had an agreement with her that if she rang us we would call her back so that she did not use up all the credit on her mobile as they had no landline. Bo was crying so were he girls and her partner was shouting at the girls to shut up, Bo told me she just wanted to die, I was frantic with worry, I rang the social worker and she called out to see Bo. The social worker and I were so concerned about Bo and the girls that we had a agreement and that was if I had not heard from Bo or had been unable to get hold of her for a day I would ring the social worker who would then call round to check that all was alright, this worked most of the time but of course fell down on the weekends as I could not get hold of the social worker.

Bo Kevin and I had sat down and talked about her situation before the girls had in fact gone home. I told Bo that if she ever at any time told me anything that I thought was putting the girls in danger, that I would inform the social worker, although she did not like this, she appreciated that I had the girls best interests at heart, and believe me I would have done anything to help Bo and the girls and to try and insure their safety.

# Renewing our wedding vows

Back in November 2001 Kevin and I had been discussing our life together and what our love for each other meant, I said to him

"Do you remember when we got married, we both said it was such a great day despite the weather, and the fact that I was sad that so many of my family were not there to share our wonderful day"

"Well come on then lets do it all again" he said to me.

We decided then that we both felt so strongly about retaking our wedding vows, we were still madly in love with each other and decided that now was a good time to think it. It was good to have something nice to look forward to. I had lost 4 stone and needed a new wedding ring as the old one just fell off my finger, and I would not wear one that had not been blessed in church. When Kevin and I got married in 1992 we could not afford a honeymoon, and not all my family were there to share our special day.

"OK then, but only if we are able to have the service in the LADY CHAPEL of ST DAVID'S CATHEDRAL"

On our next visit to Pembrokeshire we made an appointment to see the Cannon of ST David's Cathedral, when we turned up at the Cannons home I knocked on his front door and it was opened by the same CANNON that had Christened Bo at Llanrhian Church in 1981. We discussed why we wanted to renew our vows and he said he would be delighted to officiate over the service and agreed that we could hold our special ceremony in THE LADY CHAPEL. Fetching his dairy he asked when we were thinking of having this great day. To be honest we had not at that point got passed the fact that we wished to renew our vows, but the three of us together set the date, it was going to be the 15th June 2002. In amongst all the uncertainty that surrounded Bo and the twins we suddenly had something positive to channel our thoughts and energy into, we had something to look forward to.

On the drive back to my parents home I said to Kevin

"This is going to be great, by the time June 15th is here the twins will have arrived, and also my eldest son and his partner would have had their new addition by then as well, they already had a daughter (my grand daughter)"

So that was that we all had something to look forward to the following June. I made the invitations and they were sent out, my wedding ring was taken to a goldsmith who melted it down and made me a new one from our original one, I had bought the fabric for my dress which I was making, and after deciding not to have any bridesmaids, I gave in and had my Grand daughter and my niece as my "special girls" for the day. Kevin went to the local wedding /formal hire shop in HAVERFORDWEST and hired his suit - top hat and tails, he looked amazing as he stood there in that shop, and fully clad in the attire he was going to wear. The photographer was already booked and the deposit paid, so it was just the flowers, I went along to a local florist that I have known for a long time and ordered a huge bouquet of sweet peas to carry. We booked a local hotel in St David's for a reception afterwards, and then all we had to do was sit back and wait.

Back home in Oxfordshire I had gone to a wedding fair in Wallingford one afternoon where I had seen the work of a clever lady who made tiara's form tatted lace, they were exquisite, I had not decided what I was going to wear on my head and I thought that one of these tiara's was just the sort of thing I would like., so I commissioned her to make me one using silver thread, it is the most delicate and beautiful piece of work I have seen, I was so delighted with it.. She rang one day to let me know it was finished so I went alone to her home to pick in up, in the tissue wrapping was not only the tiara she had handmade for me but also she had made me two small silver butterflies One day I hope that Hope and Morganna may choose to wear my silver tatted lace tiara, they sometimes ask me now if they can see my "special crown" and they smile broadly as I place it on their heads and let them have a look in their pink bedroom mirror.

I started work on my gown and had settled on a two piece, which consisted of a long skirt with a flowing short train on the back and a corseted top, the fabric I had already chosen I had seen months before it was lovely a shade of blue that was electric to look at. It took me many hours of cutting and sewing to make that gown, but when it was finished I loved it, it was perfect. I was so pleased it had turned out so well. I hid it away from Kevin until the big day; he had no idea what I was wearing. Soon it was time to turn my attentions to what my special girls would wear, I found two white cotton dresses and added to these some blue sequins that matched my dress, and then I bought some white ballet shoes for them and spent more hours sticking sequins onto those as well

As the months rolled on I went through some pretty awful and worrying times with Bo and looking forward to "our special day" kept me going. We wanted to have a few days alone after we had retaken our vows so we had asked my Mam and Dad to have Oliver for us so that we could get away somewhere nice - just the two of us.

I think someone up there really had it in for us, as to this day Kevin and I have not been away together alone without the children.

Christmas came and went and so did the New Year, which was followed quickly by Valentines Day, and then my world, began to crumble and fall apart.

Events overtook us as Hope and Morganna's early arrival into this world threw us all off course, we considered cancelling our special day, but decided against it, we had by this time paid for everything that needed paying for, everything was set in place and it seemed a shame, so we decided to go ahead, working on the theory that by then Bo and her partner would have settled down into the role of parent's.

Neither Kevin nor I had any idea what the following months were going to bring us.

Kevin's mother was very ill she had breast cancer and it was now terminal. This was yet another thing that would put pressure on us. We went to the Heath Hospital in Cardiff to visit her taking Oliver with us. One day in May Kevin was told that his mother was dying, she had very little time left, and he so desperately wanted to get back to Wales to see her before she died. The farm that Kevin was then managing the dairy herd for was silage making they had about one day left before it was all in and sheeted down. Silage making is a busy time on the farm, it is when the grass grown to feed the herd over the winter is harvested and brought in to the farm and stored in specially built silage clamps, as the tractors bring in trailer after trailer of grass, which they unload into these clamps a tractor rolls it, which basically means that a driver skilfully drives a tractor over and over the pile of grass, which compresses it into a solid mass, this process is repeated until the clamp is full and then it is sheeted down with heavy gauge black plastic to protect it and then it is weighted down using old tyres - a laborious job, which has to be done. It is important to get the sheeting down all finished as soon as possible as the last thing a farmer wants is for his silage to be rained on. Kevin had asked if anyone could cover him, we even rang the manager who was in charge of the contract for the agency Kevin worked for, he had explained how desperately he needed to get away and see his mother before she died, but no one would cover for him. I have always felt pretty annoyed at the response he got from the agency that day, really the manager should have done the decent thing and come out and covered Kevin's absence, he did not, and by the time Kevin was able to leave the farm his mother had passed away. That manager for the agency managed to completely loose any respect Kevin held for them that day.

We went home for Kevin's mother's funeral, coming back to Oxfordshire the following day. Kevin became difficult to live with as he struggled to cope with his bereavement, and his increasing work load. I tried so hard to support him but I too was going through hell, the twins had arrived and were surrounded by uncertainty. Both of us were trying to cope any way we could with our own individual pain.

We were both as determined as each other that come what may our day was going to happen.

The month of May left us and flaming June arrived, Bo had told me that she couldn't afford to buy the girls a pretty dress each for our special day. I had told her not to worry and that if she did not mind I would go into Oxford and buy something for them, she was thrilled, so the following day I rushed into Oxford and bought two of the tiniest pink dresses that I had ever seen, they were for small early newborn babies up to 7lb, Bo had never worn such a small dress as a baby. I also found a couple of small white cotton hats. My Mam had crocheted them a white cardigan each, so they were kitted out as well.

We had a leek in our roof here last week, our attic room is the girls playroom, we lost most of the girls toys as they have been contaminated with a mixture of rainwater and the horsehair padding that was used many years ago to insulate the roof. When I was going through our things up there I came across a box which contained my wedding dress that I had worn when Kevin and I got married back in 1992, and the bridesmaid's dress Bo had worn. Also in the box were the pink dresses I had bought and the cardigans my Mam had crocheted for the girls to wear the day we renewed our vows. I have now washed them and stored them in the girl's special memory box, which is where we put all kinds of special things that they will enjoy looking at when they are old enough, there are lots of special things tucked away in the memory box.

# "NO PLEASE GOD NO"

On June 6<sup>th</sup> 2002 a very tearful Bo rang me and asked me to ring her back

I rang her back immediately

"Whatever is the matter" I asked her, not daring to think as goodness only knows what had happened this time.

"Mammy help me" she said through her tears

There was a lot of background noise; I could also hear the girls crying. She did not say anything so I shouted at her trying to keep calm

"what's the matter with the girls Bo, why are they crying?"

Bo went on to tell me that she was at a mates flat, this usually meant that everyone there was drunk, stoned and possibly both. She told me that she had left the girls at this flat with her partner whilst she had gone off with a friend and that when she had returned she found both the girls crying and their baby slings were wet through with cider. I was really cross with her and told her to get the girls out of there immediately and get them back to her flat, and then to change and feed them and put them to bed. I also told her to lock her partner out, as I feared what would happen should he go back to the flat worse for wear. She had calmed down a little and agreed that she would take the girls, but then she said she couldn't cope on her own as it meant carrying both of them, I replied

"Well get your friend to help you she is there isn't she, if she will go back with you she can help to carry one of the girls and to help change and feed them?"

Bo replied that she was and that she would ask her, she did and this girl friend had agreed to go back to her flat with her and the girls. I told Bo I would ring her in half an hour, which would give her time to get back to the flat and secure the door.

"Its OK mum I will ring you as soon as I get into the flat"

Bo did not ring I was going frantic, worried that she may have run out of credit I kept ringing her mobile but it was switched off and going straight to answer phone.

"Bo, please ring me back" I cried as I left yet another message.

I was worried sick, I asked Kevin what I should do and we agreed that if I had not heard from her in half on hour I was to give her local police station a ring and ask them to go and find her an the girls, this would have had devastating repercussions for Bo as the girls were both still on the Protection Register. All kinds of awful scenes were running through my mind, I was imagining terrible things, and I was now beside myself.

At 11pm that night Bo rang me she was screaming,

"Mammy, Mammy they have taken my girl"

"Who has taken the girls, what the hell are you talking about"

"I'm going to get them"

She was making no sense; I was by now imagining that the girls had been taken by her partner or someone else that had been in the flat.

"Who are you going to get Bo, for Christ's sake talk to me, what the bloody hell has happened"

Bo went on to tell me that her partner had attacked her in the street earlier that evening, she told me that he was hitting her whilst she was pushing the girls in their pushchair, she also told me that she had self mutilated again cutting her leg this time.

None of this mattered; all that mattered was that I found out who had taken the girls and where they were.

"Bo where are the girls, who has them?"

Fear was gripping at the pit of my stomach and twisting it into a knot, my blood began to run cold and in the few seconds that it took before she answered me I was beginning to imagine all sorts of things.

"Christ Bo answer me what has happened to the girls Bo" I screamed at her.

"The police have taken them, Mammy they have taken my babies, they won't give them back or let me see them and they have taken them up to the hospital. Please help me Mammy, please make them give my babies back, or I shall kill myself"

I was shaking, I wanted to be sick, and I don't know what I feared more, the fact that the girls were in hospital, were they hurt? What had happened? Or had Bo's threat to kill herself frightened me?

"If anything has happened to the girls Bo or anyone has hurt them, so help me I'll"

I stopped there, remembering her threat I knew it would be useless to continue, I couldn't let her hear my fear, couldn't be angry, not yet, must get the facts first, must check on the girls. My head took over from my heart and I said to her

"I will ring the police station see what I can find out"

I did ring the police station in her town, they told me they had attended an incident and that they had taken the girls on an emergency protection order and that they had placed them on the children's ward at Withybush General Hospital, they also told me the girls were unharmed, and asked me to give the children's ward a ring to let them know which twin was which and

79

of any medical needs they may have had. The duty sergeant also gave me the telephone number of the duty social worker and told me to ring them to see what was going to happen to the girls.

Ringing that children's ward broke my heart. I spoke to the staff nurse, who was lovely, I told her how to identify each of the girls. Hope is the very fair one, she is the smaller of the two, Morganna (Morgan) is the one with the tiny ears, and she also has a strawberry birthmark on the outside ankle joint on her foot. As I spoke to her tears were streaming down my face, Kevin was stroking my back as if trying to comfort a child, and the pain I was feeling was so intense it was crushing me.

"Try not to worry too much the girls are safe here," said the staff nurse.

"Please give them a big cuddle from me, tell them Grandma loves them so very much"

"I will go right now and give them both a hug from their Grandma she said"

Bless those nurses who on that night took care of my precious girls. I was so many miles away, and it frustrated me, I wanted to be there, to hold both of the girls and let them know ii was there for them, that they were not alone and to tell them over and over again how much I loved them - I loved them more than life itself.

I then rang the duty officer for social services; she tried to reassure me telling me to give the girl's social worker a ring first thing in the morning. There was nothing more I could do so I said I would ring them first thing in the morning, I also told her that I had spoken to the hospital and would be doing so again before I went to bed and again first thing in the morning.

Then I had to ring my daughter back, God alone knows how I managed to hold it together throughout that call, I was so angry with her, but I daren't tell her as I was so worried that she would put the phone down and harm herself - or worse carry out her threat to kill herself. I told her I would ring the social worker in the morning and then give her a ring straight away. She was crying and angry, she was after the world, telling me that the police had no right to take her girl's from her. Everyone was her enemy, even me.

I cried all night that night, my world came crashing down around me as I realised that this was what I had feared most.

"We can't loose them now Kevin we just can't. What can I do?"

Kevin held me all through that night; it must have been terrible for him to watch me breaking. I am such a strong person, it's always me that in a moment of need is the one who can see through a problem and think clearly, but not this time, this was one time when I couldn't see through anything.

Throughout the night I lay in the comfort and security of Kevin's arms, the warmth of him, and the familiar smell of him - even this brought me no sleep.

That night I thought about my daughter, I tried to work out where I had gone wrong with her, where did I fail that part of motherhood? You know the part where you teach your children to love as they have been loved, to respect and to treasure, to value all they have.

How could she let this happen, why couldn't she for once put her children's needs before those of her or her partners? Why hadn't she taken the girls home that night when I told her to. Why God Oh Why? I have never been able to find the answer to these questions, no matter how hard I tried.

At 4.30am Kevin went out to work, he really didn't want to go, he knew I was in hell, and he wanted to be there with me.

"Its OK love go on I will be alright" I lied as he tenderly kissed me and ran his fingers through my hair.

"Ring if you need me" he said as he quietly walked out through the bedroom door.

I lay there in the dark willing the dawn to break. They say don't they that things will look better in the morning, well as the dawn broke and the birds started singing nothing in my world looked any better, the uncertainty and worry was still there.

I wandered what the girls would be doing, had they slept at all, were they fretting for their Mammy? I know I will ring the hospital I thought at least that will give me something to do for a minute. I rang and spoke to the nurse who told me that the girls had had a comfortable night, Oh Christ not that old cliché I thought, and then remembered that I had said that to many patients family members who had rung in to enquire how their loved ones were. I made myself a promise there and then that if ever I went back into caring I would never say that to anyone ever again. "Please give them a kiss and a hug for me, thank you for looking after them" I said to her as I replaced the receiver. I hope she did realise just how grateful I was.

I waited all night for that clock to reach 9am, and had at one point walked around the house checking the time on all the clocks and decided that the one that was fastest was correct! Even so 9am was a long time coming. At last it was 9 o clock and I rang social services only to find out that they were all in an emergency meeting.

"Don't worry" she told me "Someone will ring you back as soon as possible".

DON'T WORRY, DON'T WORRY, what the hell was she thinking off saying something like that to me; I was beside myself with worry. I wanted someone to speak to me right now, didn't she understand that.

I rang Bo and told her that I was now waiting for social services to ring me back and that I would ring her again as soon as I had spoken to them. She was calmer, but I was seething inside as in the background I could hear her partners voice calling to her, asking her who she was talking to.

"What the hell is he doing there Bo, are you completely stupid"

"Don't start Mum, he has a right to be here, this is where he lives"

God damn and blast her, where was her common sense, why the hell was she behaving like this? Try as I might I could not understand her behaviour at all. Maybe she needed him to be with her, maybe in some way it brought her comfort. I will never know, I will never understand, never.

I went into the kitchen and again I wiped down the kitchen worktops, again I walked out into the garden and aimlessly wandered around the garden, walking through the archway that led form the back garden to the front I made my way to the flowerbeds and dead headed the few flowers that were dying. I stood there listening to the birds singing and the traffic passing down the road and I can remember thinking that it was wrong, my world was falling apart and yet everyone else was carrying on as if there was nothing wrong, to the rest of the world it was just another June morning.

I went back into the house, dropping the dead flower heads off into the rubbish bin on the way in, making a mental note that the bin bag was full and that I would have to change it later. I put the kettle on again, tipping the contents of my coffee mug into the sink, ah well that's another on I didn't drink. Making myself yet another mug of coffee - well it was something to do, something to occupy a few minutes of those endless hours, till the clock struck 9 o clock

Every second that blasted kitchen clock ticked by I felt, every tick got louder and louder, it was like a bomb ticking away in my head,

TICK,

TICK,

TICK,

How I never took it down from the wall and threw it against something and put an end to its ticking once and for all I really don't know.

Eventually after what seemed like a lifetime the phone rang and the familiar voice of the girl's social worker was on the other end.

"Keri, I am so sorry, this must be hell for you"

Well she was getting pretty close to how my world felt, but I felt sure that hell couldn't be this bad.

She went on to tell me what had happened and why the girls were taken from Bo.

"Keri, there's something I have to ask you."

I knew her tone well enough by now; she was finding this as difficult as I was.

"Ask away" I replied.

"Can you come and get Bo and the girls, we have spoken to Bo and she has agreed to come back to Oxfordshire with you that is if you still wish to offer Bo your support with the girls"

What a stupid question of course I wanted to help and of course Bo and the girls could come here.

She went on to explain to me what had happened the night before, she told me why the police had placed the girls on an emergency protection order, and as usual Bo had only given me a few of the facts, she hadn't told me the full story, but that was not so unusual for her, Bo had made accusations to the duty social worker that her partner had been flicking one of the girls in the face until she cried, and apparently my daughter had gone on to say that it was alright because she used to cuddle her until she stopped crying I was annoyed to the point where I was ready to explode at my daughter, and at that moment would have gladly served the time for what I felt like doing to her partner, how dare that animal do such a thing to them, how dare my daughter let him do it. I could neither do or say anything not if it put at risk Bo changing her mind to stay with us. It all had to be left unsaid, but inside of me it festered away for years.

The social worker went on to explain that the hospital would only be allowed to release Hope and Morganna into my care, those were the instructions that social services had given the hospital.

"How will they know who I am, do I need to take proof of identity with me?"

"No that won't be necessary I have given them a description of you, they will know who you are. Try not to worry too much Keri, I know that wont be easy, but I also know you can do this"

I decided to be prepared and make sure I had my driving licence with me just in case. The alterative to the girls returning with me was to have them placed into foster care. Now there was no way on God's earth that I was going to allow that to happen. I had already put up quite a fight on the girls behalf, but this was to be nothing compared to what the next 10 months were going to demand from me, and the more the situation was going to demand from me the more I found of myself to give.

"Right, I can't leave here until I have arranged for someone to care for Oliver, as he is on half term, but that won't be a problem. I will have to travel back to Pembrokeshire on my own as Kevin is working and there is no one to cover for him"

"That's alright she said, just give me a ring later and let me know when you think you will be here and I can inform the hospital. I will ring you first thing on Monday morning; see how things went over the weekend"

Poor Kevin came in for his lunch to find me frantically trying to pack a bag. We had not even discussed this part; we had not sat down and talked over what we would do if push came to shove. I knew that whatever decision I made he would fully support me, when I told him he said "its OK cariad, just go and bring them all home, we will manage somehow, and we always do.

I also had my sister coming over that night, she was coming over with her children for the weekend, blast I thought what can I do, and she will be on her way by now. I rang her mobile and quickly explained to her what was going on.

"There's food in I told her, everything's here"

"You go" she said "I will sort tea out for everyone, and I will make the beds up, you just go and do what you have to do, Ker, please take it easy"

I couldn't think straight, my head was all over the place. What the hell was happening? God why was this happening?

Kevin asked if I would be alright driving back to Pembrokeshire on my own. I said I would manage somehow, I had to do this, and the girls needed me more than ever now.

At the last minute as I walked out of my dining room I picked up a handful of CD's to listen to on the way. I never did listen to them; they remained in a pile on the floor of the car.

The motorway was busy and I was in a hurry why does that always happen? Then I got caught up in a traffic accident that had happened just minutes before I got to the scene, and then it poured down with rain, just like every other time when I go home to Pembrokeshire. This was not going to be an easy drive. Mam was in Carmarthen shopping and I had rung her to say

I was on my way home. I have to stop in Tesco's I said as I will need to buy baby milk and bottles etc for the girls. I will meet you there she said. I arrived at Tesco's about 6.30pm, exhausted, after an awful journey.

I did not need to ask Mam how I looked, her face told me

"Oh Ker, come here love"

I did not need asking twice and I couldn't have cared less if the whole world was watching me I needed my Mam to hold me, I needed someone to take care of me. We sat and drank coffee and ate biscuits, there was no other food available on the café counter, and I hadn't eaten all day. We walked around the store picking up nappies, baby milk, bottles, sterilising tablets. I had nothing at all for those poor little girls; you name it I had to buy it, as I was worried that Bo might not have all the things the girls needed. Now looking back I think deep down inside I knew she was not going to make that return journey with me.

That drive home was the most heartbreaking one I thought I would ever make

Little did I know............... Little did I know.......................

Mam and I arrived in Haverfordwest and I rang Bo to tell her to meet me outside the local cinema, I had no intentions of going to her flat, as I feared that her partner may have been there, she had already been told by the social worker and by me that when she met me her partner was not to come anywhere near me. My hatred of him was intense, I was also afraid of what he was capable of doing.

When I spoke to Bo she told me that she had decided not to come back to Oxfordshire with me and the girls, saying that she needed to be with her partner. At that point I could have really lashed out at her, the stupid girl I thought. Instead I quietly asked her why she wasn't coming, pointing out that her coming with me was part of the plan that she had drawn up with the social worker earlier on in the day, had she not given any thought o the fact that the girls needed her?. As I tried to coax her into changing her mind, my head was racing ahead. What if she didn't come back with me, what should I do? The social worker were not available on the weekends, OH MY GOD what should I do? Calmly I began to think, there was only one thing I could do, and I would have to take the girls back to Oxfordshire with me. With or without Bo Hope and Morganna would be coming home with me.

Bo agreed to meet me, but when walked around the corner and walked towards my car, she was holding the hand of her partner, he was with her, they both got into my car I was furious, she shouted at me that he had a right to be there. I told her that he had no right at all and that she had already been told she was to meet me alone. At this point my Mam got out of the car opened the back door and told him to get out.

I asked her once more to reconsider coming with me, but she was refused to come. I told her that I was going to fetch the girls from the hospital and needed her to give me the girl's car seats for the girls; she said I would need to go to the flat to pick them up. I arranged to meet her at the flat in 20 minutes. Pulling myself together I started up the car, I had to stay strong, I could do this, I had to do it, the girls were depending on me. It was me or foster care. Shaking that thought from my head I put the car into drive and pulled away from where I had been parked.

I was so worried about Bo's partner being at the flat and feared a confrontation with him and Bo that I decided to call at the local police station and ask them to attend with me, which they did. Bo was furious, she handed over the car seats, the girls Moses baskets, and a small bag of their things, the police helped me load the few possessions Bo had given me for the girls into the car. It was an awful situation to be in. To have to take the police to my own daughters flat was the most unthinkable of things to have to do, but I was to have to endure many more unthinkable things before this was all over.

My heart was breaking, this was not what I wanted to happen, I wanted Bo to coma as well, but still she refused, not even the police could persuade her. She asked me to bring the girls for her to see them before I set off home to Oxfordshire with them later that night, I said I would think about it, but the police told me not to, they said go straight home to Oxfordshire with the girls, as they felt the situation with Bo and her partner was too volatile, they did not want me caught up in anything. They asked me what time I thought I would be leaving Pembrokeshire, they were going to let the station know, so that if I needed any help, it would be at hand.

I arrived at Withybush General Hospital and made my way to the children's ward, and met the staff nurse; they were expecting me as I had rung them to tell them I was on my way.

She led me into a small side ward and there were my beautiful little girls, they were wearing the clothes that they had been wearing the night before when the police picked them up, little blue pinafore dresses and navy blue tights, the hospital had them laundered for the girls. I picked Morganna up and just held her so close to me I could hear my Mam gently saying

"Come on Ker, it will be alright, you can cope with all this you are so strong"

I knew I was strong, already in my life I had lived through so much, but this time I felt so small, this time I felt so ashamed.

Shame was beginning to touch my life with its ugliness. I was choking back the tears as I explained to the staff nurse on the children's ward that Bo was not coming back to Oxfordshire with me. I was so ashamed.

I was also beginning to understand the true feeling of lasting sorrow. But a much deeper and bitter sorrow was still to touch my life.

I put Morganna into her car seat and picked up my little Hope, she has always been "my little Hope", when I held her the images of one weekend flashed through my mind. We had arrived at Bo's flat to find things a little fraught Hope and Morganna were both crying, Bo had Morganna in her arms, Hope was in her chair, Bo and her partner favoured Morganna over Hope. I picked her up and she was like a rag doll, she had been crying for so long, I took her into the bedroom and cradled her in my arms singing to her until she eventually fell asleep. Here I was again with this tiny precious bundle in my arms. I looked at both Hope and Morganna wondering what their future held for them. They did not ask to be brought into this world, they had done nothing, they were tiny and vulnerable, and they didn't deserve this. I looked at both of them trying to see if they had any marks on their faces. Which one of them had she accused her partner of flicking in the face? To this day I have never been told - and if I ever asked her she always replied that she had lied to the duty social worker that night just to get her partner into trouble.

My words came back to me

"I will be there for you no matter what"

Well Mam you were right I am strong, but this was bigger than me, this was bigger than all of us. Sometimes over the months and years that followed I often wandered where I got the strength from.

Mam and I walked away from the children's ward and towards the lift hand in hand, each one of us carrying one of the girls, as we walked through the hospital we were greeted with admiring glances from people, who smiled at us, I couldn't smile back. How could they have ever known the pain behind the tears that were rolling freely down my face. That walk through the hospital was the longest walk of my life, and although the tiny baby I carried weighed no more than a few pounds, it felt as if I was carrying the weight of the world in my arms that night, so heavy was my burden.

As we reached the main doors leading out of the hospital my heart started pounding, What if Bo and her partner were outside, what if they tried to snatch the girls. I tightened my grip on Morganna's seat, and on my Mam's hand, explaining my fears to my Mam, we decided that it might be safer if I went and got the car and brought it up to the main doors. Leaving Mam in the safety of the hospital foyer I went to get the car.

I left that hospital with a heart torn in two, and a head that was racing ahead of me, so many questions -not one answer.

We put the girls in the car, I fastened car safety belts securely around their seats, got into the drivers seat and drove away into the darkness.

We went to Mam's home, Dad was there waiting, he was in an awful state, I don't think any of us could really work out why this was happening. Mam was concerned about me driving back home again, it was late, I had been driving all day, but I had to get back, Mam, Dad and I decided it was best for Mam to come back on that return journey home to Oxfordshire with me, we were all concerned about how I would manage with the girls as well. I was so grateful not to have had to make that journey on my own as goodness only knows how I would have coped if I had needed to do any of the practical things on my journey home like go to the loo.

The responsibility of having the girls was just beginning to sink in; I was beginning to see what was lying ahead of me.

We left Pembrokeshire; I drove home to Oxfordshire on autopilot. I had to stop at one of the service station along the way, as I pulled up I was comforted by the police car that was parked outside. Mam stayed in the car with the girls whilst I ran in to the loo and to get us both a coffee. Whilst I was waiting to be served I asked the police if the road ahead was all clear, and how long it would take me to reach my junction off the M4, they knew who I was where I had started my return journey home to Oxfordshire, and exactly where I was going.

Hope and Morganna slept all the way home to Oxfordshire

Someone was watching over us all that night.

Over the following years, that someone whoever it was watched over me many, many times.

I am so grateful; that they did watch over me

I arrived home in Oxfordshire to be greeted by my wonderful husband, and the rest of my family.

I placed the girls on our pine farmhouse table in their car seats, just like I had done hundreds of times with Oliver when he was a baby, but this time was so different, and I fell into Kevin's arms and cried.

We fed the girls, washed and changed them and then tried to get them to settle for the night in the Moses baskets that I had brought back with me from Pembrokeshire. The girls were both restless and would not settle each time I placed them gently into their baskets they awoke and cried. The poor little mites must have been terrified. In the last 24 hours they had been taken from a rowdy, smoky party in a small flat that was overcrowded with people who were drinking, smoking and taking goodness knows what, put into a police car and taken to and left on the children's ward of the local hospital where they had spent the night, then the following day they had been picked up by the only familiar person they had seen in 24 hours, me, I had then put them in my car and driven them 5 hours down the M4 to my home. Quite a journey for such tiny babies they must have been shattered, confused and anxious. What should I do? It had been 9 years since I had had a baby in my home for anything more than a day. My head was swimming, come on old girl think, I told myself. Well I could try walking and singing them to sleep that sometimes worked with Oliver, but Oh God, I was so tired, I was emotionally and physically shattered, every part of me aches. All I wanted to do was sleep, but I couldn't sleep, not yet.

OK then, there was nothing else for it, they would have to come into bed with us, that never failed to work with any of my own children, but these were not my children, oh God what should I do. Oh to heck with it I thought I can only try. So we gently placed the girls in between us side by side so that they could touch and smell each other. Eventually they both drifted off into sleepy land, Kevin also drifted nervously off to sleep, and he was afraid he would roll over and squash Morganna who was nearest to him. I lay in our double bed, half hanging off the edge next to Hope, she was so small. Morganna was just 9lb 9ozs and Hope was 9lb 6ozs when they came to me, they were just over 3 months old. When Oliver was born he actually weighed 9lb 10ozs, at birth he was 1oz heavier that Morganna was at 3 months old

I lay there for hours just watching the girls; I was cuddling up to Hope. To this day when the girls awake they always come into our bed for a cuddle, and if Kevin is not at work Morganna gets in his side or clambers over me so that she can get to him for a cuddle, and Hope gets in my side and cuddles up to me, inevitably we will be joined by Oliver who is now nearly 13 years old and he too will get a cuddle off both of the girls, they absolutely worship him, and the feeling is mutual. You will be pleased to hear that we did buy a new bed, our expanded family outgrew the old antique double, so we replaced it with a king sized sleigh bed. Now the girls think this bed is fantastic fun as they bounce on it, and use its tall footboard as an imaginary horse and sit akimbo it shouting with glee giddy up horsy - there is no such thing as a quiet lie- in in this house!!!

## June 6th 2002, on this day my life changed forever.

*"My darling girls this was how you came to us. This was how I brought you to the place you know as home, just two tiny babies, their car seats, their Moses basket's and a few clothes. This was when you began to fill my life, all our lives, and our home. I was sad, very, very sad - I wanted you to be with your mum, with my Bo, but it wasn't to be. From the very first day that you came into our home you took over in the nicest possible way, our home became a place of safety, a place to grow, a place to learn to love and to be loved, a place where you and I together have learned so much and shared so much. I no longer wore a suit and went to work; I no longer had time to put on any makeup. I stayed at home with both of you and Oliver. It has all been worth every tear, every lost nights sleep. I love you both so very dearly."*

# *I DON'T KNOW WHY*

I was totally shattered, I had lain awake for hours just watching the girls sleeping, watching their tiny bodies move in their sleep, their chests rising and falling gently in a rhythm.

Until I drifted off to sleep. I was woken by the sounds of babies crying, my mind was far away then, I realised the babies I could hear were the two little bundles I had brought home in the early hours. I lay there holding you both crying my heart out, it was a while before the three of us stopped crying, I'm not sure which one of us stopped first, eventually all three of us lay there calm, I watched you both, your tiny hands were waving around as if painting imaginary pictures in the air, I watched the expressions on your faces, Hope was screwing her face up tight and Morganna staring into midair, probably wandering where on earth she was, her eyes had focused on the light shade above our bed. Looking at you both I felt an overpowering sense of protectiveness, I could have lain there with you for ever, all the heartache and uncertainty seemed so far away. For what seemed like the first time in weeks I found myself smiling, it was the most serene of moments, and I shall never forget it as long as I live

## Saturday June 7th 2002

Hope and Morganna - This was the first day of the rest of our lives together.

I should have been at work, but as Bo never came back with me to Oxfordshire, I had to take unpaid leave, a minor detail in the bigger scale of things, but that did not make me feel any the less guilty that I had to let my work colleagues down, this was going to be the first time of many that I would have to let them down over the next few months that followed

I could hear the noise downstairs as my sister Deb's was sorting out her children, the house was beginning to wake up, the familiar footsteps of my Mam made their way across the landing and down the stairs to join my sister, and the upstairs of my home fell silent again, the only sound I could hear was the synchronized breathing of the girls as they lay either side of me. I realized that my breathing had also fallen into step with theirs.

Deb's, my sister brought me a cup of tea, the two of us sat there on my bed as we have done so many times, the only thing different this time was that  my bed had two pairs of eyes staring up at us from two most beautiful perfect little heads.

Deb's and I have always been very close, she is eight years younger than I am, and we shared everything, even our bed when we were young. I can remember feeling this huge sense of pride and responsibility when as a baby she was put into my small bedroom, we shared that room for years. I think we both felt the same on that morning in June 2002. We watched Hope and Morganna and both knew what a special relationship they would enjoy as they grew, it is such a wonderful thing to love somebody else so much that you treasure them through thick and thin.

Eventually Deb's and I took the girls downstairs, much to the children's joy. Oliver was waiting to greet his two nieces, and Deb's children Abigail and Adam were excited. Between the three of them they kept the girls fairly amused as I got their bottles and then once they were fed Oliver, Abigail and Adam ran around collecting the things that Deb's and I would need to change the girls nappies. Deb's and I washed and changed the girls and then sat them in their chairs, under the watchful three pairs of eyes that had placed themselves around the chairs, now it was time for my breakfast. After I had eaten I rang Bo, I did not get through her mobile was switched off.

Saturday was fairly easy; apart from being exhausted I had plenty of help with Deb and my Mam there. Meals were prepared and cooked by one of us and the girl's needs were just shared out between the three of us. One of the reasons that Deb's had come over was so that Abigail could try on her dress for the renewing of mine and Kevin's wedding vows. This much awaited day was now just a week away. A part of me wished that we had postponed it, but another part of me was excited, this was a day that was about me and Kevin, and we were both looking forward to it, it was just going to be a little different to how we had planned it, but then aren't the best laid plans subject to change. Everything was in place, Kevin or I had contacted everyone and double checked, then checked arrangements again.

On Sunday 8th June 2002, Deb and her children left to return to their home in Pembrokeshire, taking Mam with them. As Deb drove away I felt this sense of loneliness, I was totally on my own with Oliver and the girls, and Kevin was at work. I had no family around me and had only made a few friends in the area.

It was as I shut my front door on the world that I broke down again, this time in absolute total despair. The enormity of the situation was only just beginning to sink in, how was I going to cope, not just on an emotion level but also a practical one too. There was no time to ponder on this for too long as two cries were soon filling our home with requests for another feed, and it hadn't been long since their last feed, now I had another problem, everyone had left and Kevin was at work, Oliver had decided to go over to see his friend who lived just across the road, leaving me totally alone with two hungry, screaming babies, who's cries were getting more and more demanding by the second I had to think about this, and fast. How was I to warm the bottles ready for the girls and at the same time comfort the girls? Mam and Debs had made sure that I had enough bottles made up for the girls to take me through the next 24 hours, so at least I didn't have to make those up as well. I checked on the girls who by now were screaming at fever pitch, but they were safe in their chairs so no harm could come to them. Picking up both the chairs- one in each hand, I took the girls with me into the kitchen. As I moved the chairs the crying stopped only to start again as soon as I placed them down on the floor in the kitchen. Looking down at the chairs two sets of tear stained eyes looked up at me longingly.

"Well then let's get these bottles on shall we"

At the same tome thinking to my self "come on you can do this" trying to ignore the wailing wall that now filled the air in the kitchen I Opened my fridge door taking out 2 bottles from the row that now filled the shelf in my fridge that was usually full of fresh fruit and vegetables.

I put the bottles into a jug and filled the jug up with hot water from the kettle that I had somehow put on to boil without realising that I had done so, with bottles warming, and the girls still wailing, I thought, ah yes coffee, I could rally do with a caffeine fix right now so I made myself a mug of much needed coffee. Right then, let's see. What else do I need? Making the short dash from the kitchen to the dining room I collected my wicker magazine basket, which had up until that morning been full of glossy magazines, now they had now been thrown into a drawer, and now that basket was full of the smallest nappies you would ever have seen, nappy rash cream, baby wipes, tissues, bibs, nappy sacks, etc. I took all the things I needed into the conservatory, placing them next to the chair I was going to sit in and then collected the girls from the kitchen, who by now were wailing on top of their voices, they may have been tiny, but my God they could cry. The crying stopped as I picked up the chairs only to start again as soon as they were placed onto the floor. Which one of the girls did I feed first, how on earth did I decide which one was most in need of feeding, which was a silly thing to think as they were both hungry, whichever one I chose would leave the other crying, so after checking the bottles were at the right temperature, were they? I wasn't too sure, I had always breast fed, but I had read a book, so maybe I was an expert now! Trusting my instinct I picked up both the girls together and somehow managed to hold them both in my arms and feed them at the same time, please don't ask me how I managed this, but I did and before long a peace  descended on my home as two very hungry little girls drank their milk. I can remember thinking how much easier it would have been to breastfeed them both, no bottles to sterilize, no formula to mix up, no reheating of ready made up bottles. Pure and simple everything on tap, much easier than bottles I thought.

When the girls first arrived as well as having no routine, they also couldn't drink the full amount of baby formula that they should have been drinking, this was partly down to how Bo had been feeding them as she would give them a bottle whenever they started to get restless, sometimes this may have been just half an hour after their last feed. It was an almost impossible task, and some days I found myself sitting down for most of the day which was something I had never done in my life, I had always been very active, and I found this so difficult.

The coffee I had made myself was to become the first of many hundred's of mugs I was to make myself over the coming months that just ended up going cold and then thrown away because I had not been able to drink them.

Somehow I managed to feel my way through that Sunday, feeding, winding, changing, singing, soothing, most of which was done through tears that seemed relentless in me, it was not easy. Kevin came in from work that night, and I had my first hot coffee all day. The girls did not actually "go to bed" with Bo, as more often than not they were out visiting their friends, which of course meant that at least her partner was drinking, and the girls were being subjected to at the very least cigarette smoke. We could not just put the girls down into their Moses baskets to settle down. On that first night alone with the girls we eventually got them off to sleep, Kevin using the "let's walk around the house method" with Morganna, until she gave in and fell asleep, whilst I wrapped Hope up into me "welsh fashion" - this is where you get a long sheet or blanket and fold it in half length ways, you hold the baby in the crook of your left arm and then tuck the sheet under her, then throw it - the sheet not the baby! Over your left shoulder across your back, down onto your right hip and then grabbing hold of the sheet by your right hip you wrap it over the baby and tuck it underneath her, between her body and yours. it's a great way of carrying one baby, I did most of my housework carrying all my own children this way, I became an expert at it Babies carried this way feel secure, they can still smell and feel you, they listen to your heartbeat which soothes them and they will sleep, it also means you have both hands free to do what ever it is you need to do. This works great on one baby, but not on two!!!!

I gently rocked Hope off to sleep wrapped up like that, I sang to her and she drifted off. One of the songs I used to sing to her was a song called "I don't know why" even today she loves me singing it to her.

"I don't know why, the sky is so blue
I don't know why I'm so in love with you
For if were is no music then I can not get through
I don't know these things, but I do".

The following week was awful. The girls had no routine at all, they were fretful, and didn't settle easily. Morganna didn't cry properly, she grunted and it was pitiful to hear, her fists were tightly clenched all the time, it was months before those tiny fists began to uncurl, I spent hours gently massaging them with almond oil into which I had mixed one drop of lavender oil. When Morganna's fingers uncurled and stayed straight for the first time I can remember looking at her fingers and thinking what lovely hands she had, her fingers are lovely, maybe she will go on to be a pianist, she certainly has the fingers for it.

96

Hope would cry, but she responded easily to me singing to her it soothed her; she would nuzzle into my neck and just lie there completely relaxed.

It must have been bewildering in their little world; I can't imagine what they must have been going through, poor little things. Together Kevin and I did our best to see to their needs we certainly did have a crash course in raising twins.

None of this was made any easier by the fact that Bo had decided she was not going to come back to our place at all. Everyday I had her on the phone, she would be shouting at me accusing me of taking her girls away from her and I would talk to her and eventually she would agree that it was actually social services not me that had taken the girls. On occasions she would be complaining about her partner, and telling me that she was missing the girls, so I would use these opportunities to try and get her to realise that she needed to be here with the girls and not there with him. I couldn't understand her at all, none of this made any sense to me.

## Monday 10<sup>th</sup> June 2002

It was getting very close to our special day, Kevin and I both wanted Bo to be there, I spoke to the social worker who said that if Bo stayed with us for the weekend. We were not allowed to let her take the girls anywhere on her own. I had also asked the social worker if they would agree to me and Kevin taking the girls away for the week after we had renewed our wedding vows, she said she would have to clear this with her manager. Later that day she rang to say it was fine, they just needed to know where we were going and when we would be back, and so it was that we changed our plans to have a quiet few days alone together, to those of spending a week at Butlins in Minehead. Bo had also agreed to come as well, so that was that a honeymoon became family week at a holiday camp for our new extended family. Silently I hoped just as the social worker did that this stay with us might just be the one that turned things around for Bo, and that she would realize what she was turning away from, and what she stood to loose.

The payment was made to the holiday camp, and social services provided Bo with a travel pass that allowed her to travel by train from Pembrokeshire to Minehead, as there was no room in our car for her as well as us and the children, let alone our luggage, which now also consisted of a double pushchair, and 2 travel cots.

I struggled to get all the last minute things together for our big day, and now I had the girls to sort out as well, fortunately I had already bought the girls new dresses to wear to the Cathedral, which was a big help. I was also on annual leave, so work pressures were removed which eased things greatly.

The daily calls to, or from social services were terrible, I did not want to talk about what was happening with anyone, but I had to. It is difficult for any mother to have to discuss her own child's failings with anyone, but believe me it is so much harder when it is a mother who is talking about her own daughter's failings in the ability to place her own children's needs before any one else's. I found this so incredibly hard.

I didn't eat and I hadn't had nights sleep for over a week, on top of all I was doing at home I was also constantly worried about Bo. Kevin was on annual leave from the Wednesday night onwards. We went to bed on Tuesday night and I lay in his arms and cried myself to sleep, waking at 3am to give the girls their night feed, Kevin got up at 4.30 and went off to work, I felt a little better as I knew that when he came in that night he would be in for 10 days, so I would have some help, but I felt guilt over that too as we had made plans for that time off, those plans had now changed. We were travelling back to Pembrokeshire to renew our wedding vows, this was supposed to be about us, now it wasn't, and I felt totally screwed up. On the Thursday I had an appointment with my hairdresser, Kevin and I had talked about it and I was going to take the girls with me.

"It's alright love. I can manage; just tell me what I have to do"

I wrote him a list of things he had to do, 10 o clock, girls feed, bottles are made up in the fridge, just warm them first, check they are not too hot and feed the girls, change their nappies, oh and don't forget to wind them!

Now Kevin was very much the hands on Dad, he was a fantastic Dad to Oliver, but Oliver was breast fed, until the girls came into our lives he had never bottle fed a baby. Oh for sure he had done his fair share of bottle feeding lambs and calves, but these were screaming babies, and there were two of them.

"Look, just go will you, we will be fine"

Now deep down inside I knew he would be, but that didn't stop me worrying

"You will ring if you need me wont you?"

He did not ring me he coped just fine and all was quiet in my home when I got back.

Bonding with Hope and Morganna was easy, I had loved them from the very beginning, and it was very much a case of love at first sight. I had also felt that overwhelming surge of protectiveness for them both and maybe this was why I instinctively would know if things were not right whist they were with Bo and her partner.

Kevin and I walked the length and breadth of our home with Hope and Morganna. I am surprised that we didn't leave permanent marks on the carpet where we had both walked with the girls soothing them. My days were filled with feeding and changing, soothing and trying to catch up on housework in the time that the girls slept.

## June 11<sup>th</sup> 2002

I had to register the girls with my GP today. I had been discussing this with the social worker  and we both felt this would make life a lot easier as if the girls needed treatment it was useless them having a GP 4 hours away in Pembrokeshire. There was a baby clinic being held today in my neighbouring village, this was going to be my first trip out on my own with the girls. Now doesn't that sound easy, well think about it for a minute, I have twins - two babies, two car seats, no help and a heart heavy with pain. When I walked into that village hall, there were quite a few Mum's as well as Dad's there, most were waiting in line to have their babies weighed, some were sat at tables drinking tea or coffee, chatting away to others, sharing birth stories, cooing over the new arrivals. When I walked in I felt every head turn towards me and stare, not only was I a new "Mum" but I also had TWINS this brought wonderful gasps of pure delight from everyone, "oh look aren't they cute," I was crumbling inside, I just wanted to run from that hall, taking my little darlings with me. I wanted to be left alone. I did not want to have to tell anyone what had happened - not yet it was too soon.

I undressed both of the girls had them weighed, re dressed them again, said yes thank you to the health visitors assistant as she reminded me that clinic was held again in two weeks and would I like to go, and then made a hasty retreat back towards the sanctuary of my car, the health visitor helping me by carrying one of the girls, she was to become a good support to me over the coming months.

Today Hope weighs 10lb and Morganna weighs 10lb 2ozs.

The admiring comments I received that day were correct of course, my beautiful girls were cute, and today they are still absolutely gorgeous.

## June 14ᵗʰ 2002

We travelled to Pembrokeshire on the 14ᵗʰ June 2002, Kevin, and Oliver the girls and me. I don't know how I managed to get everything in the car, but I did, poor Oliver had to sit squashed between the two girl's car seats in the back of the car, he never complained. Bo came to stay with us at my sisters and over the next two days we all rallied around and whilst everyone ignored their urges to "have a go" at her they all instead joined in with Kevin and I trying to  get her to see sense and come back with us to Oxfordshire and to look after the girls. We all stayed at my sisters, and it was intended that Bo should have the girls in the bedroom with her overnight, I was hoping that this would give her the push I felt she needed to come round to my way of thinking. However, in the early hours of the morning I ended up having Hope in with me

# I DO

Dawn was beginning to break as I got up to make the first of the days feeds for the girls, Bo and I sat together and fed them, we talked about all kinds of things, of me, of her life and the girls futures, and of what she wanted to happen. But what she wanted was for the girls to go back to her and her partner, well that just was not going to happen not without absolute proof that he had turned his life around. I told her that the only chance was for her to come to us and be with the girls and for him to go into a rehabilitation unit, and that when he had succeeded in making his life changes and they no longer posed a threat to the girls maybe, just maybe they could all be back together, but in the meantime she had to be strong, she had these two most beautiful little girls that needed their Mammy. I told her that I needed to be a Grandma not a Mammy. I thought I was getting somewhere, but I wasn't, as before the end of the day she was going back to be with him again, leaving her little babies with Kevin and I - and on our special night as well.

My Mam and Dad took responsibility for Hope and Morganna that morning so that Kevin and I could be together, to be able to get ready without having the worry of the girls. Bo went with them. Kevin and I were to be at the Lady Chapel in ST David's Cathedral at 12 o clock. We had arranged to go to our dearest friends Heather and Raul in Solva to get ready. We arrived there late and it was rush, rush, rush. Until now what I was going to wear was my secret, no one had seen it. Kevin's face was a picture of pure delight when I walked out of our friend's bedroom. We drove together into ST David's, and walked hand in hand towards the Cathedral. ST David's Cathedral is the most magnificent building, I had spent many hours their as a young woman, I love it for its peace and serenity we walked through the Cathedral and its beautiful long corridors and onto the Lady Chapel. Kevin's fingers were entwined in mine and I felt 6ft tall and for the time that it took us to walk to the Lady Chapel I forgot about the heartache that was surrounding us both.

All our guest's were there, chatting away happily, the Canon ushered our guests into the Lady Chapel to take their seats and then once they were all seated Kevin also went in to wait for me. As he walked away I can remember feeling how lucky I was. My Dad walked me in and as I walked down the aisle, smiling at my family and friends, I was also thinking why this was happening to us, why was our special day being tinged with a great sadness?

It was a beautiful service; I remember as I was retaking my wedding vows I was also trying to make sense of what was happening to us. Here I was standing at the alter in the Lady Chapel where it feels so peaceful and yet at the same time there was a great sorrow in my heart. We all stood to sing the last hymn "All things bright and beautiful" and today we all smile as we recall how fast the organist played his way through the whole hymn, it was almost as if he had to finish dead on time, it was hysterically funny.

In the week leading up to the service Kevin and I had spoken to the Canon, we had told him about Bo and the girls and of the weeks developments, we asked him to mention the three of them in his prayers that day and he did, what he said was lovely. I think all of us who were there that day offered up our own prayer as well, hoping that somewhere someone was listening and would help Bo.

Afterwards within the grounds of the Cathedral the photographer David took some amazing photographs, he took Kevin and I over to the small bridge at the back of the Cathedral and then away from he eyes of our guests captured some truly magical photographs of us together. If one thing did shine out in those photographs, it was the love that Kevin and I hold for each other. When I look at them now I don't know how I managed to turn out so well that day, having had no decent sleep since before the girls came to us, I was emotionally messed up and my heart was crying inside. One thing that saddens me when I look at those photographs is the changes in other people's lives that were there that day. I guess most of us can look at our wedding photographs and see at least one couple that are no longer together, or look at a familiar face that is no longer with us.

When I stood in that Lady Chapel, that day I knew I stood next to a man that would be by my side forever no matter what, he is strong, he is true and he is mine.

Afterwards we all went to the Ocean Haze Hotel in St David's, for a buffet lunch. During our speeches Kevin and I both said how proud we were of Bo, and although not everyone there that day had the full details of what was occurring, they all shared with us the hope that Bo and the girls would soon be back together. It was Oliver's 9th birthday two days after we renewed our wedding vows so we arranged a surprise for him too as we felt he had been brilliant over the past few months. A birthday cake was brought out and put in front of him and as he blew out the candles, we all joined together in singing him happy birthday.

I did not want that day to end, everyone who was important to Kevin an I were there and I felt cosseted and comforted by that, as if life had for a while cocooned me in a safe place.. As the afternoon drew to an end we all got ready to leave, we had originally planned to go out in the evening with our family and friends, and then to go on from there to be alone, just Kevin and I for a few days. Now all that had changed, but our friends decided it would still be nice to all get together again later that night, so we met at the Harbour House in Solva for a meal and some fun. I was incredibly sad that yet again the chance of Kevin and I being able to spend some time alone together had escaped us, I was also annoyed at Bo, even if at the time I did not say anything to anyone, I was annoyed because yet again her life choices had once again crept into and overshadowed something that was special to Kevin and I, and something we both deserved. Our day was still beautiful, it was still something we will remember always, it just won't be remembered by anyone for the true reasons we would have liked it to be remembered for.

Whenever I look back over the photographs of that day, I don't see a perfect day, I look at Kevin and myself and not only do I see the love we have, I also see the pain we were both going through at the time. I look at the group photograph and I see my daughter looking so sad and miserable, and my twin grand daughters not being held by her, but being held by Kevin, I and members of my family and our friends, who throughout that day shared the caring of them.

Bo had gone back to her partner later that afternoon; she was so keen to get back to him. She had agreed to travel down to Minehead and meet up with us there when we arrived with Oliver and the girls. Once again at the last minute she changed her mind and said she would be down on the Wednesday instead. I was disappointed in her, but what could I do. Kevin, Oliver Hope Morganna and I left Pembrokeshire and travelled to Minehead without Bo, she did turn up on the 19th June, and we picked her up from the train station. All the time that Bo was with us she was short tempered and miserable, she did not want to be with the girls and us at all. It was our intention to get Bo to care for the girls whilst she was with us and we encouraged her to do so, but it was short lived and it wasn't long before Kevin and I took over the care of the girls completely whilst she stayed with us in Butlins,

One afternoon Bo and I took the girls for a walk, they were lying quietly in their pushchair. Bo pushed them around the camp and I watched her face beaming as complete strangers came over to look at the girls and commented to Bo just how beautiful they were, and how fortunate she was to have twins, she began to relax and for the first time I saw my daughter as a Mum, she loved the attention she was receiving and was enjoying being there with the girls, but as quickly as the moment appeared it was lost again as her mobile rang and she answered it only to begin yet another argument with her partner. God he was miles away, but still he managed to get to her, still he managed to rile her, her mood changed and she became sullen and argumentative. He had spoilt everything - damn him.

Bo wanted to go return to Pembrokeshire, back to her partner. I was cross with her, I could not understand her at all, and all I wanted was for her and the girls to be together. I tried so hard to be supportive, but I couldn't understand her need to be with him instead of with the girls. Frustrated I said firmly to her "No you are not going back, you promised us and social services that you would stay with the girls until the case conference on June 25th" She was furious and screamed back at me

"I deserve a life; this is not fair on me"

"And what about me and Dad Bo, don't you think we deserve a life, this time was supposed to be about us, the only ones this isn't fair on is Dad and I"

She stayed, but boy did she make us suffer. Every day was hard work, and she did very little with the girls, who were also sharing our room now as Bo was unable to cope with them at night, those were truly difficult days.

We left Minehead on 21st June. In amongst the bad times over that couple of days I had also seen something that I had not seen much of lately, Bo really did love the girls, and when she felt like it she it was really lovely to watch her with the girls, during the day and with support she handled the girls well. Sadly this all served to make the whole situation even more frustrating. Somehow I had to reach inside her head, to get her to see just how much she would get out of being with the girls, how their love could and would if she allowed it too give her the courage and strength to go on and to do this alone without her partner, but that was part of the problem, she did not want to do this without her partner, she wanted him and the girls and couldn't understand why everyone was so concerned. I had to make her see just what she stood to loose, potentially what we all stood to loose.

Kevin went to Oxford train station to pick Bo up as she had to travel from Minehead to Oxford on the train. Over the next few days back at our home in Oxfordshire Bo manages quite well with the girls apart from when they are crying, this is when she gets agitated with them and starts shouting. She is in daily contact with her partner, sometimes 2 or 3 times a day, inevitably they end up arguing with each other and its not easy to listen to, I cant help but hear as she argues loudly with him, the language is disgusting, and it is having an effect on Oliver, who hates to hear his sister shouting down the phone. Bo is often tearful, and I am the one who sits and listens to her as she tells me what they were arguing about. I tried so hard to make her see that this is not a good relationship, that it certainly is not going to be good for the girls to be brought up within such a volatile relationship, and of how much harm it could do them both emotionally, and God forbid physically, because as they got older they too would be at risk of being hurt. Her response to this is that she will keep them safe. I replied that she hadn't kept them safe the night they were taken from her by the police, at which point she got up and walked away from me-this was always Bo's way of not hearing what she knew was true. I really cant understand what the attraction is for her, it is almost as if he has a hold over her, as if there is an invisible thread between the two of them, which every now and then he tugs on and then reels her in, Bo instead of putting up a fight against him, turns her fight onto me and the girls instead, and regardless of the fight I put up on Hope and Morganna's behalf, she meekly gives in to his requests.

We are travelling back to Pembrokeshire tonight; Oliver is staying with a friend for the next two days so that he does not have to miss school. This also means that instead of travelling back to Pembrokeshire on the train Bo can make the journey with us in the car. When we Leave Oliver at his friends we

I promise him that we will do everything we can to keep the girls with us, and I promise to ring him tomorrow night. I felt bad about leaving him, he is our son and yet we are leaving him behind to go to Pembrokeshire and try to sort out this mess.

We leave our home to travel back to Pembrokeshire again for the case conference with social services; I am terrified of the outcome of this meeting as things are not looking good. I am also nervous, the last meeting I had attended had scared me half to death and I was on my own, at least this time Kevin is with me, I draw comfort from that, but I am still scared.

# ONE STEP FORWARD, TWO STEPS BACK

## June 25th 2002

Bo decided to return to her partner as soon as we arrived in Pembrokeshire, leaving me and Kevin to pick up the pieces yet again. The girls are fine and at this stage I am grateful that they are babies, as God alone knows what they would be going through if they were old enough to understand all that was happening to them.

There is no time to experience my own feelings, I am far to busy trying to hold us all together, I am also having to endure my families viewpoints, they are not as accommodating of Bo as I am, and they freely express their views, which in one way is good, but in another it only succeeded to make me feel even more of a failure as a mother, at this time I was still holding myself responsible for my daughters apparent failings. The peace I was to find once I had realised it I was not to blame for my daughter's failings was to elude me for a long time yet.

The morning of the meeting arrives and I am a nervous wreck. I fumble my way through a morning fog of feeding and bathing the girls. I had also made an appointment with a solicitor in Haverfordwest as Kevin and I both felt this was the best way forward for us now that things were moving fast. Thanks to The Grandparents Association we knew it was best to have legal representation, we also needed to find out whether or not we would be entitled to legal aid. Mam had agreed to have the girls for us whilst we attended the meetings with the solicitor and the one with social services. Kevin and I kissed the girls goodbye.

I found the meeting with the solicitor difficult, she was brilliant, it was what I had to discuss with her that was the hard part for me. After filling in all the relevant forms and telling who was now "our solicitor" about the situation we found ourselves in it was decided that she would accompany us to the meeting with social services. It was during this initial meeting with our solicitor that we discussed for the first time a RESIDENCE ORDER on Hope and Morganna, and what it would involve. Once again someone up there was looking over us that day. Bo and her partner were already there, they had arrived together, just before we did. I am shaking inside, I have been holding inside me a silent fear that social services may decide to place the girls with a foster family closer to Bo to make contact easier. I am all too aware now that Kevin and I may be the girls Grandparents, but in law we do not have automatic rights to our Grandchildren.

The meeting with social services was awful, Kevin and I sat there listening to what everyone had to say, then it was my turn, I was feeling sick as I had to recount the events of the last 9 days. I had lived through it, Kevin had lived through it, and somehow we just got on with it, there had been no time to sit and turn it all over with each other, now I was sitting there telling complete strangers and that for me was the most awful of things to have to do. Knowing that your own daughter has not been able to commit to her children is one thing, but telling others who can influence the outcome is terrifying. I found watching her difficult, her mood swaying from anger to tears, I wanted to hold her, to tell her everything was going to be alright, but I couldn't, none of the decisions that were made that day were down to me, all I could do was to offer to continue to support Bo, to offer the girls and Bo a home. My heart was crying out for me to say to everyone there "please leave the girls with us, please don't take them away" but I daren't I had to stay calm.

Then we were asked to leave the room that meant me Kevin, Bo and her partner. All four of us waited outside in the reception area, after a little while Bo spoke to me

"Mum what do you think they will do?"

"I don't know sweetheart, we are just going to have to wait and see"

She went outside with her partner for a cigarette. How can she be so removed from all of this does she not realise what the hell is going on here, how can she just walk off with him and go for a cigarette? After what seemed like hours we were all called back into the room where the meeting was being held.

The chairman spoke breaking into the silence that had fallen on that room "we have reached a unanimous decision, it has been decided that it would be best if the girls return to Oxfordshire with their Grandparents, and that we draw up a contract which gives clear guidelines for us all to follow. All of us who were involved in that contract sat and spelt it out, it was felt that this way Bo was being given the best opportunity to move forward. It was decided that Bo and the girls should reside with us in Oxfordshire. That I should continue to work and whilst at work Bo should be responsible for the care of the girls. Bo was told she could request travel passes from social services to travel back to Pembrokeshire to see her partner whenever I was able to accommodate her requests to look after the girls for her to go back. Bo agreed to the contract and it was signed by me, Bo and social services. Bo's partner did not approve of this decision; he wanted the girls returned to him and Bo.

It was also agreed in this meeting the Bo's partner should have supervised contact with the girls if he requested it, this we felt was good, and we agreed to bring the girls back to Pembrokeshire for contact meetings and also for them to attend their hospital appointments at Withybush hospital. Social services agreed to pay our travelling expenses to cover these visits back to Pembrokeshire, up until this point we had borne all our expenses ourselves and it was crippling us financially, so this for us was good news, they also said that they would contact me weekly to offer support and for us to share information. These weekly contacts between the social worker and myself were to prove to be useful, they also allowed a picture to begin emerging regarding Bo's behaviour, it was to prove crucial, we left that meeting together, Bo was angry, she said it was so unfair on her and her partner, and that we were all against her, which of course was totally untrue, what we were all trying to achieve was to give her support, and at the same time afford the girls safety, which for us was so important. Whilst I, and I am sure Kevin silently hoped that during the time she was with us that the bond would develop between her and the girls making it impossible for her to want to leave them again. That bond never formed strong enough, despite everyone's best efforts.

Bo said that she wanted to come back to Oxfordshire the following Saturday as she wanted to spend time with her partner, I was disappointed with her, had she not taken anything on board in that meeting After pointing out to her that I actually had work in the following week, we agreed that she could stay with her partner as long as she did return to Oxfordshire on the Saturday. Once again on my return home to Oxfordshire I found myself ringing work and taking more unpaid leave.

# June 26ᵗʰ 2002

Back at home in Oxfordshire, its baby clinic again today, so off we go me and the girls.

Today Hope weighs 10lb 13oz. Morganna weighs 11lb 1oz. They are doing fine, and there are no concerns at all with either of them. This was good news for me as I was very concerned that I may not have been doing everything I could have been doing, but I was, the girls are doing well and are healthy.

Bo returned to us on July 1ˢᵗ 2002, she really does not want to be here, she is sullen and moody. I have by now got the girls into a fairly workable routine, they are not constantly crying to be given a bottle all the time, which is what they were doing and they are now able to take most of their feed when they are given it, they are also going down for a morning and an afternoon nap, which gives me a little time to catch up on things. Aware that Bo may not approve of what I have achieved with the girls I decided that it may be easier to write the girls routine onto the board in our kitchen so that she can see for herself what the girls day is like and then she can work with that routine without feeling that she has to keep on asking me, I was trying to make everything easier for her, she did not see it that way at all, she accused me of interfering, and it hurt. I tried so hard to make her understand that having a routine for the girls was a good thing, but she dispelled it.

I had the next three days back at work and leaving the girls for the first time with Bo I found incredibly hard, I worried about not only the girls but also Bo. I knew that Kevin was close at hand, but he could not keep running back to the house all the time to check that things were OK. Over those three days Bo rang me in work, on my return home Oliver was meeting me as I pulled up outside,

"Quick Mum, Bo is shouting at the girls"

When I got back into the house both the girls were fretful and crying

"Bo why are the girls not in bed, they usually sleep most of the afternoon"

She looked at me and screamed,

"They are my babies; I will do what I like with them".

I tried to explain to her that following the routine was what the girls had done, it was what worked for them, and it would make life easier for her in the long run, she refused to listen, and what could I do.

That night the girls cried endlessly, Bo shouted at them and I found it hard not to interfere, but I had to stand back a little. The next day was pretty much like the first, and the evening was no better, that night I was awoken by Bo shouting at the girls, I lay in bed crying, it tortured me to stay in my room, I closed my eyes trying to shut it out but all I could see was images of my beautiful grand daughters, eventually they stopped crying and all went quiet, too quiet, I went to her room to find both the girls sat in their seats with their bottles in their mouths being propped up by a pillow. Bo was asleep; I was furious, I woke her and told her I was taking the girls back into my room with me. I couldn't let this happen again, so the following day I rang the social worker from work and left a message for her to call me back, she did and we discussed how things were progressing, or rather not progressing as we had hoped, she told me that the routine I had established with the girls was good and that I had to get Bo to follow it, this I felt was going to damn near impossible, I had seen the way my daughter opposed anyone who tried to tell her what to do, then would dig her heels in and whoever was on the receiving end of her fury would be well advised to batten down the hatches. I knew that this time this person was to be me! I was also told that Bo had already requested a travel permit and it would be arriving tomorrow in the morning post. Bo had not actually told me herself that she was intending to return to Pembrokeshire.

Bo left on July 4th, she had spent just 3 days with the girls, she is due to return tomorrow, I took her to the station and as we made the drive there I asked her if she thought the journey there and back was worth it for such a short amount of time to spend with her partner, I was told to mind my own business.

I don't know why I am surprised but Bo hasn't come home today, the girls are very settled, partly I think because they are so tired, they settle back into their routine well and I even managed to get some housework done. I managed to get hold of Bo late that afternoon; she told me she would be home at 6.30 in the morning. The girls went to bed that night at 11pm after their last feed, they slept through until 5.30am. Bo did not return until late evening on July 7th.

## July 7th 2002

Today is Oliver's school fete; this will be the first time that we have taken the girls out to a school event. By now news has filtered its way around the small village where we lived, most of the people we knew expressed a mixture of sadness that we were going through such an awful thing and admiration that we being so supportive towards my daughter.

We had a great time at the fete. All our friends got a chance to nurse our beautiful grand daughters, and it was nice to be out enjoying ourselves. Oliver and his mates were off doing their own thing which involved getting wet through as they tried to knock each other off a bar with plastic poles. The girls slept through most of the cuddles they got that afternoon. Just for a short time we allowed ourselves to chill out. The atmosphere in the house was also better, but that was all about to change yet again.

Bo returned home to us late that night in a foul mood, this mood stayed with her for all the time she was to stay with us on this visit

During the month of July Bo was with us for just 11 days, the rest of the time she was back in Pembrokeshire with her partner. The contract Bo agreed to is failing, I have taken more days unpaid leave than I have actually worked this month and I am devastated, it is beginning to have an effect on me, I feel that I have to try and pull this all back together again, but how, where do we go from here?

I rang social services again, the first week in August I am working everyday as I am covering my colleagues annual leave, I can't do this and look after the girls, and Kevin is also at work. I have one other option and that is to put the girls into a nursery, after discussing this with social services I made arrangements to take the girl along to a nursery I had already made contact with for a visit on Thursday afternoon. On Friday 2nd august, the girls stay at the nursery for the day. The girls have been with me everyday for the past 8 weeks and it felt strange not to have them with me. They will be at nursery everyday next week, while I am at work.

The week that the girls were at nursery was exhausting. The mornings found me meeting myself coming backwards as I tried to get Oliver off to school, get the girls ready for nursery and myself for work, on top of that I also had to cope with the phone calls I was getting from my family and from Bo. Whilst I was at work I was busy there. The social worker would ring me at work as it was the only time she could get hold of me, by now she was sharing my concerns about Bo. During July and into August there had been a rise in the amount of domestic violence that Bo was being subjected to by her partner, or was it possibly a rise in her telling me about these incidents, some of these incidents had resulted in the police being called. I was worried out of my mind for her safety.

This week in August also saw some other things happen in our home

# "DARLING WE MUST TALK"

August is here and it is beautiful, on Sunday 4th we took the girls shopping in MOTHERCARE for some clothes, they are growing fast now, I also need to go up a size in their nappies, until now the girls have still been wearing the premature baby ones that fit up to 11lb! Can you imagine that? They are five and a half months old and they weigh what Oliver weighed at 2 weeks old.

A t long last Kevin and I get the chance to sit down and talk about what we would like to see happen in the future. This is not easy for me as I feel so guilty and ashamed that my daughter can't do what is right. I have taken so much for granted in expecting Kevin to feel as I do about the girls being in our lives, not to mention the possibility of bringing them up. As far as I was concerned it was a decision that I did not even have to think about before I made it, for me it was an automatic decision, if Bo failed in her part to be a mother to the girls then there was no way I would stand back and loose them, they are my Grandchildren and being without them is unthinkable. I would fight to keep them within our family with every ounce of strength I had. Over the past few days I had begun to think about what I would do if Kevin said that he could not commit to bringing up the girls, and I had decided that if he felt unable to be by my side in my decision that I would leave, taking the children with me.

Reading that back it scares the hell out of me that I could have even thought that way. But do you know, if I am honest I knew Kevin would stand by me whatever decision I had reached. But this was not just about me it was about Kevin, Oliver and the girls as well.

114

As we talked that evening, we talked as we had never done before completely open and honest. During our married life we have been in some pretty awful situations that had tested both of us and the strength of our relationship. This was a situation that was to demand a lot from Kevin. I knew that this time I was going to be the one that would need supporting, it was me that was going to need a rock. Up until not it had always been me that was the strong one in our relationship, I did not have the energy to be strong for all of us, the day to day caring of the girls was heavy, and with the added emotional stress of the situation that we found ourselves in and still trying to be there for Bo as and when she needed support was beginning to take it's toll, I was shattered by the time the evening would arrive. We talked about Bo's lack of commitment, and how she seemed unable to place the needs of her babies before those of herself and of her partner. I need not have ever doubted that Kevin would have done anything other than support me, I knew my man and he was as committed as I was, maybe that was why I had let such an unthinkable thought even enter my head that day, looking back on it though I think if Kevin had made the decision that he couldn't commit then I would have been driven to leave, so strong were my feelings of protectiveness over Hope and Morganna. So that night together we decided that we would apply for a residence order on the girls. Another thing we spoke about was me working, I was being torn in so many pieces and I couldn't go on like this, something had to give. It was becoming increasingly difficult for me to take time off, it was not just me that was looking for commitment, my employers were also looking for that in me, and at that time they were certainly not getting commitment from me, besides which this was not fair on Oliver, he was so young to be living through this event with us and I know how much he hated seeing me being torn apart and crying. Over and over again in those horrendous of years, my young son was often to give me a glimpse of the fine teenager he was to become. So once again together we made the decision that I would resign from the job I loved doing the following day and for the first time in my life I was to become a stay at home Mum. This was important to me for two reasons, firstly I felt that Hope and Morganna deserved continuity of care, there had been enough upheaval in their little lives, they deserved to be settled now, and also if we were to have the girls with us then it was only fair on Oliver if I was home, he had so graciously shared his Mammy and Daddy with the girls, at least I could be here for him when he got in from school. If I was home then I would be able to give him a little more time.

Kevin and I talked about what was important for both of us, and it kept on coming back to just one simple thing. And that was, no matter what somehow we all had to stay together. In the beginning both of us had thought that this arrangement was only going to be a short term thing, just long enough to provide Bo with the support she would require to build a life for her and the girls. As the days turned into weeks, the weeks into months both of us had begun to take on board the more serious side of what was occurring - that the girls may well need to be with us long term. As these months slipped past I had completely missed recognising a change that was happening within me, then one day it slowly began to manifest itself and I became aware of what I was feeling. Something had grown inside of me, I had been taken over by an overwhelming maternal feeling towards the girls, and along with that maternal feeling came the knowledge that I could no longer imagine my life without my beautiful girls, they were now a part of me. They had truly grown in my heart, and they along with Oliver filled it.

I had not expected this to happen, naively I guess I had just thought that when Bo had got her life sorted out, and the issues that social services were concerned about had disappeared, that the girls would go to live with their mother, my daughter, and that I would just slip back into the role of Grandma. I had not even given a thought to what I would be feeling; there was never time for that. How could this have happened? When did it happen, over and over again I had asked myself those questions.

On a more practical level we also agreed that some other changes were needed. firstly we were going to turn our guest room into a nursery, up until now we had not done this as Bo used the room when she was staying over, the girls needed this space more than she did, they needed to be in cots and not in their Moses baskets in our bedroom ,and we needed to have our privacy back, we had become like ships that passed in the night, and the intimate part of our loving relationship had just vanished, we were both too physically and emotionally exhausted. This part of mine and Kevin's life together I was missing terribly, it is something that no Grandparent who is placed in our position talks about.

So with our frank and open discussion mostly over, it was time for bed, I felt better that at least now we had been brave enough to talk about our fears and our feelings and both of us knew we were singing form the same song sheet . I believe Kevin had recognised the maternal feelings in me a long time before I did, he just hadn't said anything.

We went into this with our eyes wide open and certainly under no illusions that it was going to be easy, but in truth neither Kevin nor I really expected this event to reach the destination it has, we expected the girls to be with Bo, even so we knew we were in for a rough ride. For one thing we were both aware that me resigning from my job was going to financially burden us as we were to become a five person family living on one pay packet, up until the girls arrival we had been a three person family with two good incomes, and this was going to test us both.

Turning the lights off in the lounge we locked up the house and sleepily climbed the stairs hand in hand to our bedroom, we looked at the girls as we always did before we went got into our bed, they were sound asleep, Morganna lying on her right side, Hope on her left, this was how they always slept, in their own baskets, but facing each other, it was gone midnight and they had slept through their 11 pm feed, they were both fast asleep.

I climbed into bed and lay there awake for a while, the moon was high in the clear summer sky and I watched as the curtains moved gently in the breeze that wafted the late evening smell of the honeysuckle in through our open window. I turned over and over again in my head the things that Kevin and I had talked about and the decisions we had made, all of which should have been happening to some one else, you know the people in the magazine article, that we may have read about, but it wasn't it was happening here and now and it was happening to us. I was aware that I would have to tell my family, especially my boy's about the decision that Kevin and I had made. I knew that my two eldest boys would probably find it difficult to understand, but regardless of their feelings I would do what had to be done, they had their own lives. I was concerned that in having the girls I would be left with no time to spend with my son's or their families, my eldest son was living with his partner and they had two lovely children, a girl and a boy, they also lived in Pembrokeshire, but now that I had the girls seeing them was not so easy. When we did travel back to Pembrokeshire the time that we spent there was always taken up with meetings with our solicitor, case conferences at social services, contact meetings for Bo and her partner to see the girls, hospital appointments for the girls or hospital visits with Bo to the A&E department as she would self mutilate and I would have a phone call to say she needed me. There was no time for us to do the things we would have liked to have done and visiting not just our family, but also our friends became impossible.

Most of all I thought about the incredible amount of strength we had in our relationship, and I knew just how lucky I was. I may have been on an emotional rollercoaster, and the ride was hell on earth. I may not have been able to apply the brakes, I may not have been in control, but I was not in this alone, or so I thought on that August night.

I curled into Kevin's arms and slept like I hadn't done for a long time, perhaps somehow us talking and making a few decisions of our own had made me feel more in control, but I was also as scared as hell that we would not succeed in our application for a residence order. I was nervous of telling the social worker of our decision, but it had to be done, that phone call was yet another thing I had to do the following day.

My sleeping thought that night set the pattern for my dreams - "Oh God what if we failed".

# "MAMMA"

## HOORAY, HOORAY

Its August 5th and the girls have slept all night, they did not wake for their 11pm feed, must have been all that shopping yesterday, after all a good rest is what all us girls need when we've hit the shops. Whatever the reason I had just enjoyed a blissful 8hrs sleep!

August 5th off to work dropping the girls off in nursery on the way. I spoke to the social worker today, Bo has not been keeping her appointments with her and so I mentioned the residence order, there was a pause before she answered and then she said "I think its for the best" so it is agreed, Kevin and I were to ask our solicitor to apply to the court for leave for a residence order on Hope and Morganna, in our favour.

In the mornings post on August 6th came the forms for us to fill in to make the application to the court for a residence order. This was it, the beginning of yet another horrendous part of my journey, filling in those forms was difficult, but once they were done I returned them to our solicitor and waited. Morganna has today discovered her voice and much to her delight, and to my eardrums pain she has discovered the most ear piercing high pitched squeal, it is almost painful to hear, but she loves it, every time she does it Hope laughs, they are beginning to interact with each other now and it is a joy to watch. Bo is missing this joy.

I have been unable to get hold of Bo for the last few days, the social worker says she has not kept her appointments with her so we are both concerned; she is going to call in and see if things are alright with her. I have never really got used to Bo's "going to earth" time it causes me great concern if I don't hear from her, but no doubt she will ring me tomorrow as if nothing is wrong.

The social worker rang me today and informed me that the case conference that was listed for December has been brought forward to August 13th. Our solicitor also rang to inform us that she has issued our application for an interim residence order and a full residence order, and that the court has listed it to be heard on the 28th August 2002 at 2.30pm. I am also told that Bo and her partner will have received their papers from the court today informing them of our intention to go for the residence order.

Sure enough on August 9th Bo rang, she was furious and called me everything, I let her rant and rave at me and then told her that Kevin and I were doing this for the girls, that it was not about her or her partner. I told her that there was no way I was going to stand back and watch my precious Grand daughters go into foster care and then be adopted, with the possibility of being separated as well. .And that for as long a there was breath in my body I would continue to fight for the girls. She rung off saying she would ring me later.

In the afternoon the girls and I were in the garden playing. I was playing peek-a-boo with them. I put a book in front of my face and as I poked t up above the book again and said boo, Morganna giggled, Hope looked at me and said "Mamma" my heart ached for Bo, she should have heard that not me, I picked Hope up and hugged her, my face wet with tears, she smiled at me, she had a smile that would melt the hardest of hearts.

## August 12th 2002

Off to baby clinic again today, I am getting quite good at this now, I am also meeting a few new mums. I still feel like a fish out of water, but I am now the fish learning to walk on dry land.

Today Hope weighs in at a staggering 13lbs 12ozs and Morganna, the little dumpling weighs 14lb 1oz; ah well off to buy bigger nappies.

I decided to go to TESCO'S on the way home as we were running short of a few things, what used to take me half an hour can now take me three hours to do. I have to park then find a twin trolley, and then the fun begins, I get stopped so often that being polite is wearing thin

"Oh look aren't they lovely, you must be so proud"

"Are they twins?"

"Where did you get them from?" now I used to love this question, my reply was always" oh just down there on the end of aisle 6, they are on offer this week, buy one get one free"!!!!!!!!!!!!!

But the most frustrating question I was asked, and I was asked it a lot was whether they were boys or girls, and what their names were. I used to reply.

"They are both girls, this is Hope and this is Morgan"

"You are so lucky, one of each, they are delightful"

"No, they are both girls Hope is a girl and so is Morgan"

I could understand what they were getting at and how the girl's names would confuse them, I also hated the name Morgan, it really did not suit her at all, so we lengthened it to Morganna, Ah bliss now more confusion. When Hope began to talk, she picked up on the Anna bit of Morganna, and that is how she became known, that is until just 2 weeks ago. I was ordering the name tabs to put onto their school uniform when she announced she wanted to be called by her "proper name" I asked her what she wanted to be called

"Well Morganna oh course" she replied whilst flicking her hair.

So Morganna it is then, she has now grown into this beautiful name, it is one you never hear, so both the girls have pretty and unusual names.

Going to TESCO'S was something I would leave and do in the middle of the night whilst the girls were asleep, it was nothing for me to leave Kevin and the children tucked up in bed and rush off to do the shopping at midnight. Ah the peace was great. I could get around the store in the dead of night without any admiring glances, and the only things that I would bump in to were the huge trolleys of stock waiting to be put on the shelves.

Now shopping in general with the girls was hell, most of the shops I needed to go into were small and I had no chance of getting a double pushchair in them, and so I developed quite a keen eye for spotting the store managers to have a whinge at.

Off to Pembrokeshire late tonight, as we have to take the girls into Withybush Hospital tomorrow for an appointment with the paediatric consultant, Bo is supposed to meet us to attend this appointment with us, and then the following day we have to attend the meeting with social services. We find it easier to travel during the evening as the girls will sleep through the journey, that is they did for most of the times we travelled down, but it did not always work, and sometimes it was me that was squashed in between the girls car seats trying to pacify them whilst Kevin drove and Oliver had the luxury of my seat in the front of the car, the pick of the numerous bags of sweets that kept us going and worst of all he would have control of the car CD player, and not only would Kevin and I be subjected to his taste in music, but also the volume at which he like most kids of his age, had to play it otherwise they seem unable to hear it. Kevin and I would have headaches from listening to the girls complaints and being in a car seat when they would much rather be having a cuddle, but also from the noise of the music our darling son would choose for us to endure, which often had my head thumping in time to the beat for hours after our journeys end.

As usual on these visits back home to Pembrokeshire my sister and her husband were awaiting our arrival, the coffee would be made and drunk and then whilst the men unloaded the car and erected the travel cots. Made up the beds etc, Debs and I would feed and change the girls, catching up on all the news form our families, whilst cooing over the girls at the same time. Deb's and I would catch up on all the family news whilst cooing over the girls. It must have been a lovely scene for Kevin and Deb's husband Geoff, even if it was sad for there before them were two sisters who had enjoyed their lifetime so far growing up together, sharing each others lives, and now those two sisters were sat together feeding twin sisters who were yet to grow up together and had so much before them. It must have been a magical sight. Two sisters looking after two very precious little sisters.

We have arranged to meet Bo at the hospital, my Mam is coming along as well, after all it doesn't hurt to have a bit of moral support, it also gives us another chance to see Bo and try to talk to her about what she is doing, when we meet Bo she looks dreadful, she is painfully thin and her eyes are vacant looking, something is troubling her, I don't know what it is but I know that it is not her conscience. All was to be revealed two weeks later.

The consultant is pleased with the girls they are developing well, he would like to have their hips ex-rayed, but has decided it would be better to have this done in Oxfordshire in the JR Hospital, this makes life an awful lot easier for us. Kevin is using up all his annual leave entitlement making these trips back to Pembrokeshire.

Today Hope weighs in at a healthy13lb 10ozs, she measures 23 inches. Morganna weighs 13lb 15ozs and measures 24 inches.

The weather is glorious so we decide to have lunch at the hospital, buying sandwiches and drinks from the WRVS, we take them outside into the patio area of the hospital and sit there in the sunshine talking to Bo, we cant get her to see things as we see them, she is adamant that she is staying with her partner,

"Even if that means you will loose the twins Bo, think about this will you, you stand to loose so much"

"Oh leave off Mum, you don't understand"

"But I want to understand, talk to me Bo, and make me understand"

Bo does not answer, I tell myself that maybe she can't see what we can see, or that maybe she is in denial

After we have finished lunch Kevin and I invite her to come back with us to spend some time with the girls, but she won't, she has to get back to her partner. So Kevin and I leave Mam in town to do her shopping, she will catch the bus home, whilst Kevin and I take the girls to Solva to see Heather and Raul, knowing that they would love to see the girls.

That evening after the children have been settled for the night, Kevin and I tell my family what we are planning to do.

"You are doing the right thing" my Mam and Dad recite.

Deb's and her husband agree that we have the girl's best interests at heart; they also say that they will do whatever they can.

I cried again that evening, my Dad, my Mam and my darling sister can't comfort me.

Mam is having the girls again tomorrow, whilst we attend the meeting.

"Emotionally this is a bloody awful place to be. It is hell. It is also difficult for all of us"

# "MY CLIENTS WOULD LIKE TO INFORM YOU THAT"

We arrived at the meeting with social services to find that the Paternal Grandparents were also present. Kevin and I are asked if we have any objection to them being included in the meeting, we reply that we have no objection, it is fine with us. Our solicitor arrived at the same time as Bo and her partner.

The meeting is absolute hell, it rips my heart out, and I can honestly say that for the first time I feel like slapping Bo. Watching her sat next to the man who is causing her so much heartache makes me feel sick. I can't believe that she can just carry on her life as though nothing has happened. Doesn't she see what is happening here? Does she not understand that everyone in this room is actually looking to her to prove in some demonstrative way that she can show even the slightest bit of hope of trying to build a future for her and the girls together. No one was looking for the perfect parent in her, just the signs of one that would do her best, God alone knows I was not the perfect parent, none of us are, we all share that common learning process, and we do our best, which is all that is needed from us by our children. I know that everyone in that room tried so hard, we all willed her to throw us a sign; we all tried so hard to see what just was not there. I think that as time went on we all felt as if we had failed in our own way. Listening to all the negative responses from the various agencies involved is crushing me, and I feel like a complete failure as a mother, I have felt like this so many times over the past months. The frustration and anger is almost too much to take and I feel like exploding , Kevin knows me well, and I feel his hand gently rest on my leg and it reminds me that I am not alone in this, it has the effect of calming me. Strangely it is me that feels as if I am the one who is the bad guy in this meeting, but I think this is because I am the one being questioned about how Bo interacts with the girls, and of how the care plan has gone, or rather in Bo's case has not gone. I am now being asked to tell the meeting of an event that has happened during the past week, I knew before the meeting that I would be expected to do so and I knew that it was going to be so hard for me, but now I am aware that I also have to re tell of this event in front of Bo's partners parents. Once again I feel that familiar hand resting on my knee and our solicitor gives me a nod of encouragement.

Nervously I tell the meeting of just one of the many times Bo has rung me to tell me that her partner has attacked her, only this time it was different. I was feeding the girls one afternoon when the phone rang, I answered it and Bo was screaming,

"Don't hit me, leave me alone"

Then the phone went dead, I discarded the girls tea and immediately rang her back, she answered the phone and as I was trying to get her to tell me what was happening, I heard a thud - No, I felt that thud and every other one as he laid into my daughter, all the time she was screaming at him to stop, I could not put the phone down, I was crying, I was calling to her

"Bo, Bo darling are you alright"

What a silly thing to say, of course she was not alright, but it was the only thing I could think of saying. His attack on her was relentless. I felt every single one of those thuds as he laid into her, I feared for her life "Get out of there, run outside, quickly" everything went quiet, and I was scared to death, there was no sound, nothing, then I heard a door slamming, then a faint voice said

"Mammy"

"OK Bo its OK,

But it wasn't, gently and lovingly I asked her where she hurt, all the time trying so hard not to let her know I was crying to, but in the end I could hold it together no longer, I sobbed.

"Bo for Christ's sake just get out of there, he is going to kill you if you carry on like this"

I did not want to ring off; I was so scared that it would be the last time I would speak to my beautiful Bo. I wanted her here so that I could hold her, to nurse her sore and battered body once again, to have her in my arms, to protect her, to mother her. But I couldn't. Even today I want my daughter, my Bo, back in my arms, even today after all we have been through I want her home so that I can protect her - but I cant.

On many more occasions over the following months, and years, I was to either be told of or listen to attacks from him on my Bo.

If I could have got hold of him at that moment I would have torn him apart, I have never in all my life felt like that about anyone, even in my own past relationships where violence towards me had been an issue, I have never wished anyone any harm, but at that moment I wished her partner was not alive. I don't think anyone reading this would feel any differently if they had heard happen to their child what I had just heard happen to mine, it was only natural that I felt that way

It must have been very hard for his parents to sit there and listen to me re-telling this event. How they must have hated me at that moment in time, indeed it must have been difficult for everyone to listen too. I was in pieces, I felt as if I was going to be sick and the tears were again rolling down my face, I was shaking inside and so the meeting had to be adjourned for a short time for me to compose myself.

For a mother to have to speak of her own child in this way is just unbearable, I just want to make it all better, and I can't. I can do nothing but stand by and watch the carnage as the two of them try to destruct each other. The reality of how little input Bo has so far had with the girls would break any mother's heart, I know it broke mine, not just from a pure numbers count, but because I feel the pain of what Bo will one day have to face when she realises what she has let go, and for the girls, as one day they will be told this story and no matter how hard I try to protect them all it is going to hurt them as they discover the reasons behind this events happenings, and my heart is also breaking for another reason, one that I have yet to identify, because I have yet to admit to myself that I am grieving.

Our solicitor breaks into my silent thoughts and addressing the chairmen, she announces that we have now filed an application with the court for a interim residence order on Hope and Morganna, she goes on to inform everyone that the first court hearing is set for 2pm on the 28th August 2002. It is decided that the girls should remain on the protection register as this affords us more protection if Bo or her partner should try to take the girls. The social worker asks if Kevin and I would accommodate a contact meeting that afternoon for Bo's partner's parents to see the girls, they would like this to take place Bo's flat. Kevin and I agree on condition that the social worker remains with them at all times, this is agreed and we leave the meeting to travel back to my Mam's to pick the girls up and take them to Bo's flat.

Bo's partner's parents have not seen the girls since before June 6th, the day they came home with me. They will be at Bo's flat, I feel so desperately for his mother.

When we arrive at the flat Kevin and I carried the girls up the stairs that lead to Bo's flat, we had seen the social workers car parked outside in the car park, so we knew she was already there. Hope looked at me bewildered when I gave her to Bo, after all by now the girls had had very little contact with Bo, and had begun to form a strong bond with me and Kevin, so much so that if either of us leaves the room, both the girls will show their disapproval by crying until we return. I felt awful leaving them both there. Walking out of that flat and down the stairs to the ground floor was like walking on glass, every step I took hurt me, I was shaking, if Kevin had not had hold of my hand then I think I would have gone back up to the flat I was scared. I knew there was no need to be as the girls other Grandparents were there and so was the social worker. My fears were unjustified, but I had never met her partner's parents before, they had never met us, it must have been terrible for them, I can't imagine what they must have been going through. I was later to discover from Bo that they had not told his parents that the girls were with us, they had told them that they were on holiday if they had asked, its easy not to tell the truth over the phone, and like us his parents also lived away from the area, the only news they got was what they were told by Bo or her partner. This was the last time that the girls were to see their paternal grandparents. They do send the girls cards and presents at Christmas etc, but we have yet to meet up with them. Neither Kevin nor I wish them to be excluded from Hope and Morganna's lives. I have spoken to the Grandma several times and hopefully by the time this book is in print we will have taken the girls to visit them, after all it is no more their fault that their son chooses to live his life as he does any more than it is my fault that my daughter chooses to live hers the way she does. His parents are victims in this too and as paternal Grandparents, it is so much easier for contact to be lost between them and their grandchildren. I know this pain too as my son and his partner were later to separate, which has strained the relationship between me and my grandchildren's mother.

As time went on I found it increasingly difficult to trust anyone where the girls were concerned. That is one hell of an awful thing to say, but in time as you read this story you will understand how the passage of time turned me into someone who distrusted all but a chosen few.

# THE FIRST COURT HEARING.

We arrived back home in Oxfordshire in the early hours of the morning, Kevin and I were shattered. The girls awoke as we carried them into the house, it surprised me as they both looked around the dining room and smiled, and it was almost as if they were saying "Home and safe"

We decided that later that day we are going to go and buy two cots for the girls and some bedding, buying things that the girls need is now getting difficult for us we are getting no help financially to help with their upbringing, I am going through aver 100 nappies a week and 2 large tins of SMA baby formula. Both the girls are eating solid meals once a day now, but they still need their formula, because of their prematurely this will continue until they are two, which according to the health visitor, is when I can start introducing cow's milk into their diet. I am making all the girls solid feeds myself and freezing them in individual pots, this is great as not only is it saving us money, but it also means they are getting the best, without any additives, they love sweet potato with chicken. When they were first introduced to solids it strange how quickly their own individual preferences began to immerge, Hope enjoys sweet things best of all. Whereas Morganna has a savoury palette, both the girls love fruit; Hope prefers apples, while Morganna can easily devour a whole banana at the age of 7 months! Today if Morganna spots a banana or a pear she will eat it, whereas Hope would rather her fruit covered in chocolate. Hope is the chocolate monster of the two girls, and would eat it all day if we let her

We have bought the girls their cots, both have the same and they are beautiful. Before the girls were born we had also bought Bo a lovely double pushchair when we in Pembrokeshire on one visit home there, we found it advertised in the local paper *THE WESTERN TELEGRAPH*, Donna, who I bought the pushchair from herself had twin girls twelve months older than Bo's, she also had a load of baby clothes for sale, I bought them all, along with some cot bedding and a few toys. Donna has been a godsend to me, to this day we keep in touch, she has become a friend, and I still buy the clothes from her that her girls have outgrown, they come to me in beautiful condition and twelve months after my girls have outgrown them they are still in beautiful condition and I  pass them on to another friend of mine who has twin girls a year younger than mine, that has to be the ultimate in recycling, and it is so nice to see the clothes being worn for another year.

So with both cots erected and made up with pretty lilac bedding the girls are to spend their first night in their bedroom. When it came to bedtime it felt strange taking them in to their own room, I had got so used to them being in our bedroom, and I must admit I loved waking up hearing their gentle breathing in the morning. I had pulled down the blackout blind, closed the curtains and put a drop of lavender oil on each of the cot blanket, I selected a CD called Angels to play for them as they drifted off to sleep. Kevin and I tucked the girls up safe kissed them goodnight and quietly left the room, closing the door behind us. We looked in on them several times that evening before we turned in for the night, they were both in the same positions that we had left them in, facing each other. Today the girls still have the same bedtime routine, at about 7pm they climb the stairs each night with Kevin. Hope will be clutching "Honey Bunny" her most treasured cuddly toy - it goes everywhere with her, and Morganna will dive on her bed and grab hold of "Peter and Molly Panda", then its PJ'S on and into the bathroom to clean their teeth, then a visit to the loo and after that its wash hands and at last after a busy day its into bed. Hope gets into bed and snuggles under her duvet as if its freezing even in the summer, she is always lying snuggled tightly into her duvet, whilst Morganna will just get into bed and leave the duvet for us to pull over her, and you could pull it back over her a hundred times a night and she will still throw it off again. We then kiss and cuddle them goodnight, telling them how much we love them, and as we leave the room we turn on the string of daisy flower lights that run along the beam in their bedroom, and put on the CD player, which now plays them either a bed time story or bed time songs instead of the ANGEL CD. As we leave their room we leave behind us a chorus of

"Mammy, Daddy I love you, lot and lots and lots"

Sometimes as we reach the foot of our stairs we are still calling back up to them that we love them too. It is such a fantastic and wonderful thing to hear each and every night. We are so blessed.

The next few days are busy ones, Oliver is on school summer holidays and I also have my friends two children for a couple of days each week so that she can work. It is so nice that we are spending most of our time out in the garden.

"Kevin, we could really do with a wooden playhouse for the girls"

I say one blazing hot sunny day, but we are very conscious of the fact that the court case is going to cost us an arm and a leg and we are really worried about it. Later that day I mentioned it to my friend when she came to pick up her boys,

"Well that funny" she said, "there is one at the bottom of my garden, it was there when we moved in and it was just resting up against the wall, it is all dismantled, and I don't know if it is any good, but Kevin is good at fixing things, you can have that if you like,"

Later that day Kevin went and collected it, fortunately my sister and her husband were coming over on the weekend so together with the help of Geoff, Kevin got the wooden playhouse house erected, with a bit of TLC from Kevin I give it a coat of paint, and after a few hours spent painting fairies on the inside walls, and making little curtains for the small windows after the girls have gone to bed at night, often finishing it by torch light, the little house has provided the girls with an outdoor play space,. When we moved we brought the playhouse with us, and it is now in our back garden full, it provides the girls and their friends with hours of fun. It's now full of dolls and dolls clothes, they play at being Mammies, taking their babies for walks in the prams my uncle and aunty bought them last Christmas. Morganna also puts her cat Peggy into the pram and that silly cat just lies there under the blanket that Morganna will have put over her and then she will go to sleep as Morganna takes her for a walk around the garden.

I have not heard from Bo for a couple of days now, I can't get hold of her, and I am worried, instinctively I know that something is wrong. I make a mental note that if I have not heard from her by tomorrow morning I will ring the police and request that they call on her and do a welfare check to ensure that she is alright, after the event of that horrible afternoon at the beginning of August I cant bear it if I have been unable to get hold of Bo. The following morning Bo at last rings me, apparently she had lost her phone, so she has now bought a new one, she gives me her new telephone number, we chatted for a short time, she seems withdrawn and quiet, but she maintains that she is fine, but she has not convinced me. After yet another two days of not hearing from her, Bo rings me again, she tells me that her partner has become very violent towards her and whereas it used to be that any violence would follow a drinking binge, now he seems to be violent most of the time. I try to talk to her about her leaving him, but I am now beginning to accept that this will never happen.

The next few days in August see the girls reaching more milestones in their lives. Morganna has now caught up with Hope and both of them are really good at rolling onto their tummies. I was told at the last visit to the health visitor that both the girls may appear slow in reaching their milestones at the same age as my children had, this she explained is because of their prematurely, she said that when looking at the stages of child development on premature babies, medical staff will always deduct the amount of prematurely from the actual age of the child, meaning that although the girls are now 6 months old, they would not be worried if they were only achieving the same development stage that a three and a half month old baby had reached, this meant that the girls were doing fine. On august 19th 2002, both the girls were able to sit up alone for a few minutes; this is great and means that they can now see much more of their little world. Today brought another tearful phone call from Bo, she and her partner have been arguing again, I am not quite sure what she wants me to do; I think she just needs to have someone to listen to her.

On 23rd August Bo rang in a dreadful state, her partner had attacked her, hitting her in the stomach, she told me that she had told him not to do it as her period was late and she thought she might be pregnant again.

"What do you mean you may be pregnant again, for Christ's sake Bo don't you think you have enough going on at the moment, how could you have been so irresponsible. Have you done a test yet?"

"No not yet, he said buying a test kit was a waste of money"

Bo had some money on her that was mine, he did not know about this, so I told her to use some of that. Bo rang me later that afternoon, the test was positive. This was the last thing that she needed and was not going to help her case with social services. The two of us talked for hours that afternoon, she rang off saying she would talk to me about it when she came over.

When Bo told me that the pregnancy test was positive I was devastated, my world was still crumbling and there was nothing I or anyone else could do to prevent it. Hope and Morganna were just 6 months old and already they had a new baby brother or sister on the way. I found it difficult to understand how such a thing could have happened. As I struggled with the news I also struggled with the fact that her partner was still attacking her even though she was pregnant. I read a lot about violence in a relationship and apparently it is quite common that a man who is abusive towards his female partner will do so throughout her pregnancy. But he wasn't only attacking my Bo; he was also attacking my unborn grandchild. Damn him to hell.

When Bo did come over, she stayed for just two days of the seven she had said she was going to spend with us. The social worker has been in contact several times a week over the past month and is as disappointed as we are over Bo's lack of contact with the girls. I have also informed her that Bo is pregnant, she says that Bo is going to need a lot of support, she also asks me if it is alright to arrange a supervised contact for Bo's partner to see the girls on the morning of the court hearing for the interim residence order, I say this will be fine, the contact meeting is arranged fro 10am on the 28th August.

## August 28th 2002

We travelled to Pembrokeshire the evening before the Interim Residence Order hearing and are staying at Deb' house again. After a tiring drive and a restless few hours sleep, Kevin and I get the girls fed and dressed ready to have them in Haverfordwest for the supervised contact to take place. The pressure of all the travelling back and fore to the court hearings, case conferences and contact meetings is beginning to take its toll and we are shattered. It takes us between five and six hours to do a one way trip as we have to stop for the girls. We arrive just in time for the contact meeting Bo turns up but her partner does not, apparently he went on a drinking binge last night and had gone off somewhere. We are furious, this is a complete waste of our time and it's also unsettling Hope and Morganna, leaving we go back to Mam's and after a quick lunch we leave Hope and Morganna with her and make the journey back into Haverfordwset for the court hearing.

134

## The first hearing 28<sup>th</sup> august 2002

I am terrified, and despite everyone trying to reassure me that the interim residence order will most certainly be granted, and that if it is not that social services will go back in front of the judge for a care order and the girls would then return to Oxfordshire with us, I am scared to death, all the way into Haverfordwset I kept going over and over it all in my mind trying to will it to happen, at all costs I have to keep Hope and Morganna safe. The events over the past few days in Bo's life have just reinforced in me that I am doing the right thing, but it still feels wrong that I may have to fight my own child in order to keep her children safe. Arriving in the court Bo and her partner are there already, they are outside having a cigarette, I speak to Bo, but I can't bring myself to even look at him, I despise him and all he stands for, how dare he hurt my daughter and my grand daughters, but I was to learn something this day. As I watched my daughter with this man I saw someone who was devoted to him, I could see my daughter became defensive if he was approached, even to the point where when he was asked why he had not attended the contact meeting that had been arranged at his request, it was my daughter that muttered some kind of response and not him, she was protecting him, whatever hold he had over her it was strong enough to get her fighting his corner for him even when he was s obviously in the wrong.

Entering that court building was terrible. This was the first time that we had appeared before the judge in our fight for a residence order on Hope and Morganna neither of us knew what to expect and we held hands tightly as we sat in the court foyer. Each time we looked at each other and made eye contact we sent each other an unspoken message of encouragement. We sat there watching as the other people were called into the courtroom and as the door to the courtroom would close I thought about what it would feel like when we had to get up and cross that foyer to the courtroom. The courtroom door was opened and the last case to go in left the court room and congregated in the foyer just in front of us. One woman was crying and being comforted by a man, a younger woman pushed her way through the party and shouting obscenities left the court buildings.

"SWAIN -V-SWAIN"

The voice of the court usher cut into the muffled whispering that was going on all around us.

Kevin stood up and taking me by the hand he helped me up, my knees were shaking and I had a thousand butterflies dancing around in my stomach as they began their flight of fear. I began to shake and that old familiar hand went around my waist and as he pulled me into him Kevin whispered into my ear

"It will be OK Cariad"

But I wasn't so sure, I was scared to death.

Kevin and I sat in that court room listening to what was being said. Bo and her partner shared the same solicitor, through her they told how they were going to separate and live apart. They also were opposing the residence order, now things were going to get tough. The judge had listened to all sides, he had read the report prepared by the social worker and he ruled in our favour for the Interim Residence Order, which meant that the girls would be returning with us to Oxfordshire. He also set the date for the next court hearing which was to be a directions hearing this meant that all the parties would be given the opportunity at this next sitting to request extra reports, it also gave the judge the chance to order further reports. That next court hearing was set to take place on 27th November - my sister's birthday.

This first court hearing was to be the first of many as I travelled along this rollercoaster.

We agreed to a contact meeting after the court hearing for Bo and her partner to see the girls, and this time he did turn up. It is agreed that Bo is to come and stay with us for a while; she is due to arrive on Sunday.

Back in Oxfordshire the girls settle back into a routine again and all is fairly quiet. There is only a week left now of Oliver's summer holiday and Kevin and I are both aware that we have done nothing in the way of a holiday, all Kevin's time off has been used going back and fore to Pembrokeshire with the girls. We have spent the odd day down on the beach and visiting Kevin's father who also lives in Pembrokeshire. Oliver has been brilliant over the fact that he has not had a holiday, which makes it easier for us to cope with. On the weekend we are going to go for a picnic to Beale Park, Oliver loves it there; let's just hope the weather is good.

# BACK TO SCHOOL - SOMETHING KIND OF NORMAL

Oliver is back at junior school at South Moreton in Oxfordshire, I have discovered that there is a mother and toddler group which meet in the school twice a week, I have made contact with the organiser and am taking the girls along, I only know one of the mum's that takes her little boy and she is much younger than me. So on that first Tuesday of the autumn term I dress the girls up in their best dresses (must make a good impression) and off we set the few miles in the car to the school. The mother and toddler group meets in the afternoon, so I get the benefit of Kevin helping me to load the girls into the car at home after his lunch, and then after the group has finished we can wait for a few minutes for Oliver to finish school and he can come home with us instead of on the school bus. This also gives me a chance to catch up with some of my friends and gives them a chance to coo over the girls. It is also doing something else and that is forcing me to get out and about, I have been burying my head in the sand a little, finding it easier to stay in and not have to answer awkward questions form people, after all you don't suddenly have twins do you !

When I arrived at the school I was a little nervous, I expected to find all the mum's there were much younger than I was and that they would have all known what was going on in my life, I felt like a window without curtains and I found this a little un-nerving. But I needn't have worried as they were great. It turned out that I already had met some of them as they had older children in the school and that gave me a bit of confidence. I had already decided that if I was asked about the girls and their mother that I would just say that she was ill and couldn't look after them at the moment and this is what I said, but in time it became increasingly hard to satisfy the more inquisitive minds, and eventually one way or another it all came out. I have to admit that at first I found it very difficult to talk about and would often break out in floods of tears. Mostly, however people were very supportive, they usually ended up crying along with me.

I have become very aware that I miss my family and friends back in Pembrokeshire. I know that if this had happened whilst I had still been living there that I would have had a lot of support, not just physically, but also emotionally, how I missed the hugs I used to get. However I am more than aware that if I had still been living in Pembrokeshire it would have made getting the girls very difficult as one of the things social services would have wanted was for the girls to be safe, the fact that we lived 4 hours away from Pembrokeshire meant that the girls were safe.

It did not take long before I used to look forward to the mother and toddler meetings as they gave me other adults to talk to, and other mothers to get ideas from

Baby clinic again today, Hope weighs in at 15lb 4ozs, Morganna weighs 15lb 5ozs Hope is catching Morganna up now, but I somehow don't think it will last; Morganna is quite a bit longer than Hope is.

It was during this first week of some kind of normality, that whilst I was out shopping with the girls in Didcot, that I met up with an old friend that I had not seen since I left Age Concern, she told me of an association called HOMESTART that gave support to families who needed a little help, this included the parents of twins.

"You look tired, I'm sure they will help out, I know its only 2 hours a week, but at least it's a start, go on try them they Have an office in Didcot"

Well, the thought of just two hours a week "me time" was tempting but alas straight up behind this thought in my mind came the ugly head of my pride, and my welsh upbringing, I didn't ask for help easily, how could I make that call, to me it seemed like an admission of being unable to cope. I had to give myself yet another of the stern "talking's to" that I was getting quite good at by now. Whilst we were living in Sussex I had worked for a company that was responsible for providing care for the elderly and disabled in their own homes. It was my job to take on the care packages from social services and with the help of the social worker, set in place a package of care at home and then place that package with one of the carer's or nurse's that worked for the agency which in turn would enable that person to remain in their home instead of going into care. So advising other people on support for themselves was second nature to me, I would just have to take a leaf out of the old book as it were, and so I made the call. And was told that a lady would com out to meet me the following week.

Oliver had joined the local youth club and so every Wednesday night the girls and I would get into the car and drive him to his youth club meeting, it was hard work as from about 5pm each afternoon both the girls were adept at making life hard work, they would become restless and grizzly, something that most of the other mum's at the toddler group were reassuring me was quite normal, but it did make for a hard time and when there are two babies being difficult at the same time life is all but easy, it was during these fraught periods that I was to understand that even I had a limit to how much I could take, but for me I could usually find a way of distracting the girls until bedtime usually Oliver and I would take the girls out for a walk along the farm track that ran behind our house, if it was raining then I would just bath them a little earlier. I had also discovered that lavender oil calmed the girls nicely, so a drop or two of that was added to their bath and as they sat in their bath seats I would wash them and sing them songs, soon enough all was quiet again, anyone outside must have thought I had lost the plot as I sang "Incey wincey spider" over and over again to the whoops of laughter from the girls. Several times Kevin came in to find that all three of us had curled up on the floor on either the lounge or the conservatory and fallen asleep.

The girls are now eating three solid meals a day as well as having milk they are thriving; they love their high chairs and will sit in them quite happily whilst I prepare theirs and Oliver's tea. Now that the girls are settled into a good bedtime routine, Kevin and I will have our meal together later in the evening. We always take the girls up to bed together, it's something that we have always done and still do apart from the nights where Kevin is at woodcarving classes.

The day of the visit from the lady at HOMESTART arrives and I have run around the house on a mission to clean every corner removing every discarded shoe and evicting every spider that has decided to take residence in my neglected house over the past few months, and there is are a lot of them. I can't have this lady thinking I am a mucky girl now can I. Arriving at the door she is greeted by me and the girls whilst the aroma of freshly made coffee wafts around the dining room. We sit chatting for a while and she asks about the girls and their background.

"Well I think I have just the lady for you, I shall bring her out to meet you next week shall I?"

She said

"Oh as soon as that ok that will be great, eh, thank you "

It seems my guardian angel is yet again watching over me, as the following week true to her word she arrives bringing along with her the lady she had spoken off. Margaret is lovely and over the next few weeks she visits every week, then on one of her visits I am brave enough to leave my precious little girls with her. Over the following weeks and months Hope and Morganna quickly fall in love with this gentle caring fun filled lady, and so do I, she is like a breath of fresh air to me, and as well as looking after the girls which gives me time to go to the Dr's, have my hair done or go shopping without carrying the girls with me, she also gives me someone to talk to. What a God send she was. I valued her then as I do now; she is now one of the girls Godmothers.

I also decide that I have to do something for myself. I have always given to others and I am beginning to resent the fact that in my time of need very little is coming the other way. When Kevin and I decided to leave Pembrokeshire the decision was primarily Kevin's, he had found work with an agency and they had offered him a long time contract in Sussex, he had little tying him to Pembrokeshire as he is originally from Shepton Mallet in Somerset, I on the other hand had all my life in Pembrokeshire and I left leaving behind my "three F's "family, friends and familiarity, it was not easy. Now I found myself giving up "me" I had no life, everything I did revolved around the children. Kevin and the home, now I know for most mum's this is also the case, but remember I was at home looking after my daughters children 24 hours of the day 7 days a week, I had no family around me and we had only moved into the area the September the year before, I had no support and no help apart form Margaret who came once a week for 2 hours. I needed an outlet, something for me, watching the TV one day I watched an advert for home learning, "I could do something like that " I thought, and so the seed was sown, and I enrolled on a distance learning course that would see me gain a Diploma in Beauty Care and Personality. I sailed through this course often using my 2 hours a week that Margaret gave me studying, the rest of the time me and the girls would sit outside in the little garden around their playhouse, and as they played I would be sitting my exam papers. Somehow I did it, I passed with a credit. Now I had caught the learning bug, and I wanted to do something else, evening classes were out of the question, for one thing we could not afford an evening class for me as well as Kevin and for another I would be so tired that I would probably fall asleep! So I saved up for a few months and enrolled on another course which would if I was successful give me a Diploma in Counselling. I had also begun to think about what I wanted to do in the long term, I have never been one to stay at home, and I had decided that if we were successful in gaining the full residence order on Hope and Morganna that it was important to me to continue to provide the children with continuity of care and part of that was to involve me staying at home with them until they reached school age, this was a big issue for me, so enrolling on the Counselling Diploma course gave something back to me, and hopefully gave me a head start on what I was then planning to do once the girls started school full time in 2006, back then in 2002 it was hard to look forward to 2003 turning let alone 2006.

I enrolled on the Counselling Course and when I opened the first set of coursework correspondence that arrived I thought "oh my God, I can't do this". Over the next week I picked those papers up time and again and one day thought "I can and I will do this" and off I went. Often on days when the weather was good the girls and I used to go out into the back garden to their little wooden house and as they played contentedly on the floor of their house I would sit outside on the veranda and study. Kevin would come in for his lunch to find I hadn't done any as I had been studying, so he would go into the house and make us coffee and a sandwich and a drink for the girls which he would bring outside on a tray, then we would sit and enjoy our lunch whilst watching as Hope and Morganna would chew away on a crust of bread that we had given them. I would submit my assignment papers for marking and they would be returned with nothing less than 95% on them. Excitedly I would show Kevin when he came in that evening from the farm, and he would look at me and say that he could not understand how I managed to get them done at all. Well it wasn't always easy, but I was pretty damn determined.

Baby clinic again today Hope weighs in at 15lb 13ozs, whilst Morganna is running away again and weighs a hefty 16lb 4ozs, Morganna has gained 1 lb 1oz in the past 4 weeks. The health visitor is also delighted with their progress both are actually reaching milestones before they would be expected to do so, which is reassuring news.

Both the girls are now crawling, and I have been taught yet another lesson by them, my home is not child proof, so I spent the evening removing breakables and giving them all new homes in the safety of the lounge where they cant be got at. Plugs are now covered with safety covers to stop inquisitive little fingers, and Oliver's bits of Lego and his game boy along with anything else he wants to keep in one piece are banned to his bedroom only, even the cat has decided to become more of an evening visitor in our cosy home, choosing to go up and sleep on Oliver's bed in the peace and quiet and away from these two four legged monsters that are now sharing his floor space and getting quicker at reaching him as the days pass, after falling asleep on the bed Nick, the cat will stay there until the girls go to bed, at which point he decides to go out again and then starts meowing to come back in about 9pm, spends a few hours with us and then goes off hunting again for the night. The most interesting thing the girls have found over the past few days are the patio doors that go out onto the steps which lead into the garden, they spend ages sitting there watching the little birds that Oliver has over the past year enticed into the garden with a beak watering array of different bird seeds.

My sister and her family also visit us as does my brother Michael and his family, its great to have the house full of children, it's nice to see my nieces and nephews and be able to spend some time with them instead of dashing about all over the county of Pembrokeshire trying to cram it all in, and usually coming away without seeing everyone we had intended seeing.

The whole of September 2002 was all about a mixture of settling down into some kind of normality and trying to cope with the demands on us to travel back to Pembrokeshire for appointments with our solicitor and contact meetings for Bo and her partner, as well as trying to tie these visits in with seeing members of my family, Kevin's Dad and our friends, most of whom were very short changed on the time we could spend with them, often our visits were flying ones, but I am sure those who it did affect understand why. The other thing that kept raising its ugly head was Bo's relationship with her partner. It had been confirmed that the pregnancy was in fact correct and that she was about 10 weeks pregnant, so now on top of everything else there was to be discussions within social services about the unborn baby as well. I had also been made aware much to my horror that the violence in Bo's relationship was not just one way, she was in fact violent towards her partner, often lashing out at him, and not in self defence which I had thought was the case the first time it had happened. The understanding of this was to have awful effect on me, I became aware of my own distrust for her, I felt unable to leave the girls alone in her company again, and so I didn't .It also in its own way served to reassure me that we were doing the right thing in our application for a full residence order.

We returned home yet again once more in September, we took the girls to see Bo and made no promises to come to see them I was devastated. She looked terrible, she was thin and pale, she also had fresh cut marks on her arms where she had been self harming Bo was angry that we were going for a full residence order, she could not understand why we were doing this to her, she still has not grasped the fact that it was all down to her and had nothing to do with me.

I have discovered an association called TAMBA which stands for TWINS AND MULTIPLE BIRTHS ASSOCIATION. I have paid the membership fee and have received my membership details along with a copy of their latest magazine. Flicking through it over a mug of hot coffee I see it is crammed full of interesting information, stories about other twins and triplets, as well as loads of adverts. I ma hooked this is brilliant, now I can read about other twins and how their families cope with the bad times as well as what to expect as they grow older. They also have a TWINLINE where you can get all sorts of advice or just ring up and speak with someone who will just listen to you, joining TAMBA also means I can save some money - always a good thing, as certain stores give discount to TAMBA members, which comes in very useful when buying the girls shoes.

# OCTOBER - MAD BIRTHDAY MONTH

"Stop the calendar and let me get off, mad month is here again"!!!!!

In my family it has been a long standing joke of everyone's that we wish we could just delete this month from all our calendar's as there are so many birthday's in my family fall over the coming 31 days that I feel that I am constantly in the card shop I bet that you also have at least one month in the year that is just like this one.

My birthday is the second one in our family in October, and falls on the 3rd, as usual I expect the flurry of birthday cards that bring my birthday wishes to my door- no I joke honestly I am lucky if I get a couple delivered by the postman on my actual birthday date, I was looking forward to having birthday cards this year from my two new grand daughters, but they were here with me, and Bo hadn't sent one either. My eldest son had also now split from his partner, they had been together for years and had two children, aged 4 years one little boy who is just two months younger than the girls, I was really upset, I had no cards from them either, as for my middle son, I knew that my birthday wishes from him would come over the phone later in the day-and they did. This birthday one that I wished I could have turned back the clock and let everyone start again, getting it right on the second attempt. No cards arrived on the day and Kevin had also forgotten it was my birthday, so on the way home from shopping, I jokingly said

"Where have you hidden my birthday cake then?"

"Oh blast he said I knew there was something, it's your birthday isn't it?"

"Well yes I have one every year on the 3rd of October"

You see even he was now falling foul of the old system that had broken down in our household over the past few month. I was the old system but I was on system overload and as a result had stopped reminding him of important things like birthdays, finding it easier and quicker to just get on with it all myself. Being like most men Kevin needs a PA everyday to remind him of these everyday events.

It was the last straw, I was in floods of tears and felt swamped by the feeling that nobody loved me and had forgotten me, which oh course they hadn't - it just felt that way because of the emotional place I was at.

"I can't have a birthday without birthday cake" I sobbed,

He drove into TESCO'S car park and ran in with Oliver, leaving me in floods of tears in the back of our car with the girls.., who were looking at me as if I had two heads and a tail.

Kevin and Oliver returned to the car carrying a cake and a huge bunch of flowers, and as grateful as I was I still felt cheated of that "spoilt feeling" that hadn't happened that day.

We went home and had chocolate cake as there was no birthday cakes left that Oliver wished to choose, so he had picked a gooey chocolate creation instead. The girls loved it and before too long they were wearing more chocolate cake than they had actually eaten.

That evening when the little darlings were all tucked up in bed I sat on the sofa and the phone began to ring, first Mam rang and wished me a happy birthday, then it was James, my middle son, followed by my sister Deb's. Kevin came back down from his shower, made coffee's sat down and fell asleep on the other sofa, and I was left alone, me and my birthday. The television was on, but there was nothing worth watching so I put on a CD instead. Sat there in the lounge with the curtains open I watched the moon as it played peek-a-boo behind the clouds. Now why couldn't everyone have made a special effort this year, I thought, but then I reminded myself that I was just feeling sorry for myself. My thoughts quickly turned to Bo, why hadn't she rung me? Where was she? Dear God I do hope she is alright, panic stricken I rung her mobile, by now it was coming up to midnight, but I knew that she would be up as her life pattern meant she was up most nights, all night and then would sleep in the daytime. I got no reply. Now I worried even more than I had already been.

Happy birthday Keri!!!!

The following day I wrapped Bo's birthday gifts up with a lot of help from the girls, I had made a special effort to make sure that I bought her meaningful gifts, especially from Hope and Morganna, I felt so deeply for her as this would be her first birthday where she was a mum, and her girls were not with her, some of you may well read this and think it was her own fault, and that she didn't deserve all the love and support she was being shown, but I felt and still feel differently. I have to admit as the years have passed and her situation has remained unchanged my attitude towards her and her lifestyle has got harder, but I still do make the effort, it just gets harder to do. I painted the girls hands with paint and placed them on the inside of Bo's card, they were too young to write their names, but his was a lovely was for her to have something special that they had done. Wrapping the parcel in brown paper, the girls and I drove the few miles form our home to Didcot where we posted her cards and gifts.

Bo's life remained in the same chaotic mess. On October the 10th the social worker from Pembrokeshire was due to visit us in Oxfordshire and undertake a home visit; he has to do this as part of the report which he is preparing for the court. Once again my house became the subject of a military operation, all corners were cleaned and then cleaned again, all spiders were evicted for the second time this year, and the house was beginning to look reasonably loved and not neglected. Everything was ship shape and Bristol fashion ready for his visit, now I knew he was visiting us not our mess, but I had to do everything I could to show him we could provide a good, safe and clean home for the girls, the fact that they have already been living here for 4 months is neither here or there, this spring cleaning has to be done even if it is October.

Along with the social worker Bo is coming as well, she is staying with us; the social worker has booked bed and breakfast in a neighbouring village. Once again there is no one to cover Kevin's work on the farm so he has to work; the social worker will catch up with Kevin when he comes in for his lunch.

Over the past few weeks Hope and Morganna have been calling me Mamma and Kevin Dadda, we are very aware of this and have been correcting them,

"No darling Grandma or Granddad2"

Whichever has been appropriate. I am so aware that this is going to hurt Bo, and I don't want that, so I have warned her, she didn't say very much, I think she has accepted how it has happened, the girls are just copying Oliver, and it is difficult and is something that I shall discuss with the social worker when he comes over.

When the social worker and Bo arrived we all sat chatting in the conservatory, which has now become the girls playroom, there are toys scattered everywhere, the girls are into everything now and are both desperately trying to pull themselves up to a standing position with the help of the furniture, Hope is having more luck than Morganna, and it is comical to watch them trying so hard to stand, I guess it wont be too long now before they will be standing, and then I shall have to move things yet again. As we are sat there talking and at the same time playing with the girls Morganna says Mamma to me, I correct her, gently saying "grandma" of course she does not understand at all and keeps on saying "Mamma", its now a game, I looked across to Bo and the tears were in her eyes, I hurt for her. I asked the social worker what I should do about it; his reply was to continue to discourage it.

Leaving Bo in the conservatory with the girls, the social worker and I go into the dining room, here he interviews me, this became one of the few times I break down and cry as I talk about my daughter, the girls and my feelings and hope's for the future, he is aware of my dedication not just to Hope and Ann, but also to Bo as well. I discuss with him my fears for Bo's unborn baby; as yet she has made no plans for her future. I tell the social worker that all I want is to be able to close my eyes at night and know that my girls are safe, loved, warm, fed and clothed, is that really too much to ask for. I also tell him that we have decided that we have made the decision that we as Bo has made little, almost no effort to spend time with the girls, we are definitely l going ahead with our application for a full residence order on Hope and Morganna.

The social worker interviews Kevin during his lunch break and when Oliver comes home from school, he asks if he can also talk with Oliver, this I feel is a good idea, we have hidden very little from Oliver over the past 5

147

months, so I have nothing to fear from the social worker chatting to him, I also see this as a positive move as I am aware that if Oliver does have any niggling problems with the girls being with us, it is highly unlikely that he is going to tell either Kevin or myself about them, and I would rather know, as having Hope and Morganna with us is having and will continue to have a great effect on Oliver's life.

We also sit down and try and talk to Bo, Kevin, the social worker and I, all of us trying so desperately to get her to see what stands to loose, and that how we all feel that with help she can actually do this and care for her girls plus the new baby, we talked about her possibly coming to live near to us, so that we can be on hand to help her out if needed, this was something that she had discussed with Kevin and I a couple of months back. The social worker also said he felt it would be good if Bo moved back in with us. I was not happy about this suggestion as I know all too well the disruptive effect it has on our household when Bo is with us, it is one thing that Kevin and I may chose to put up with, but allowing her disruptiveness to turn the children's lives upside down is something we won't allow. We would need to be pretty convinced that this time she meant what she was saying and was going to try her hardest to rehabilitate with the girls. I was not prepared to put Oliver and the girls on this rollercoaster with me unless it was for an extremely good reason, and up until today nothing she had done or said had convinced Kevin or I that she had anyone's interests at heart other than her partners and then hers.

The following day the social worker was meeting with the girls health visitor, he was then calling back to see us before he left. Bo had decided to go with him back to Pembrokeshire, despite all our pleas to stay and spend some time with the girls. In the whole month of October she spent a total of just 24 hours with the girls, which did nothing to help her case in trying to get the girls back with her. She has told us that she is determined to fight our application for a full residence order on Hope and Morganna until the bitter end, always pointing out to us that they are her girls not ours, to which we always reply.

"You are right Bo, so you do what is right and put them and their safety first, rebuild your life and prove you are making an attempt to provide them with the love and safety they need and deserve, We will gladly step back and support you if social services are convinced that the girls coming back to you is safe"

We received a letter from our solicitor on 14ᵗʰ October informing us of the firms costs, which are £100 per hour plus VAT, We are also advised in the letter that we will have to hire a barrister for the final hearing, which will hopefully take place in April 2003, the cost of hiring a barrister is £750.00 per day for a one day hearing with costs of £500.00 for every day after that. This is a shock, but we have to go on, we will find this money somehow, we have to.

Also in the contents of the letter is some bad news our solicitor advises us that if the social worker were to recommend to the courts in his section 7 report that they were still looking favourably at rehabilitation for Bo and the girls then in reality the judge would not grant the residence order in our favour, and whilst we could in fact state that we were still concerned about Bo's ability to care for the girls as well as the unborn baby when it arrives, if we did not help to try and support Bo in an attempt to rehabilitate her with the girls, we may end up loosing them as well, as social services may feel it best to place the girls with foster parents. I feel numb at this piece of news.

I feel damned if I do and damned if I don't, what a no win situation, all we want to do is keep the girls safe, and the last thing I want is to put them within the reach of harm. I have also become more than used to having the girls around me, and I am beginning to feel as if I cant be without them, try as I might they now feel part of our family unit, and the thought of loosing them now is almost to much to bear, it brings a lump to my throat to even think about it. This can't happen, we have to fight and keep the girls safe, for me it really is "off with the gloves and come out fighting"

Any Grandparent reading this who is bringing up their grandchild/ children will identify with the emotions that I am feeling, they will understand the drive that keeps me going, and they will know all too well the feeling of absolute fear that I was beginning to feel should my daughter win her fight to have the girls returned to her in the situation she is at present. How could anyone sit back and risk that happening, especially when they know as much as I did about the world my daughter lived in, and I only knew part of the bigger picture, there was a lot that I didn't know. As much as it would have torn my world apart, over the months that had passed and the ones that were to follow, if my daughter and her partner had tried to convince social services and the other agencies involved that they were trying, if they had made the life changes required of them which showed us all that Hope and Morganna's welfare and safety was the forefront of both their lives then I would have had no choice other than to let social services hand the girls back to Bo. Even after just those few short months doing so would have broken me, today I am sure I would die of a broken heart if the girls were not here with us, they are my life. In Hope and Morganna, I have a little bit of my beautiful Bo, in them she lives on, in them I see her everyday in some of the things one or the other of them says or do. She has given to me the greatest gift of all.

Sadly Bo makes it easier and easier for everyone to reach a decision, by her total lack of commitment, and the continuing level of violence in her relationship, over the next few months. During one incident she told me that she had attacked her partner with a knife, I was totally shocked and bewildered, was this really my child that was doing these bizarre things I took this incident to heart and I was worried about where it was all going to lead. For the first time I was also beginning to fear Bo being left with the girls alone and I spoke to the social worker about this, I have now said that never will I leave the girls alone with her. So far the level of violence she was displaying was as far as I was aware restricted towards her partner, what I did not know was that already there had been incidents where she had been violent towards others. I was to later discover that she had the capability when roused to be extremely violent towards another woman.

We were sitting talking over lunch one day when suddenly we could hear water running, I went into the kitchen to discover the washing machine was leaking and water was flooding out our kitchen, for me this was the straw and it broke the camels back, unfortunately I was the camel this time, I couldn't speak, I was unable to get my words out, my whole body was shaking and I couldn't move, I tried to walk, but my legs would not move, I tried so hard to talk, but Kevin couldn't understand what I was trying to say, the harder I tried to make him understand, the more jumbled up my words became. I was so frightened; I did not know what was happening to me. I can remember looking at Kevin and seeing the horror I was feeling reflected in his eyes, somehow he got me upstairs and into Oliver's bedroom where he gently lay me on the bed he lay next to me, stroking my hair and telling me it was going to be alright, I remember him telling me that I had just had enough and that he would look after me. I tried to tell him I was terrified, he understood, its ok you will be alright, you have to be. After what seemed like hours (it wasn't, but to me it felt like it was) he said he was going to check on the girls who were asleep in their cots and on Oliver who was downstairs watching TV. I remember no more, he told me later that when he came back up he had found me in a deep sleep, so he let me sleep and I slept for hours. It was the girls crying that brought me back from my world of peace I heard Kevin climbing the stairs and opening the door to their bedroom, I wanted to get out of bed, but my head was too heavy I couldn't lift it from the pillow it was resting on, I was confused, How had I got there, who had got me there, my last memory had been of the water on the kitchen floor, what water, why was there water on the floor? Kevin brought the girls to me and I lay there with tears rolling down the sides of my face for a long time as the girls stroked my face and tried to cuddle me. Slowly I began to regain the strength that I so took for granted. I didn't know what had happened to me that day until about a year ago, and I have not told a living soul about it either, in fact many of my family and friends will be reading this and learning of it for the very first time .

I learnt something about myself that awful day, I was taught that I was not invincible, and that even I had a breaking point, I had reached it that day, and believe me it was something I needed to learn. All of my life it has been me that has been the strong one, it has been me that held others together, and held them up, whenever there was a problem, good old Keri would be the one to listen and the one to help, I still am this person, its just that on that awful day of reckoning I was to start a new journey within myself, one that was to teach me to say "NO" occasionally. It was the wake up call that both Kevin and I needed. I came back from my peaceful world. That day my mind and body just "shut down" it went into a period of total rest, if it hadn't I would have in all probability broken further than I could have ever repaired. Every time I thought of that day after that it scared me as I would worry about what would happen to everyone if I hadn't "shut down"

But I had and when I came back from my "rest" I came back fighting.

How lucky was I and everyone else in my family that I recovered, some people find themselves going through what I had and they don't recover as I did, they need specialised help.

All I had was sheer determination, my fight for Hope and Morganna became my driving force, and I had the love of a strong man. I was a little unsteady for a couple of weeks, and for a while after that awful day I would get the occasional wobble, but now installed in me there was an acceptance that I was not invincible, I was now able to recognise the signs if I was beginning to struggle and I would remove myself from the situation or take some time out, I stopped being Bo's emotional punch bag, and all of the small things that would give me cause for concern I put to one side, I concentrated on the things I could change. One other major thing I tried to do was each day when I woke I would focus on one positive thing that had happened, instead of feeling overwhelmed by the insurmountable negative-ness that Bo's life choices surrounded me with. It was easy for me to find my positive, it was Hope and Morganna, everyday I woke up with them was a positive day, every smile, every chuckle, every touch of their hands as they explored my face, reinforced in me a positive that was to see me through it all.

# THE RECOMMENDATIONS

November is just as October was apart from the flurry of birthdays and the lack of a visit from the social worker, but this month was to see Kevin and I make a big decision that was to improve our quality of life.

News had reached us that the farmer who owns the farm that Kevin is managing has decided to get out of milk production and sell off his dairy herd. This news makes it easier for Kevin and me to reach a decision that we have been talking about and throwing back and fore between each other for a while now. Kevin is really feeling the pressure of work and has become pretty impossible to live with. There has to be a better way than this, we have to sort it all out and look to our future.

The following week another letter arrived from the solicitor, this time with some good news; she had received the copy of the social workers report to the court which also contained his recommendations for the girls. He was recommending to the court that the girls should reside with us on a permanent basis, I wanted to jump through hoops, but it was not all good news, Bo was contesting the residence order, we would need to engage a barrister for the final hearing. We were not home and dry yet, but the social workers recommendations were good news, the best we could have wished for, and it strengthened our case.

The day before the directions hearing in November I had a call from Bo, in the background I could hear her partner shouting, he was threatening to kick my head in, this he shouted along with some choice swear words, he also said that he hoped that we would have a car accident on the way home to Pembrokeshire for the court hearing, and that all of us were killed including the girls. There had been several incidents of him making threats and displaying aggressive behaviour towards Kevin and I, we were strong enough to take this on the chin and he could threaten me until the cows came home, but there was no way I was letting him get away with threats involving any of the children. Our solicitor was instructed to send a letter to his solicitor stating that any further incidents would be reported immediately to the police and that I unlike my daughter I would not be bullied by him and that I would press charges against him.

When we attended the directions hearing in Pembrokeshire on 27th November Bo turned up, her partner did not. Once again we were asked through Bo's solicitor to accommodate a last minute request from Bo for her partner to see the girls, this visit was to be a supervised visit as that was the only way social services would allow contact for her partner to see the girls, which in effect meant that the social worker also had to change any plans he had and arrange a place for us to meet and a supervisor to be present. After we had changed our plans for the afternoon and agreed to the visit, the social worker found a meeting place and a supervisor, the meeting was all planned. After everyone's efforts he did not even bother to turn up. Again we instructed our solicitor to contact his solicitor saying we were angry that he had not shown up for the contact meeting especially as it was requested at the last minute, and that we had to change our plans to accommodate this request. We also asked her to point out that up until now we had always made contact easy for him by informing Bo of any visits we planned to make to Pembrokeshire, this was now going to stop, and in future if he wished to have any contact with Hope and Morganna he would have to make the request himself.

Kevin and I knew that we had a battle on our hands, but we also knew that it was looking favourably towards us, which in no way brought us any reassurance; we still had an uphill struggle. I was fighting to keep my daughters children safe, and within their birth family. I found it difficult to accept that whilst she knew she was up against it she still chose to fight us. If she had supported her fight with efforts to build a relationship with the girls and displayed some kind of commitment to them that would have been easier to accept, but she did nothing to show any of us that she felt any commitment towards Hope and Morganna, she did nothing at all to better her position, if anything her position was worsening as the days went on.

One day I was talking to her on the phone, when she suddenly started crying and asked me why I hated her, and why I was doing this to her. I told her that day, and on many other occasions that followed, that I loved her no matter what, that I would always love her, but that I did not like her or what she had become. I also tried to explain to her that I was not fighting her, and that her fight should not be with me as all I was trying to do was to keep the girls safe for her, her fight was with social services. It was not me she had to prove herself to, or to convince that she was making an effort; it was social services and all the other agencies that were involved in her life. Although in a way she did have to prove herself to me, it was not me that was judging her ability to parent, and I was not the one calling the shots or making the decisions on Hope and Morganna's future. I was the person trying so desperately to hold it all together; I was the one who was committed to providing the girls with a safe home around people who loved them unconditionally as I indeed loved Bo. This question I was to continue to be asked many times over the coming years by my Bo, I always answer it the same way. Bo I love you, you are my daughter, my only daughter, I just don't like you and the way you have chosen to live your life, I will always be here for you and will help where I can, but you have to understand that Hope and Morganna are my priority now.

# CHRISTMAS 2002

Any of you reading this will remember and identify all the important "first's" in our children's lives, most of which as we think about them bring a smile to our faces and possibly a tear to our eyes, so far Bo had missed all the girls first's. I had been the one to see them both do so many things for the first time. I nursed them as they cut their first teeth. Gave them their first haircut and slipped the hair safely into a photograph album for safe keeping, I saw them both crawl for the first time, I took them to their first toddler group, and for me the most heartbreaking of all was that it was me they had called "Mamma" and not my daughter.

As Christmas began to approach Kevin and I tried to persuade Bo to come to us and be with the girls on their first Christmas, such a big thing in any new child's life, that very first Christmas is such a special time. I can remember each and every one of my own children's first Christmas's. I actually begged her to come, telling her that this was time she could never recapture and live again, that once it was gone that was it, it was gone. She chose not to come saying it would be unfair on her partner, my response to that was to ask her if any of this was fair on anyone, she did not reply.

On Kevin's weekend off we took the children along to the local garden centre and let Oliver choose our Christmas tree, it was huge, That night when the children were all asleep in bed, Kevin trimmed about two foot off it's base and brought it into the house after rearranging the furniture in the lounge to accommodate the tree I decorated it, soon with the heat from the open fire blazing from the fireplace the familiar and cosy fragrance form the

156

Christmas tree was filling our lounge, much to my delight, it was also stirring in me memories of my past Christmases, and as I decorated the tree so I went on a mental trip down memory lane, this was my 27th Christmas in my own home, it was also the 6th year that I had not been home in Pembrokeshire to celebrate a family Christmas with my family and friends. On that Christmas tree I had hung decorations that I have had for so many years, I had hung all 4 of my children's first bauble, they had each been bought one fro their first Christmas. Now this year Hope and Morganna too would be able to hang their special first Christmas bauble on our tree. When the children got up in the morning I took the girls in to see the tree, their eyes lit up. Hope is now beginning to try and talk and I am greeted with "ook, ook" she is trying to tell me to look, Morganna has a look of wonderment on her face, and yet again I feel that familiar sadness in me, that it is me and not Bo that is experiencing yet another "first" with the girls.

As the house took on its creative festive look (something I spend hours doing every year - this year trying to get it done when the girls are napping in the daytime) so the Christmas spirit began to descend on our home. The usual flurry of Christmas cards were posted through our letterbox by the postman and fell onto our doormat, and as usual Oliver took great delight in going through them to see if any were for him. The realisation began to dawn on me that that many of our friends knew nothing about what we were going through as we had not had the time to tell them all yet. Every morning when the girls woke up I would take them downstairs and they would sit for ages just watching the twinkle of the fairy lights on one of our three trees, yes we had three in fact we had four if you count the one out in the garden. There was the big one in the lounge that nobody was allowed to touch - but they did if they got the opportunity. There was one in the dining room which we always have had, this was always the children's tree, and it is covered in their decorations. Then this year we bought a small fibre optic one for the conservatory so that the girls could watch it as it changed colour, and of course the one outside in the front garden, which twinkled its lights to welcome our visitors as they walked up the path to our front door.

I somehow managed to make our Christmas cake, but it had not been made in late October and fed brandy for 6 weeks before I iced it as I had done in previous years, this was a last minute rush job, however, it was a Christmas cake, and it was homemade, even if the icing that adorned it was straight out of a ready rolled packet! This year for the first Christmas since Kevin and I had been together my own jars of homemade mince meat, which would have contained most of a bottle of good brandy were not neatly placed on the shelf in the pantry awaiting to be blanketed between a pastry so light, you would have to eat them one after the other until they were all gone - and Kevin would eat his way through more than his fair share of them. So instead I sent Kevin to the local TESCO'S store one night to track down a couple of the few remaining large jars of mincemeat on their selves, and over the following two nights turned those jars of mincemeat into mince pies. I got fed up of hearing Kevin saying

"Not as good as your usual ones cariad"

Blast him, he was lucky to have any mince pies at all that had not come out of a cardboard box!! There was however one thing that did not change in our household in the lead up to Christmas and that was me driving Kevin mad from about early December playing the collection of Christmas CD's I have accumulated over the years, he would never really know what he would be subjected to when he came in from work, I could be doing anything from joining in and singing along with the angelic voices of the Winchester Cathedral Choir to blasting out on top of my voice the lyric's of SLADE'S "Merry Christmas everyone"- this year I was often dancing around the dining room or the kitchen with one or both of the girls in my arms, singing along as they both smiled and giggled. Now four years later I still play the same old CD collection (I have added to it - but don't tell Kevin!) only now it's not just me that dances around the house, its my apprentice Christmas rock chicks as well, because Hope and Morganna also join in, poor old Kevin came in last year and found all three of us covered in flour, busy rolling out pastry to make mince pies that did in fact contain my home made mincemeat and singing "When Santa got stuck up the chimney". All thoughts of tea had slipped my mind as I had tried to concentrate on keeping most of the pastry on the table as the girls cut out holly shapes from the leftover pastry to go on top of the pies, so Kevin and Oliver were banished form the house and sent out to fetch some fish and chips for supper - he doesn't stand a chance does he? Now don't go feeling sorry for him as he loves it all really he does, he just likes to play the part of the neglected husband. So determined was I that we would have a Christmas of sorts this year I had even ordered our free range bronze turkey from our local butcher.

Before we knew it Christmas week was upon us. I left Kevin in charge of the girls one evening and taken Oliver to his youth club meeting, I had said I would stay and help out as the youth club were planning to go around the village singing carols and instead of asking for everyone's hard earned cash, they were offering the people who's homes they had graced with their limited singing ability chocolates from a tin, a real twist to carol singing, and I have to say a really nice one as well. So with coats and hats on and warm scarves wound tightly around our necks to keep out the winter chill off we set into the frosty night. We needed all the Christmas spirit we could muster to keep control of the excited, rebellious youngsters who appeared to have forgotten the correct words to the carols along with the ability to read them from the song sheets they had been given. Christmas arrived for me that night and I returned home to Kevin full of a mixture of festive spirit and a feeling of overwhelming sadness. The girls were asleep and once we had managed to get Oliver off to bed, I got on with packing into freezer bags the beautifully decorated holly leaf mince pies the girls and I had spent all afternoon making, once they were in the bags I hid them at the bottom of the freezer before Kevin had a chance to eat any more!, I'm sure he thinks that I lose the ability to count when it comes to mince pies, or maybe that is why I am offered a large glass of wine to warm me up on my return home from carol singing!

The last minute provisions were collected by me with the girls in tow, and put away and Kevin and I took Oliver and the girls to church in the village where we lived for the candlelight carol service. This was the first time many of the people in the village had seen the girls, until now a lot of the older people in the village had only heard of them, most of them were overjoyed to see our two contented bundles of mischief. They were so well behaved throughout the service. I had Hope with me and she had taken a shine to a gentleman sitting in the pews behind us and kept smiling at him, much to his delight. After the service we all stayed behind to share mince pies and coffee, it had a true sense of community spirit that is not seen much these days and it was great to be a part of it.

On Christmas eve not long after Oliver had settled for the night Kevin and I had placed beneath the Christmas tree in the lounge the children's Christmas presents that I had somehow managed to get wrapped, Hope woke up which was something she never did at night time. Kevin brought her downstairs as he couldn't settle her back to sleep. I think she was preparing to give us a special Christmas present that night, it was about 11pm when he brought her down, her face was a picture as she looked around her at the tree and the presents which lay beneath it wrapped in shiny paper. I had just changed her nappy on the floor in the lounge and was watching her as she pulled herself up at the pine blanket box which had on top of it my beautiful hand carved calf that Kevin had bought me many years ago, it is quite large and when Oliver was a baby we used to have to keep it on the floor as he would pull it down from wherever it was placed and then sit on its back, using its ears as reins, I often wondered where he was riding off to in his mind when he sat on that calves back, now Hope and Morganna would do the same, "horsy, horsy" Hope would say, my poor old calf has got quite a collection of small dents on her head from where Oliver and the girls have tried to use it as a teething ring. Once she had pulled herself up to standing, she worked her way towards the end of the pine blanket box and towards the tree, when she reached the end of the box she let go and took her first unaided steps, she walked to the Christmas tree. My beautiful little girl was walking, what a fantastic Christmas present for Kevin and I, tears were shed and I held her so close telling her what a clever girl she was, that night Kevin and I spent ages getting her to walk from one of us to the other, it was magical, she made my Christmas. It was as if she wanted to share that moment just with Kevin and I. Morganna started walking two weeks later, I was in the kitchen when I felt a tug on my skirt, expecting to find Hope by my side I found Morganna stood there looking up at me with a huge smile on her face. Now I had two clever girls, I had seen yet another two first's. Kevin came in that day for lunch, and as always the girls were waiting for him to come in, they used to wait by the conservatory doors waiting for him to walk around the corner, then when he did they would crawl through the kitchen and out to the back door as fast as their little legs would let them, by now Hope was quite quick on her feet and would rush off ahead of Morganna, well today I stood there holding Morganna's hands, when Kevin came in I said to him "call Morganna love" he called her and she let go of me and walked to him with the biggest smile on her face I had ever seen. He was thrilled.

Everyday from that day onwards they waited for Kevin by the conservatory doors and when they spotted him they would race each other to the back door to see who could get to him first. Now years later when they see him crossing from the milking parlour to the front of our house they run out the back door, up the side of the house to the gate that Kevin made high enough so they couldn't get over it. Morganna climbs up the gate and undoes the special lock (which most adults struggle with) in double quick time. Hope then swings the gate open with her sister hanging onto it for grim death, Morganna gets off the gate and they both run up the garden path that takes them out to the front. It is the most blissful of sights to watch as they hold his hands and the three of them walk back down the path again.

Christmas morning arrived and Kevin was out milking when the girls woke. Over the years Oliver and I have got used to him not being in on Christmas morn, when he gets in we have a special breakfast before we open our presents. This year was to give us a taste of what our future Christmas's were to be like, I think the word manic, springs to mind, as before very long our lounge floor resembled that of a packaging company, and there is an assortment of toys and clothes lying everywhere. Not to be outdone in flurry of Christmas activity, Hope decides to show Oliver her brand new skill, and walks over to him, he is chuffed to pieces, but she isn't after him, the chocolate monster has spotted his selection box!

We also had a guest for Christmas, my eldest son who was now on his own, having split with his partner, had rang a few days before Christmas and asked if he could come over, I was thrilled, it had been years since my eldest son had shared a Christmas with us. Having him with us provided me with a welcome distraction in our home that year, but I know it was very difficult for him as it was the first year he had not been with his own children for Christmas, it must have been made even more difficult for him because Hope and Morganna are the same age as his son. I have some wonderful photographs of Oliver sharing that Christmas with not just the girls, but also with the big brother who he worships so much

I rang Bo first thing on Christmas morning, she was understandably quite tearful, she was missing the girls, but we had done all we could to try and get her to come over to us, even when I knew her older brother was coming over I tried to persuade her to travel over with him, but she would not. She told me that her partner had invited a friend to come and stay with them for Christmas, she was angry about this and told me that her partner and his friend had been drinking, she was in very low spirits, but what could I do, there was nothing apart from ring her several times during the day.

On boxing day I rang her again, she was in a dreadful state and told me that her partner had hit her, she said that she had a bruise which was covering half of her breast, I told her to go to hospital, she refused telling me that if she did it would only make things worse for her as by now social services knew about her pregnancy and she feared that this would worsen her position, she was of course right. I talked to her trying to get her to understand that she had to work with social services not against them if she hoped to be able to keep her unborn baby, she understood this, but it made no difference, she would not seek help. Bo knew we were coming to Pembrokeshire the next day.

This year was also to be different for another reason as well, usually in the past Kevin and I would try to get back home to Pembrokeshire to visit our family and friends during the lead up to Christmas, this year we were not, instead we were going to make a mad dash to Pembrokeshire on the 27th

December returning to Oxfordshire on the 30<sup>th</sup>, this was so that Bo could see the girls over the Christmas period, I felt strongly about her seeing them and as Kevin was actually working over Christmas we could not get away. Travelling back and fore to Pembrokeshire was now also causing a problem for us in that it was disrupting the girls routine, and when we would return to our home in Oxfordshire it would take between three and four days for them to settle back into their routine again.

Because Bo was not coming to us I spoke to Kevin, and so off we went again. Bo was thrilled and we agreed to meet up and exchange Christmas presents. I had spent the past month buying little bits and pieces to make up a nice box full of gifts for her from us all, including some special framed photos of the girls that we had had taken by a photographer. When we arrived with Bo she tried everything she could to get us to take the girls to see her partner, we refused, she had already been told by the social worker before our visit that if he wanted to see the girls he would have to contact the social worker himself so that a supervised contact could be arranged, his contact visits had to be supervised, there was no way given his threats towards us and the continuing violence between him and Bo that we were going to put the girls safety at risk. Bo hated us for this.

The remainder of our visit home to Pembrokeshire was busy as we travelled from one home to home of our family and friends, to say that I was exhausted by the time we got back to Oxfordshire would have been an understatement. Christmas had turned into the new year, I rand Bo on new years day and she was full of high spirits, she was at a friends collecting sausage rolls for the party they were having that night, I said I would ring her that night to wish her a happy new year. I did not ring anyone that night, I was ill, I had lain huddled up in a duvet on our couch in the lounge, feeling pretty miserable, and as the bells of BIG BEN rang in the new year I closed my eyes and silently wished for a better year ahead of me that the one I was just saying goodbye to.

# *HAPPY NEW YEAR - OR IS IT?*

January had arrived and it was already looking like being a busy month. The wish I had silently offered up as the old year was rung out by the new one has already been forgotten as I had eventually got hold of Bo only to discover that her partner had spent most of new year's eve in a police cell, so not only did she not get a call from me, she also saw the new year in without him. It seems as if this fresh New Year is set to become just like the old one, already the worry is beginning.

It is Kevin's birthday on the 3rd January, so Oliver and I have been busy planning a tea for him, we have been out and Oliver has chosen a birthday cake. Oliver is a little sad as he hates the Christmas decorations being taken down after Christmas, he knows that I always leave them up until after Kevin's birthday, when I take them down and pack them away until the next Christmas, which at the moment seem like a long time away. Although I expect somehow that the year is going to fly by all too quickly.

We have been told that the case conference that was due to be held on January 10th in Pembrokeshire has been rescheduled and will now take place on the 23rd January; this is a bit annoying because we had also made an appointment to see our solicitor on the same day. Bo also knew we were coming down as she too was to be at the case conference, so she had asked me if her partner could see the girls when we were down, I had said that he would have to ask the social worker to arrange it. Well the social worker has now been in touch to request the supervised contact between Bo's partner and the girls, we have of course agreed to this. So once again we are off to

Pembrokeshire, we will have made the round journey to Pembrokeshire and back three times in five weeks.

During the first week of January a lot has been happening. Oliver is back at school for the new term, and I am taking the girls off to toddler group. I have also rejoined my slimming group to try and shift the weight I have been gaining since the girls came to us; I know I won't be able to do so on without support, so it's back to slimming classes.

## January 8th 2003

The girls and I went off to baby clinic today; the health visitor was surprised to see Hope walking. Both the girls are doing well, they are gaining weight, and don't I know it as carrying them both in their car seats is now getting a little difficult for me, I am convinced that I am going to end up with arms that scrape the floor!

Hope weighs 18lb 14ozs, whilst Morganna I think has been helping Kevin to finish off the mince pies, she weighs 20lb6ozs!

Kevin an I are getting a letter from the solicitor at least twice a week now, this is indicative of the impending court case, which will we hope be listed for early in April. When we see our solicitor in January she needs to have our completed statements, I deliberately put off writing mine over the Christmas period, so now I have to knuckle down and get it finished, a lot will hang on what I say in my statement as I am probably the one person in this who knows more about Bo's relationship with her partner and with Hope and Morganna. The statements will need to be typed out and then filed with the court by the 20th January. I have found writing my statement an arduous task to say the least. I am not sure what it is I am supposed to be writing, and when I do begin to write it, it feels wrong, like some kind of betrayal towards my daughter, after all she is my child and for the past 23 years I have done everything I possibly could to try and protect her, now I find myself needing to write this statement with another thought in the forefront of my mind, and that is to protect Hope and Morganna. Bo and her partner also have to have their statements filed with the court by the 20th January, as do social services and the Psychiatric reports.

When we visit our solicitor in January, she informs us that she is leaving the firm she currently works for, this unsettles me, as I do not wish to start all over again with another solicitor, ours has been fantastic right from the outset of our case and has not only looked after us as clients, but as friends too. Kevin and I discuss what we want to do; it takes us both no more than a minute to decide that we will move with her, she can take our case with her when she leaves. Fortunately for us she agrees to do so, and Kevin and I start to breath a little easier, knowing that she is still going to be the one looking after us all.

Returning to Oxfordshire once again we settle back into the girls routine, before we know it the time has come yet again to travel back again for the case conference on January 23rd .

The case conference was not as bad as I had anticipated it being, there can never be a good one of these, because the very nature of them wrings out your insides, and emotionally it screws you up for day's, as you spend most of your time going through what was said over and over again in your head, often it will keep you awake at night as you try to remember who said what. I have been to quite a few of these meetings now, but I don't think I will ever get used to sitting in a room in which other people have gathered to discuss you own child. The strange world that my daughter lives in just gets stranger by the day, I do not understand this world of hers at all, in fact, in truth I don't want to as it scares me to death. In the case conference we received some good news, it was decided that Hope and Morganna were considered to be safe enough with Kevin and I to remove their names from the protection register, it was an unanimous decision by all the agencies present, this was really good news. I no longer would have to worry that if I had to take the girls to the hospital for any reason, I would not have to explain that they were on the protection register. I knew that social services were recognising the fact that the girls were safe.

Now you may remember that earlier on I wrote that our move from Pembrokeshire was to have its benefits later on, well one of these benefits were to be the distance that the move afforded Hope and Morganna's safety, because we lived so far away it was not easy for Bo or her partner to cause any concerns as regards to the girls welfare, if Kevin and I had still been living in Pembrokeshire, I believe we would have experienced great difficulty in trying to keep the girls safe. These miles apart from my family and friends were also providing Hope and Morganna with safety.

Bo decided to come and visit us for a week in January, she did come, but stayed for just one and a half days, again she needed to return to her partner. I am growing increasingly concerned about her. The pregnancy is growing, but

Bo looks ill and tired, she has been telling me that her partner is subjecting her to sleep deprivation; she says that he keeps her awake all night so that he has company whilst he is drinking.

## February 2003

At last the solicitor gives us the news we have been waiting so long for, and in some respects dreading, she has now received the dates from the court for the full hearing to be heard, it has been listed for hearing over three days April the 14th, 15th and 16th 2003.

We are yet again we will be on our way to Pembrokeshire in the next few weeks, we have to attend a directions hearing at the court on the 3rd March. These direction hearings are ordered so that the judge can look at all the statements that have been filed and to enable any of the parties to request further statements etc to be prepared. I hope and pray that when we all attend the direction hearing that everything is ready to go on to the full hearing date as it would be awful to loose that date now. Although it will only have been 8 months since we applied for the interim residence order, it feels like a lifetime.

But before this trip back to Pembrokeshire there is a celebration in the Swain household. On 23rd February 2003. Hope and Morganna celebrate their first birthday. There was no big party, no other family there apart from Kevin Oliver and I who share yet another first with our little darlings. We had a chocolate caterpillar cake with just one candle on it, Hope and Morganna took it in turns to try and blow out the candles as Kevin Oliver and I sang "Happy birthday" to them, it was a far cry from the family event I would have liked it to be. The girls first birthday somehow got mixed up with the events that were going on in all our lives. I was the one who yet again shared this wonderful time with them both, and yet inside of me my heart was breaking, I was hurting for Bo. Again I had tried to get her to come over and be with them on their special day, again she refused to be a part of this other special day in their lives.

When Kevin and I had put the girls to bed the night of their 1st birthday, after clearing away the toys and clothes, Kevin and I had our tea. Later I sat and wrote a letter for each of the girls. In this letter I told them how we celebrated their 1st birthday, I wrote about the fun we had with them, I also write about my feelings. I sealed each of those letters into an envelope, and wrote girls names on one each, and then I tied a piece of ribbon around each envelope, and placed them into the pine blanket box, which has become their memory box. I have never opened those letters, I never will. One day we shall sit and open them together, and I will relive their first birthday with them.

The day of the directions hearing is here and we arrived at the court, we are worried that the judge may decide to change the date of the full residence court hearing to a later date, and we do not want this to happen. Fortunately the judge decides that the date of the full hearing will remain unchanged, this is good news but it gives us just two weeks to have our updated statements filed with the court. We are also aware that because Bo is contesting the full residence order, we now need to appoint a barrister to act for us.

On March 12th 2003 a solicitor's letter arrives informing us that we have an appointment in Bristol to meet with our Barrister on March 18th 2003. There is no one that I can leave the girls with for a day in Oxfordshire as all of my friend's are working, so I give my Mam a ring and ask her if she will come over if we send her the rail fare, she agrees to do this and at least one of my worries are put aside. Mam coming over means that Oliver can still go to school, and as Bristol is not too far away from us; Mam won't be on her own with the girls for too long. I am increasingly aware that being with the girls for a whole day is not for the fainthearted, they are busy and demanding.

Now I focus on the more everyday things, what should I wear; I need to make a good impression on this Barrister. Aware that I have nothing suitable in my wardrobe, now that I find it easier to just throw on a pair of trousers and a jumper in the mornings, my wardrobe is basically everyday wear, so there is nothing else for it, I have to go shopping for a new outfit. On the weekend Kevin and I load the car up with the double pushchair and the children and much to Oliver's dismay we go "girlie shopping". four hours later and with one new outfit in a carrier bag we begin the journey home from Swindon back to Oxford, in our car there are two screaming worn out babies, and a rather fed up 10 year old.

Mam arrives and the girls are loving the attention they are getting, Oliver too is enjoying having some time with Grandma. Kissing them all goodbye we travel over to Bristol for our meeting, on the way there we talk about what we want to say to her and what we would like to ask her. We arrive at the Barristers chambers in Bristol and for the first time meet the Barrister who is to represent us in court. She is lovely and as the meeting with her progresses our confidence in her grows - of course it did help that she said she felt our case was a strong one. Kevin and I were aware that Bo was to attend a child protection conference on March 24th, this was to discuss what should happen to her unborn baby, we told our Barrister about this conference taking place, she told us that a lot could depend on the outcome of that child protection conference, going on to say that should social services place the unborn baby when it arrives on the protection register, that would strengthen our case even further. The baby is not due until late May I said. "Well lets just wait and see what happens" I was still nervous about our position and of course fearful of the courts decision on the full residence order after all you never can tell with court cases can you, we all think we know which way it should go, but sometimes it doesn't.

Bo rang me one afternoon, she was very distressed, she told me that at the conference for her unborn baby, and the outcome had been that if her baby was born now it would be placed on the child protection register. I asked her why; she said she did not know. I was devastated, as I am now starting to realise that we could be going through the same thing again now with the new baby when he or she arrives.

Kevin and I spend a couple of evenings updating our statements for the court hearing as the Judge had requested. Once again I find reliving the events that have happened heartbreaking. It tears me apart having to write about my daughters lack of input in the girls life, and actually writing it brings home to me just how little she has in fact done with them. The other thing it has brought home to me is how alone I have been with all of this, I have had no day to day support with Hope and Morganna, apart from Margaret, my wonderful Homestart lady and friend. We have finished our updated statements so I post them off to the solicitor by recorded delivery, once she has received them she in turn will get her secretary to type them up, and then they are sent back to us for checking and signing before we return them to. Our statements are then filed with the court on the agreed date, and then on 26th March 2003, a letter from our solicitor advises us of yet another directions hearing, which thankfully this time, we do not need to attend.

## 31st March 2003

Baby clinic today, the puddings are growing. Hope weighed in at an inpressive21lb1oz, whilst Morganna weighed in at 22ld 6ozs. All is well and they are both meeting their development targets. I have been told today that I need only take them in once every two months to be weighed.

Throughout March Bo's relationship still continues to be plagued with incidents of domestic violence, and I understand why social services consider the unborn baby to be at risk, if I am honest I have since the day I found out about the new pregnancy been worried sick about the unborn baby and of what will happen to him or her. I have spoken to my Mam about this and she and Dad have views of their own, which later I was to discover.

April is here and so is the worry, each day I keep getting niggling doubts in my head, "what if the judge does not grant us the residence order" as the days roll on this niggling doubt turns into a full blown swamping worry, I am worried sick, I am not sleeping and I am tearful I hate the phone ringing and I don't want to talk to anyone. I guess it is only to be expected. On 4th April a letter form our solicitor informs us that the judge has not changed the full residence hearing date it is to go ahead as scheduled.

We are now in the final week leading up to the court hearing. I have arranged for Oliver to stay at his best friend's house for a couple of days so that he does not miss any school. I visit the school and update them on what is happening so that should Oliver be worried or anxious he can talk to this teacher, I am reassured by them that he will be fine, like us the school have been very impressed with the way that Oliver has handled such a major change to his everyday life, he has grown up so much in the past year.

I go to ground a little in this final week leading up to the final hearing, I just want to spend as much time with the girls as I can, all our friends are sending us good luck wishes, and a few have hugged me and we have cried. My biggest fear of course is that Hope and Morganna wont return with us to Oxfordshire. I just can't even bear to think about this side of it all, I can't imagine my life without the girls they are such a part of everything I do.

We pack up the car drop Oliver off at his mates. Promising to tell the judge that he has to leave Hope and Morganna with us and as he hugs and kisses the girls goodbye, I see for the first time tears in my son's eyes. He was such a brave boy that day, it must have been terrible for him to watch Kevin and I drive away with the girls, not knowing if he will see them again.

Kevin and I talked all the way down to Pembrokeshire; I think we tried to envisage what was going to happen the following morning in the courtroom. But neither of us dared to venture down the path of what we would do if the judge did not grant the order, or worse said they had to be returned to my daughter.

Nothing could have prepared us for what did happen

# *RESIDENCE ORDER FINAL HEARING.*

Today is the 14th April 2003; it's the morning of the full hearing for the residence order. What happens over the next two days is going to change mine, Kevin and Oliver's lives forever. The birds are singing and the sun is shining through a gap in the curtains. Kevin and the girls are still sound asleep. When we arrived at Deb's last night it was very late and we were exhausted, so we took Hope and Morganna into bed with us, we placed them in between us and waited for sleep to kiss our eyelids until morning. I needed to have the girls next to me; I needed to feel their little bodies next to mine, to smell them, to wrap them up in the protectiveness of my arms - to keep them there forever. Few will understand what it is I am trying to tell you, I had never in my life felt anything as powerful as what I was experiencing that night. It was a strange and yet beautiful night, another one of the experiences I had with the girls that will remain with me until the day I die. Kevin and I talked for hours last night, he knows how I feel and I am sure he feels completely helpless as to what to do or say to me. Eventually Kevin followed the girls off into sleepy land whilst I lay awake all night just watching my precious girls, drinking them in as they slept, I was too afraid to close my eyes and sleep, I needed to be awake, I needed to know that I had spent those last hours just with them, nobody else was there, just us. I had stroked their hair, and their faces as they slept, I had held them so close that we must have been breathing as one. I had whispered into their ears as they slept that I loved them, over and over again I had done this, and I needed them to know. I read somewhere in a book that if you whisper into your sleeping child's ear, that they would hear you in their sleep. This is something I have done ever since the day they came to us. Every night I have tiptoed into the girls room, tucked them both back under their duvet's, stroked their hair and whispered into their ear's that I loved them more than anything else in the world. Sometimes one of them will be stirring as I whisper in their ear and will tell me back

"Love you to the moon and back Mammy"

I don't know why I love them so much. I have and still do love my own children with a love so strong that I cant imagine not loving them, no matter what they have done I have still loved them, I became a mother for life not just for the good times. I wonder if the love I feel for Hope and Morganna is so strong because they did not grow inside me, they grew in my heart, and that had started when Bo first told me she was pregnant, it was a love that just kept on growing. I have never taken for granted that they will love me back, as all my children have and do, my children love me because I am their mother. But with Hope and Morganna, it is different. I would imagine that the love and protectiveness an adoptive parent feels for their children must be similar to what I feel for the girls. I never wanted to tell the girls that they are special, but they are they are so very, very special. They are a part of me. I live and breath for them and Oliver.

Lying there that morning, I felt so close to Kevin and the girls, I wanted that feeling to last forever, would the judge see it that way.

Oh my god, THE JUDGE! For a while in the early hours of that new day I had completely allowed myself to forget about him and everyone else that was in some way involved in Hope and Morganna's life, for those special hours that were mine and mine alone, no one else had been allowed to intrude, they could wait. But the reality was that this was the day. How I hated the day that crept into my life that morning sending away the night and bringing me back to that harsh reality. I wanted to shout out loud "Go away, leave us alone. Please leave us alone". As the morning began to light up the bedroom and the girls began to stir, so did my fears. I gathered both the girls into my arms and the tears began to flow down my face, just as they had on the very first morning we had woken up together, and silently I prayed. I had prayed throughout that night to a God I felt had disserted me a long time ago, I was tired of asking him to help me to see my way through the fog of pain that would not go away. I had asked him over and over again to help us all, but no matter how hard and sincere my prayers were, the pain still remained, maybe that was all part of me learning about who I was, maybe it was all part of his plan, I don't know, as yet I haven't reached a conclusion on that one. I know that my Mam would, and has said to me on many occasions that it is God that has been there by my side throughout this all; oh I wish I had her faith just at this moment.

"Kevin wake up love, I have to go to the bathroom,"

My stomach was churning and I needed to be sick. I dashed off to the bathroom and was so sick that my body ached, I felt as if I had been kicked in the stomach, this feeling stayed with me throughout that horrible day. When I got back into the bedroom Kevin was on the floor playing with the girls, "Well then, best make a start" he said.

We went downstairs and fed the girls their breakfast cereal and left them to eat their toast happily, without a care in the world, I watched them wandering who would be giving them their toast, and all the other things they loved so much the next day, but if they were not with us whoever they were with would not know what they liked and disliked, "Oh Christ go away negative thoughts, leave me alone, stop tearing me apart". Tears filled my eyes, I can't do this to myself I thought, I have to be strong, but I could not be strong, I can't imagine my life without the girls. Another silent prayer "Please God, keep them with us".

As we dressed the girls Kevin and I talked about how we thought the day would go, at this point we thought we were going to be in court for three days. I know that Kevin's fears are the same as mine, he hasn't said, but I can read him like a book, he isn't saying anything, he is trying to support me. My sister leaves to take her children to school and then she is off to work. Hugging me she to tries to reassure me that it will be alright. I wish I had her faith.

Right now I wish I had some faith, anyone's faith.

Hidden away in the bathroom on the pretence of getting myself ready I sat on the floor and armed with paper and pen began to write a list of the girls likes and dislikes. I was to cry over every single word I wrote, each word felt as if it was draining the life out of me.

For breakfast Hope likes to have Weetabix with cold milk and sugar on and toast with chocolate spread on, she has milk to drink which has to be SMA formula. Morganna enjoys Weetabix as well, but likes her milk to be warm; she too likes a little sugar on top of her Weetabix. I will then wash and dress the girls, they will play until nap time, and they love playing with a saucepan and a wooden spoon. Nap time for both the girls is 11am; they will sleep until 12.30pm. When you take them to bed Hope sleeps on her left side, she has to have Croc her little green crocodile with her, and she loves to be snuggled under the blankets. Morganna sleeps on her right side, she too has her bedtime cuddly, and it is a black and white panda, Morganna hates being under the blankets and will kick them off. Every nap and bedtime the girls listen to music as they drift off to sleep, I play them a CD called ANGELS, and I also put one drop of lavender oil on each of their bottom sheets.

For lunch the girls will eat a sandwich, cheese being one of their favourites, they will also have a piece fruit, Hope likes apples, Morganna prefers bananas, or a pear. After lunch we usually go for a walk, and then I will read to the girls or play a game with them. They will sit quite happily in their high chairs with something to chew on as I prepare our evening meal, they are now eating whatever we eat, but as Kevin and I do not eat until later I will have kept enough for the children from our evening meal the day before, this I reheat for them. Both the girls love jelly of yogurt.

I bath the girls every night before bed; usually I will do this any time from 5.30 onwards, depending on whether or not they are beginning to get fractious. Kevin and I always put the girls to bed together.

By the time I had finished writing I had compiled quite an extensive list, as I read it back to myself I cried as I thought about the girls likes and dislikes. They certainly were my life and reading it brought that home to me.

As I signed the letter off I added

"If you are the one who is lucky enough to be putting my precious little girls to be tonight and every other night, please give them a kiss and a hug from us and tell them that we love them so much"

I folded the letter into four and placed it in my pocket. I never did tell Kevin about that letter, he never knew, and I had completely forgotten about it until a few months ago when we had a leek in our loft room. Amongst all the things we lost as they were badly water damaged were all my clothes that were stored up there in cardboard boxes. Going through my suits before they were thrown away I checked all the pockets, which was when I came across the letter. Reading it sent a chill down my spine and tears fill my eyes.

Returning back downstairs Kevin and I packed the girls bag full of the things they would need at my Mam's and we set off the couple of miles down the road in the car. I didn't want to leave them that day; I wanted to keep them with me I wanted that moment to last forever. I can't describe the pain I felt that day as I walked away from my Mam's front door. It felt as though I was leaving behind my heart. My Mam was also crying that morning as we set off, trying to be strong I told her that we would ring her later to give her some idea of when we would be home, we knew that we were going to have to go through this all again tomorrow.

I was in pieces by the time Kevin pulled up the car into the court car park. He came around to my side of the car, took my hand and tenderly held me in his arms. Kissing me and whispering words of encourage he led me towards the court. I was shaking; I wanted to go to the toilets to be sick. It was too late, we were inside the court foyer, and our solicitor had seen us, she came over to greet us and then led us to the consulting room we had been given for the day where our Barrister was already waiting. She was sat at the table with paper work strewn across the top of the table, she looked calm and important sat there with her black robes on, and she was important, she was the one who was going to be fighting for us on our behalf, we had every confidence in her. She got up from her chair and greeted us warmly,

"Try not to worry, you really do have a strong case" she said,

But I wasn't so sure, my daughter was still contesting the order, she was going to fight it all the way. I was worried that she would not emotionally be able to stand there and be cross examined by our Barrister, she would have been ripped to pieces and she was not strong enough for that besides, Bo was now heavily pregnant, and I was concerned about this too, she looked awful. How would she cope with being cross examined? I somehow thought this nice, gentle woman who was our Barrister also had a side to her that I wouldn't like to be cross examined by. Even now, despite all I was going through, I was still worrying about my daughter, it did not matter what she was putting us through, and she was still my child. When we had arrived at the court I looked for Bo, but I couldn't see her, it was as we were walking past an open door leading into a small room that I spotted her sitting at a desk, she was chewing her fingertips- something that she had been doing lately out of habit. I felt this sudden urge to go to her, to hold her. I knew that she was breaking; I could tell by the way she was sat in the chair. As any mother would have wanted to do I wanted to take my child into my arms and make her world better. I wanted to rescue her from this dark and soul destroying place she had chosen to live in, but the devil hadn't finished dancing with my Bo, he was to continue to dance with her, in this strange dark world that I didn't understand for a long time yet. Their last dance was a long way away.

Later I had bumped into Bo in the ladies, I had to smile as when I met her in the ladies toilets she was actually helping herself to the spare toilet roll, which she put into her bag.

"Is that wise" I had asked her.

"Well I don't have any at home" was her reply.

Here we all were as nervous as hell and she was still up to her old tricks. Once again I was to see yet another part of her that I did not understand, my daughter had no scruples at all, at any other time seeing someone walk off with a toilet roll would have made me think "flipping check" and I probably would have smiled to myself at their nerve, what I had just seen my daughter do and knowing why we were all there, just made me very sad. I had gone back and fore to that ladies toilet several more times whilst we waited in that court that morning, partly because I needed to go, and partly because I was hoping to catch a glimpse of my daughter.

Then it all began. We were all sat in that small consulting room when the door opened and Bo's Barrister stood in the doorway, entering the room he told us that his client (my daughter) was standing by her decision to contest the full residence order, and then he disappeared again. We were preparing ourselves to go into court and face the hardest battle we had ever had to fight. Rising to her feet our Barrister asked our solicitor to find Bo's Barrister and ask him if he would come to see her. When he arrived again at the consulting room door our Barrister asked us if we would leave the room and wait outside. There was a row of seats outside the room so Kevin and I sat there quietly talking to each other, trying to guess what was going on inside that room, we became aware that our Barrister had raised her voice, whatever she was telling Bo's Barrister, she was not mincing her words, we were unable to hear what was being said. The door flew open and a rather flustered looking Barrister strode across the court foyer from our consulting room to the one that had been given to Bo, her partner and their Barrister. We were called back into our room and we sat there as the Barrister went over some last minute details with us, she was giving nothing away, but one thing was sure she was not in the least concerned about the fight that lay ahead.

Then there was a knock on the door and Bo's solicitor came in and asked our Barrister if she would come across to see Bo's Barrister, picking her files up from the table she breezed out of the door behind Bo's solicitor leaving Kevin and I alone. Our solicitor had left us for a while as she also had another case being heard that day, and the Judge had called the other case in to be heard. Kevin and I sat there not knowing what to think; we held hands and just hung on to the hope that it was all going to be alright.

Our Barrister returned, dropped her files back onto the desk top, sat down and relaxed, then she looked at us "Well" she said, as the door flew open yet again and she told by a court usher that the Judge would like to see her. Rising from her chair and picking up her paperwork, she turned to us and said

"It will be just fine, you wait and see"

What did that mean, and why was she going to see the judge? Kevin anticipating what was going through my mind calmly reassured me that the Barrister had said that she would at some point before the case was heard be called before the judge to lay out the case. I remembered then that she had in fact said that the day that we had first met her.

Kevin and I sat alone in that consulting room for what seemed like an age

Again the door opened and our Barrister entered. I remember thinking how cheerful she was a she was smiling at us

"IT'S ALL OVER" she announced as she placed the thick files of case notes onto the desk.

Kevin and I looked at each other and then at our Barrister

"What do you mean it's all over" I said, fearing that at that moment we had lost our beautiful little girls.

"CONGRATULATIONS TO THE BOTH OF YOU, YOU REALLY DESRERVE THIS, YOU HAVE BOTH WORKED SO HARD TO KEEP THOSE LITTLE GIRLS SAFE, AND IT'S PAID OFF. THE GIRLS ARE STAYING WITH YOU"

I felt as if all my Christmas's and birthday's had come at once. I felt as if someone had given us the world. Kevin held me and I sobbed.

The Barrister broke into our thoughts.

"We still have to go into court, but don't worry it is just a formality, your daughter has decided to agree to the full residence order"

"Why, what changed her mind" I asked

"I think her Barrister just talked to her, he realised her case was very weak"

That little room was the centre of much rejoicing, I wanted to give Mam a ring, but I couldn't, not yet, we still had to go into court and stand before the Judge.

Sensing my apprehension, she said "Don't worry, honestly it is just a formality"

Although the court hearing was only short, it felt like my entire lifetime was flashing quickly before me, my mouth was dry and I was shaking, tears rolled down my face. Fumbling through my pockets trying to find a tissue to dry my tears my hand found the letter that I had written in the bathroom that morning and for safe keeping, just in case it was needed, had tucked away deeply into my suit pocket. I wrapped my fingers tightly around that letter as I breathed away the crushing pain of rethinking what I had gone through that morning as I had written that letter. Nobody else was going to need to read that letter as nobody else was going to care for my girls but most importantly for me, nobody else was going to have to tell them for me how much I loved them as I could do so myself every day until the day I died. Looking across the courtroom I could see my Bo, she was crushed, she looked like a small child again and I wanted to run across and take her in my arms, I wanted to take her home with me. Most of what the Judge said that morning, passed straight through me, all I heard was the part about the girl returning with us, it was all I needed to hear, after eight log months of agonising, heartbreaking anguish, back and fore to court, the decision had been made, my girls were coming home. Through our Barrister we confirmed the arrangements for contact, and our Barrister made a request on our behalf that we retained the social worker for six months, so that he could monitor the contact. Kevin and I had both been concerned about what would happen with contact once social services were no longer involved in the girl's lives. We were aware that once the full residence order was given that social services involvement with the girls ended. This was good, of course it was as it meant that Kevin and I could get on with life, up until now there had always been an element of us feeling as though we to were on some kind of probationary period where social services were concerned. I know this may be unfair to have said, but it was true, I constantly felt that I was being watched, I felt as if I was on eggshells. Social services were always there, although I have to point out that both the social workers who were involved with Hope and Morganna were brilliant, they were supportive and caring, towards not only the girls but also, to me and especially towards Bo, they both tried so hard to help her. We were both relieved when social services agreed to oversee contact until October 2003, at which time we would be on our own. Kevin and I both felt that it was important for the girls to see both Bo and partner, but we both also knew that in reality we were both going to find the contact with Bo's partner extremely difficult. Many of our family and friends have said to us on many occasions that they don't know how we ever coped with being in the same room as him. Yes it had been difficult, but for Bo's and the girl's sake we just tried to get through it.

And that was it. ALL OVER. The Judge dismissed us all. I couldn't take it all in. I was numb, and so was Kevin.

We were all standing outside in the court foyer talking through the events that had just happened. Our Barrister was congratulating us, she knew how strongly Kevin and I felt about what we were trying to achieve, and she had been ready to fight for us. Our solicitor was as pleased as we were, she had shared all the bad times with us, over the past eight months she had shared every part of what had happened to us, I had leant on her several times when I had to make an agonising decision where the girls or Bo were concerned. Now she was sharing the joy, and I am so glad that she did. I glanced over to where Bo was standing, she was with her Barrister, she was crying, but her partner was not holding her, nobody was, and in that instance I felt this enormous sense of her pain, what had I done to my child, of course deep down I knew I had in fact not done anything to my child, but at that moment it felt as if I was the one responsible for her pain. I broke free from the protective arm that Kevin had placed around me as we had walked from that courtroom, leaving him to continue thanking our Barrister and our Solicitor; I walked away from them all and towards my daughter. I opened my arms and she walked into them, just as any child who is hurting will do when their mother opens their arms for them, no matter how young or old that child may be, enclosing her in the arms of a mother that loved her daughter I rocked her gently as she cried, I cried too. I stroked her hair just as I had stroked Hope and Morganna's throughout the night, and I told her that I loved her, that she was my daughter no matter what, and I promised her that day that I would look after the girls forever. I begged her to come back with us, (I knew this question was a waste of time, she just closed herself off to it, bit I had to ask) She asked me to love the girls as I loved her, she knew I did, but I think she had to ask, cradling my broken daughter that day I told her that I would love both her and the girls until the day I died. I told her to look after herself, I knew she wasn't. Turning to her partner, I stood in front of him, until now I had never said anything to him about the way he treated my daughter,

"You" I said, and he looked up at me, defiance in his eyes, God how I detested this man,

"You look after her, she is my child and she hasn't chosen to be with you so that you can hurt her"

I asked Bo where they were going to go and she told me they were going back to their house, they had recently moved out of the flat they were in and into a two bed roomed house which they had been allocated after concerns had been expressed over the suitability of their 1st floor flat, considering that they had twins.

When she had left the flat the local council gave them 28 days in which to empty it of their belongings. One day she had gone there to collect some things after the 28days had passed and the council had taken it all away and destroyed it. I was so upset as amongst some of the things she had left there were the photographs of the girls as tiny babies, those photographs were so precious as now the only photos we have of the girls in the Neonatal and SCABU units of the hospitals are the ones I have, along some we have taken. We have hundreds of photos of the girls and Oliver as they have grown up together. They left the court and walked away, and as they did so I felt as if a part of me walked away with her that day, but it was not a big enough part of me to protect her, it never would be.

I don't think there were many dry eyes in that courtroom that day. Even the social worker must have felt it. I know form talking to him that although this is what he did day in and day out, it is something you never get used to, and that the best result for him is to see a mother and her child stay together. Well if he does read this book, which I suspect he, will I want him to know that the girls are fine, they are wonderful.

Saying goodbye to our Barrister and our Solicitor - the two women that had fought so hard alongside Kevin and I, and to whom we will all be so indebted to forever, we walked out of that courtroom arm in arm. I felt as if someone had taken a huge weight off my shoulders, so why was my heart heavy? I wanted to stand on the highest mountain and shout out load

"WE WON"

I wanted to celebrate, but it didn't seem right. How could I celebrate?

It was raining when we left the courtroom, even the sky is crying. Kevin helped me into the car as by the time we had walked that short way to our car, I was shaking and sobbing, getting in the drivers seat he turned to me, took me in his arms and held me as I sobbed my heart out, I hadn't cried like that since I had left Singleton hospital in Swansea, the day the girls had been born----the sky had cried with me that day as well.

We didn't go straight back to my parents house, I couldn't, I did not want my Mam to see me in the state I was in, I needed to be alone with Kevin for a while, we needed each other. That morning in that court I had felt as if I was being stabbed with a double edged sword, my whole world was going to come crashing round and down on me, I was so scared that we would loose the girls, afraid that the Judge would decide to place them back with their mother instead, or with a foster family. I also knew that if our application was successful that I would be watching my daughter being crushed as her world fell down on her. Mam was not expecting to see us until late afternoon and she knew that we would still be in court, so Kevin and I decided to go down to NEWGALE and sit in the car watching the sea and the world go by, we went onto SOLVA from there to share our news with Heather and Raul. We arrived back at my parent's house later in the afternoon. I felt wrung out and drained. I didn't think I could cry anymore, but as soon as I set eyes on my Mam, stood there in the doorway of her home it was too much I cried again. Once again my Mam held her own daughter in her arms as I broke all over again. Knowing what I had gone through with Bo so far, I knew it must have torn my Mam apart inside to watch her daughter being caused so much pain.

"Mam, I need to see the girls" I said

And as I went into the room two little faces looked at me with smiles so broad I thought they must have known. Hope ran over to me and Morganna followed, I gathered them both into my arms like a mother hen does to her chicks and said

"Girls you are safe, you are staying with us forever". We all cried, Mam, Kevin and I.

Later when my Dad came home he expected to be told of the day's happenings, one thing was for sure he was not expecting to hear that it was all over, again we all cried, tears of pure joy.

But inside my heart was still breaking for Bo.

Kevin rang Oliver and told him that it was all over and that the girls were coming home with us, this time for good, that there would be no more court hearings, and no more social workers in our lives, he was delighted and couldn't wait for us to get back to Oxfordshire with the girls so that he could give them a cuddle.

All that remained now was to tell the rest of my family, who all greeted the news with happiness; it was good news, the best news.

When Kevin and I began this battle to keep the girls with us, all we wanted was to keep them safe and to keep them within the bosom of their family, so that they would never loose their roots and their identity, they would always know who they were and where they belonged. When we won that battle on April 14th 2003, it was not just Kevin and I that were going to be able to watch the girls grow up, it was all my family, for they too are able to watch Hope and Morganna grow up, they too can share their lives with the girls. I am very aware that at the moment Hope and Morganna have little idea of their true identity, I guess they are suspended somewhere in the middle, but they are slowly learning, they are being told the truth as they ask questions. One day they will understand exactly who they are and who I am in relation to them, they will become aware that Bo is their mother but they will know her, she wont be a stranger with a name and a photograph, tucked away in a box somewhere, to the girls she is a real and everyday part of their lives. Although Bo has very little to do with the girls, she never rings or visits them, she relies on us ringing her and us taking the girls to see her, I talk to Hope and Morganna all the time about her and about what she was like when she was a baby, just as I talk to them about Angharad and Rhiannon, often it is a conversation that is started by something one or the other of the girls have said.

Today Hope and Morganna have made the connection between Angharad, Rhiannon and Bo, but they have never connected themselves with her in any capacity, she is Bo, nothing more and nothing less. They love her.

We may have won that day on April 14th 2003, but that day was also the beginning of me loosing something that I tried so hard not to loose.

We did not celebrate, I was quietly hoping that my family would have planned something, I really wanted to mark this wonderful occasion in some way, but I did not have the energy to arrange anything, it would have been so nice if someone else had done that for us. When Kevin and I renewed our wedding vows, we were given a bottle of really good champagne, we kept it unopened, promising that one day we would crack it open and celebrate.

As a family we have celebrated several special things over the past 4 years, those years have seen us celebrate the christening of Hope and Morganna. We celebrated when my journey to trace my Mam's sister and brother resulted in uniting the three of them in my home. It has seen us share the joy of Anwen, Deb and Geoff's baby arriving safe into the world, and it has seen us celebrate as my brother David married Clare, giving me an additional nephew Josh and a niece Millie to love.

To this day that bottle stands on the shelf unopened. Perhaps if this book is published we will crack it open then. Or is that bottle to remain unopened for some other event far into the distance of time which has yet to happen?

# THE GOOD NEWS SPREADS

Kevin and I arrived back in Oxfordshire in the early hours of the morning. Leaving everything in the car apart from the few things we needed for the girls, and picking the girls up out of their car seats we go into the house. The house was quiet, and strangely still. Our cat had come in with us, when we had pulled up outside the house he was sat on the step outside our front door. As I was busy in the kitchen making up bottles for Hope and Morganna, the cat was rubbing himself on my ankles, meowing loudly as if to say "and where the heck have you all been again" poor old Nick (our tabby cat) must have been totally confused by all the coming and goings over the past eight months, he had also been a great comfort on times as he would sense when I was thoroughly miserable and would come and sit on my knee, which was something he never did as on the whole cats are not my favourite, I am a dog person, I miss my old dog a lot and have lately found myself giving a lot of thought to having another Newfoundland, when we can afford one. The girls had both been quite happily sat on Kevin's lap, until they spotted the cat, they scrambled down and rushed over to make a fuss of him, at which point I think poor old Nick would have gratefully gone back outside and sat on the step. The bottles ready, Kevin and I sat in the lounge feeding our girls, then after changing their nappies we took them upstairs to their bedroom, put them into their cots, tucked them in and turned on the CD player, then as we always do we kissed them goodnight and told them we loved them, but when we did so this time we knew we were going to be doing this forever, and it felt so good, it was simply amazing, they were home, THIS WAS THEIR HOME AND WHERE THEY WOULD STAY. With tears of joy filling my eyes Kevin and I quietly turned away and tiptoed out of their room, and closed the door.

Outside their room Kevin took me into his arms and held me, he knew what I was thinking; he didn't have to ask,

"Yes Cariad, they are home, this time for good"

Returning downstairs I put the kettle on and made us both a mug of coffee, which we took up to bed with us. It's hardly worth Kevin going to sleep as he has to be up in just a couple of hours to go out and get the cows in ready for milking. We are both totally shattered; setting his alarm clock we cuddle up close and fall asleep. I woke to find the morning sun shinning in through the curtains and Kevin gone already.

*Christ the girls!*, it was nearly 8 o clock in the morning, worried that I had not heard their cries for a feed; I went across to their bedroom. Quietly I opened the door, and saw that they were both still sound asleep, they must have found their last couple of days as exhausting as Kevin and I had. I left the door ajar, crept back across the landing and got my dressing gown down from the hook on the back of our bedroom door, sneaking past the girls bedroom door trying to avoid the creaking floorboards as I did so I went downstairs and made myself a mug of tea, which I took into the conservatory and drank, whilst sitting in my favourite chair, which happens to be Kevin's Grandfathers old chair, Kevin has had that chair in his home since before I met him, I had sat in it every night in our bedroom as I breastfed Oliver when he was a baby, when we moved the chair came too, despite it's weathered look. When the girls were small, I used to sit in it to feed them, today the chair resides in our bedroom, and both the girls sit on it and chat to me as I am getting dressed in the morning. From that chair I  watched the birds in the garden. All of this seemed such a world away from what we had all gone through over the past few days.

I had finished my tea and got breakfast all laid up ready, Kevin would be in for his breakfast shortly. Still there was no sound form the girl's room, so I went upstairs had a shower and got dressed. After making our bed I once again tiptoed into the girls room to sneak a peak at them, they were still asleep. Kevin came in for breakfast, and for the first time in ages we both sat down and had breakfast together alone without any of the children around us. The girls woke before he went back out to work so he went upstairs and brought them down, they were smiling and laughing when he reached the dining room with them, they loved it so much when Kevin was the one who went to get them up out of their cots after they had been sleeping. He brought them to me and as he placed them both onto my lap he said

"There you are girls, home at last"

Again unguarded tears fell from my eyes, tears of exhaustion, tears of joy and happiness. Tears of worry and fear.

I didn't have to worry about Oliver that morning as he we still at his friends. After Kevin had gone back out and the girls had finished their breakfast, I rang Oliver's school to let them know the good new's Oliver's teachers were all eager to know what had been the outcome of the court hearing. Oliver had beaten me to it and they all knew by now and so apparently did most of the mums and dads. Telling the school secretary that I would surprise Oliver by picking him up that afternoon, I hung up the phone. It did not stop ringing all that day as people rang to say they were so pleased to hear the new's.

That afternoon arriving at the school gates to meet Oliver, the girls were the centre of much fuss and celebration. Oliver spotted us and ran to the girls with tears in his eyes, he was so happy, he cuddled and kissed them both not caring at all who was watching him.

The next ten days were pretty hectic. The postman brought the mail as usual and in amongst the array of different envelopes was the one I had been waiting for. A letter from our solicitor also had enclosed a copy of the Judges rulings on the full residence order. Now I knew I could relax; now it was in writing. I sat there reading that order over and over again, it was like reading pure magic, just like having a dream come true. Now I allowed the reality to sink in and I cried again. Hope and Morganna sat there surrounded by a selection of their toys and looked at me as if to say," What on earth is the matter with her now"

I had a lot to organise now as I had to let various people know that we had been successful in being granted the residence order. I rang the Drs, the Health Visitor etc, and agreed to drop a copy of the order in to the GP'S Practice so that it could be kept on file and there would be no confusion later on, they all shared our joy.

The girls and I went along to the GP'S surgery later that day and dropped the copies off with the receptionist, then we went to the Post Office and mailed a letter and card to Bo, and picked up some Passport application forms, as now that the order had been granted we could apply for a passport for each of the girls. We were planning to take them abroad on holiday as soon as we could afford it - we got their passports but as yet we still haven't been abroad for a holiday.

# ANGHARAD

The morning of April 25th 2003 was just like any other morning in our house, the girls and I had walked Oliver to the bus stop from where he caught his bus into school, this was part of our everyday routine now, something the girls and I had done every morning since the 6th June 2002, the girls used to love seeing the other children at the bus stop, and they in turn would fuss over the girls, as the girls got older they showed more interest in the other children who waited for the school bus. The other mum's would greet the girls and I with smiles and say how well they thought Hope and Morganna were doing, and they were doing incredibly well. Once Oliver had got onto his school bus, he along with all the other children on the bus would wave a frantic goodbye to Hope and Morganna, and when they had discovered they could wave too, they would sit in their double buggy waving until the bus had gone out of sight. Morganna hated Oliver going to school and would often cry as soon as the bus would arrive.

Depending on how well the morning had gone up to getting Oliver off to school, if I had succeeded in getting the girls dressed sometimes I would take the girls for a long walk around the village. They loved to see the horses in the fields. Today was one of the good days, the girls were dressed and I had even managed to get the dishwasher loaded, so off we set, we walked around the village, visiting the horses in their paddock, then we went onto the cricket field which also had a play park for the children, after a short stay at the park we trekked back home again. Kevin was just on his way in for his breakfast, so we took the girls along to see the calves and the cows before we went back into the house. The girls have always loved visiting the baby calves and the cows on the farm, and is they spot a cat so much the better as they can shout after that as well.

Whilst Kevin and I had breakfast together, the girls sat contentedly in their high chairs munching away on the toast fingers that I had given them. Later once Kevin had gone back to work, I put the girls down for a morning sleep, they were still having a short nap in the morning at this stage, probably only for half an hour, but it was enough to recharge their batteries and for me to get the washing pegged out, and boy did I have some washing, most days between us all there was at least two machine loads for the washing machine to get its teeth into. I have lost count of how many visit's the washing machine repair man has made to my house and of how many machines I have burnt out in the past 5 years, but I think it is three the one I have at the moment I bought last July and already I have had to call the repair man in to look at it twice, thank goodness it is still under warranty. I still get through at least two loads of washing a day, and as most of it is the girls clothing it needs ironing as well! The girls are proper little girls I love to dress them in pretty dresses, and today they will demand to wear the same as each other, and it is usually a dress.

The girls slept for longer than usual on this morning, perhaps the country air they had had on our walk earlier that morning had done them good, so with a few spare minutes I sat in Granddad's chair in the conservatory with a mug of coffee and a magazine. I was busy reading an article about curing migraines when the phone disturbed my quiet moment. It was Bo's partner. "Bo's gone into labour" he told me, she was in her local hospital. I asked him if everything was alright and he said that although she had gone into labour prematurely she was going to be fine and that the hospital had said that she would not need to be transferred to Singleton Hospital in Swansea this time, as she had when she went into labour with Hope and Morganna. I told her partner that I would give the ward a ring, and I did, I needed to know that Bo and the baby were going to be alright, I did not trust her partner to tell me correctly what was happening as on past occasions he had told me she was fine when indeed she was not, and I was also very aware that the incidents of domestic violence between the pair of them had got much worst recently, giving cause to speculate that he had yet again attacked her, resulting in her going into premature labour. It was as I rang the ward that I began to shake and fear the worst. The ward sister confirmed that Bo was in fact in established labour and that so far there were no causes for concern, I was comforted by what she had said and I did get to speak with Bo which was nice, she promised to give me a ring later on and I promised to ring the delivery ward later to check on her progress.

Every time the phone rang that day I would answer it and if it was not Bo I would apologise and ask whoever was on the other end to ring me back in the morning as I had to keep my line free. The phone rang again for what seemed like the hundredth time, only this time the call brought the news I was waiting for.

"IT'S A GIRL" the excited voice on the other end of the phone told me, my daughter was beside herself with happiness.

Angharad arrived in the world six weeks prematurely, she weighed 4lb 8ozs

Bo's partner was with her at the time of the birth, and Bo had told me how brilliant he had been.

It was not until the afternoon that I suddenly thought, Bo had told us and social services that she and her partner had actually separated, so how come he was with her? I came to the conclusion that mine and Kevin's fears were in fact warranted and that they had not separated at all. Bo's behaviour had a definite pattern to it and it was now one that I was recognising easily, I was beginning to understand the on /off relationship she would have with her partner, it was frustrating to watch and painful to be around especially when violence was such a major part of their lives together.

In the months leading up to Angharad's birth Bo had had a lot to do with social services as they tried to come up with a workable plan that would enable Bo to keep Angharad and at the same time mean that the two of them were safe. We had even considered the possibility of her coming to us, knowing deep down that if that were to happen the girls would have been compromised, and that our mostly peaceful home would be sent once again into disarray and become the centre of much heartache as Bo would spend her days arguing with her partner over the phone, just like she always had on the rare occasions when she had stayed with us. Bo decided that she did not want to come to u; she wanted to be near her partner. Kevin and I both knew that to have Bo with us would have caused so many problems, but despite our fears we let her know that this was her home and it was here for her to return to if she wanted to do so. Somehow Kevin and I would have coped with the problems that would cause as they arouse.

Bo had rung me one day weeks before the final hearing for the residence order on Hope and Morganna, she had told me that social services had held a child protection meeting where it was agreed that had the unborn baby arrived on the day of the meeting it would have been placed onto the child protection register immediately, this news was devastating and proved to me that nothing in Bo's life had changed, she had not learnt anything from what we were all going through with Hope and Morganna's case. This was the worst news and spelt out for me further heartache and trouble ahead. It also strengthened our case for the residence order to be granted on the girls in our favour.

Angharad was born just ten days after the full residence order was granted, I sometimes used to wonder if what Bo had gone through that day in court had in some way contributed to Angharad's premature birth, and I felt in a way partly responsible, but we also were aware that Bo had been subject to continuing incidents of domestic violence from her partner, and Bo had told me of at least two incidents where these had involved blows to her stomach which were so forceful that her knees had buckled under her and she had fallen to the ground. What animal could do such a despicable thing to any pregnant woman, let alone to my daughter? God how I despise that man. We were also by now very aware that she too was more than capable of being violent towards her partner and to others. So it was more than likely that Angharad's premature arrival had more to do with this than the court case.

When I think about Bo being violent towards others I wonder when and why this happened to her, she had not been aggressive as a youngster, but drugs, alcohol and the world in which she lived have all played their part in transforming my daughter from the carefree teenager she was to the broken and sad young lady I see today. I find thinking about this part of Bo's life so painful.

Bo was so thrilled when Angharad arrived, and for the first time in ages, I heard in her voice a glimmer of hope. All my family began to wonder if this new baby might just be the one thing that would turn her around. Kevin and I began to realise that she might just have a chance with baby Angharad, thinking that loosing Hope and Morganna would drive her on forward, and that she would now focus on proving to social services that she could bring this new baby up, and that she could work with the social worker who has been there for her every step of the way rebuilding her life and focusing on a future with Angharad.

Kevin was now back at work and was working over the weekend that followed Angharad's birth,, so Kevin and I somehow found enough money to make that drive to Pembrokeshire and home again, by now we were financially struggling, and although we had no debt to worry about and no credit card either we had found the past twelve months financially difficult. After all we were now effectively a five person family an one wage, whereas before Hope and Morganna had come to us we had been a three person family with two good incomes, times were certainly hard now, and this was something we struggled with alone, we had no one who could help us financially. On one or two occasions just after the girls had first come to us Bo had given me the milk tokens she had been given for the girls as part of her family allowance and social security payments, as she was still claiming for the girls, I used to wonder what she did with the milk tokens she had not given to me, Kevin has said that she probably went and got the milk and sold it on to raise extra cash, the idea used to infuriate me, once she had given me £30.00, but it was just the once, she continued to claim their child benefit until October 2003, the girls were eighteen months old by then. I have received their child benefit since then. Bo and her partner have never given anything towards the girls keep, and apart from a birthday and Christmas present they have never bought them anything else. I do not expect or want anything from them for the girls as when we took the girls on it was to provide them with all the love, care, safety and everyday things they would require, we were and are totally committed to them.

We arrived in Pembrokeshire to see Angharad on May 2nd 2003, Angharad was by now a week old. I think by now our car must know its own way there and back again, we have put thousands of miles onto the clock of our Volkswagen Passat over the past 12 months, not to mention thousands of pounds in the fuel tank. I have tried to explain to the girls that they have a brand new baby sister, but they are only 14 months older that her, and they don't understand as they are too young. So when we all went in to SCABU to see Angharad for the first time I was amazed at the response the girls gave to greeting their new baby sister. Hope and Morganna cuddled and kissed her, it was almost as if none of us needed to say anything, they just seemed to know that this tiny baby was special to them. Kevin and I took some photographs of them together and the love that was there between them right form the start really show in those photographs. Angharad was a truly lovely baby, she looked nothing like Hope and Morganna had when they were born, but all the girls have had the same big blue eyes. Angharad had big blue eyes and a dusting of strawberry blonde hair, just as Bo had had when she was born.

Angharad also had chubby red rosy cheeks, she still had those chubby red rosy cheeks the last time I saw her, and I expect she still has.

There was a strange thing I noticed on the day that we visited Angharad in that SCABU unit, and that was how calm Hope and Morganna were, I know that they do say that studies have shown that babies that have spent time in a SCABU unit seem to be calmed by the constant "bleep, bleep" sound of the life saving monitoring machines in the unit, I can honestly say I think this is true as it certainly did have that effect on both Hope and Morganna. Bo was so proud of Angharad and she was looking forward to taking her home to my parent's house. I had brought a lot of things back to Pembrokeshire with me for Bo. I had brought one of the girls Moses baskets, the bedding and some clothes that the girls had outgrown. I also brought the bottle sterilizing unit as well as a baby monitor, in fact all the things we had bought for Hope and Morganna that we no longer used. These things I left at my Mam's.

Hope and Morganna can still remember going to meet their tiny new baby sister in that hospital; whenever we look at the photographs which were taken on that day they will say "that's our sister, that's Angharad"

My parents had already been in to see her, and my Mam was spending a lot of time with Bo at the hospital. Social services had called an emergency child protection meeting soon after her birth and Angharad was placed on the protection register. We were all horrified and feared what was going to happen to Angharad. My Mam rung me one day and told me that her and Dad were intending on putting themselves forward to have Bo and Angharad come to live with them. My Mam asked how I would feel about this and my reply was that it was nothing really to do with me, knowing full well that my father would have done whatever it was he wanted to do. My concerns were that my parents would go through what I had been through and I really did not want that to happen. They were now both nearly 67 year old when Angharad was born, they had reached the time in their lives when they should not have been looking after children long term, they should have been out and about enjoying life. I told Mam of my concerns and left it to them to make up their own minds as to what they would do.

Prior to Angharad's release form the hospital it was agreed that if Bo were to agree to go and live with my parents that Angharad could go home to her there. We had considered having Bo and Angharad here with us, but we knew that this would never have worked, and would have caused no end of problems and confusion for the girls; social services also agreed that it was not the answer this time. So Bo and Angharad went to live with my parents. Part of the conditions laid down by social services was that Bo was not to see her partner, (or ex-partner, as she was now stating they had separated again)

## May 21ˢᵗ 2003

The girls and I went off to baby clinic today. Hope weighed in at 21lb 3ozs, Morganna was 22lb 4ozs. Both girls are doing well, and there are no concerns.

Travelling back and fore to Pembrokeshire was a regular thing for us. Not only did we want to go and visit Angharad, which we felt was really important for Hope and Morganna; we also had to take the girls back to have contact with Bo's ex-partner. On the first few visits before Angharad was born we used to go to Bo's home her partner would be there. On the first occasion after the residence order was granted, the social worker met us at Bo's home, satisfied that he felt we could cope he left, not long after he went some of Bo and her partner's friends turned up. Kevin and I were so cross with Bo and her partner as to us it felt as if they were using the girls as some kind of trophy. These contact visits were about them seeing the girls not about their friends calling around to see them as well, it was only a 2 hour contact and those 2 hours should have been quality time for the four of them. The next time I spoke to the social worker I told him what had happened and he agreed with us that in future all contact visits were to take place in a public place.

Around this time Bo was allocated a flat in a neighbouring town, this was to have given her a break away from the people who she had been mixing with, her ex-partner was to stay living in the old town she was leaving, this would  hopefully give her a fresh start away from her old life, so that when social services decided that it was safe for Angharad to go home to Bo's home with her there actually was a home to go to, this was an important part of the plan of rehabilitation that social services and Bo had agreed to. When I discovered where this new flat was I was absolutely mortified, it was in an area that was full of alcoholics and drug abusers, she had been given a flat right in the heart of yet another unsavoury part of the county, what chance did she have there-very little I feared. My parents greeted the news of where her new flat was very much the same as I did; to say we were concerned is putting it mildly. My Dad and my brother did as much as they could to turn this flat into a home for her. She was not on her own for long, her partner moved in as well.

I tried telling my parents that he was still on the scene, but they wouldn't have it. On one occasion my Dad went to her flat to help her by putting up some curtain tracks and laying a carpet. Dad told me that she was alone in the flat and that there was no sign of him being around, so my fears were unfounded. Months later I asked Bo about this and she told me that for all the time my Dad had been in her flat, her partner had been hiding up in the loft space.

We had once again during May made the journey back to Pembrokeshire to visit Bo and Angharad; she was now gaining weight and the hospital were preparing to release her from the hospital. It had all been agreed that Bo and Angharad were to go and live with my parents. I was deeply concerned about my parents taking Bo and Angharad into there home, there was no way I wanted them to suffer firsthand the same pain and heartache that I had gone through, but my Dad is stubborn and talking him around once he has made a decision is neigh on impossible, together Mam and Dad stood firm and I had to respect their decision to do what they felt they had to do. I know that Mam had said to me on many occasions that I had done more for Bo than could ever have expected of me, but I too have a small degree of Dad's stubborn streak in me, and failure was never part of my make up. My Brothers David and Michael as well as my sister Deb, must all have sheared my concerns, but they also shared in my belief that Dad will do what he feels he has to do. Watching it all going pear shaped was torture for me.

What happened over the next six months drove a wedge between me and my parents, something I found so incredibly hard to go through. I had already been through a time when I had lost contact with all my family for eighteen months and I feared going through anything like that again.

Bo had come over to stay with us one weekend; I had arranged it with social services that she could come over with Angharad. That weekend was lovely, to see all three of the girls together was magical, Hope and Morganna certainly did love her, they enjoyed helping Bo to change her nappy, trying to feed her with her bottle, and all the time Angharad lapped up the attention she was receiving from her two older siblings. It was such a special time for all three of them; it was to be the only time they were to sleep under the same roof.

Over those six months I had received phone calls from friends of mine back in Pembrokeshire

Who had seen Bo and her partner together, I had told my parents about this, as after all they were the ones who had given Bo and Angharad a safe place to stay. But part of Bo's commitment to Angharad was supposed to have been that she was not seeing her partner, but she had been secretly meeting up with him in the local town. My father refused to believe what I was telling him and ended up arguing with me over the phone, he eventually put the phone down on me, we were both in tears. Then one day I received a phone call from a friend who told me that Bo was with her partner in one of the town's pubs and that she had Angharad with her. I was livid. I had spoken to Bo about how I felt about her abusing my parents trust, she knew that I was aware that she was meeting her partner, he was no ex, he was very much a part of her present. Bo also knew that if I was to discover that she was in any way putting Angharad at risk I would not turn a blind eye to it, I couldn't as this would mean that I would effectively adopted one attitude toward Hope and Morganna and completely another towards Angharad, in no way was I going to do that. This time she had pushed it too far, she was not placing Angharad's safety before everything else. I knew it was only a matter of time before social services found out. I rang them and they knew anyway and had sent someone around to the pub to see what was going on. As a result of Bo's actions that day, and those leading up to it social services were so concerned for Angharad's safety that she was taken from Bo and placed with a foster mother.

The day that Angharad was taken from my parent's home was for my parent's one of the worse days of their life, if not the worse. They had tried so hard to make the situation work; they had supported Bo and helped her out in what ever way they could. Everyday my Mam had been there helping Bo with Angharad and babysitting for Bo to go into town, during which times she secretly met up with her partner. My Dad has never been one for tiny babies, he finds them interesting about the same time as they find him interesting, he never has nursed any of mine or my siblings babies, until Angharad went to live with them, Angharad had captured a part of my Dad that all his other Grandchildren had not done until they were much older than she was, so when Angharad was taken away I watched as my Dad's heart wept for the little girl he loved so much, even today he can not bear to hear her name spoken so deep is his pain.

I was so distraught, I now had Hope and Morganna being brought up by me and Angharad was in care, but there was worse to come

When Angharad was taken into care Bo left my parents home and went to live in her new flat, her Partner moved in with her about the same time. Social services set up contact meetings for Bo to see Angharad everyday and it was all going alone well until she started missing her contact meetings, she said she had been unwell. I was beginning to get concerned about her being "unwell" and had asked her on several occasions if there was something more sinister going on. She was insistent that my fears were unfounded.

Social services were by now running out of patience with Bo's situation, they had warned her that they were now considering adoption as a possibility, they also told her that they had begun the process of "twin tracking" which means they had actually begun the process of looking for prospective adoptive parents for Angharad. There had also been another development, because of the erratic pattern of Bo's attendance at contact meetings social services had begun to phase out some of the daily visits and Bo was only seeing Angharad three times a week, then it became two, and eventually as time went on it fell to just one weekly visit, they had made these decisions to reduce the visits as Bo not turning up had been having a great effect on Angharad's routine, it was also tying up valuable social services resources. I was at my wits end; I could not believe that my daughter was once again placing her partner above the needs of her own child. I was soon turning my thoughts towards social services plans to have Angharad adopted. I knew that they were going to have to get a court to agree to a "freeing order" for Angharad because Bo was contesting their plans to have her adopted. I found it so difficult to support my daughter emotionally through what was now going on, but I had to support her as I feared for her safety, she was not strong enough to get through it all. I was being torn apart; the thought of loosing my precious Granddaughter was more than I could bear. I had to do something, but what?

Kevin and I sat and talked for hours, he knew what was burning inside me, and he said that I was the only one that had to make this decision as it would be me that would be caring for her as well as Hope and Morganna, but I knew that deep down he was worried about me. I sat for hours and did nothing but think about Angharad and the girls, I turned it over and over again in my mind, it drove me mad, I couldn't think of anything else. As I sat feeding the girls I would envisage what it would like to fed another toddler alongside them, I thought of everything, I even thought about it in my sleep. I spoke to Bo about it and she wanted me to go and get a residence order on Angharad too, because by now things were looking bad. We had spoken to my family and friends about the situation and they had all said that I could not take Angharad as well, but the more they told me I couldn't, the easier it became for me to see what I wanted to do, so a couple of days later after a lot of soul searching. I knew there was only one possible answer for me. Over breakfast on a sunny Friday morning Kevin and I stated to talk again. We talked about the more practical side of Angharad being with us, each time one of us would think of a problem the other would dispel it with an answer, it was the practical things that we sought answers for. How would we manage if she were to come to us? We could change the car and buy a people carrier instead, so that was that problem sorted, and so it went on. Kevin asked how I would feel about staying at home for another year, and I said what was another year of my life, if it meant all three of them being together

"Kevin I cant let her go; I have to keep all three of the girls together. I have to do this, please say you will be there with me"

"It's alright Ker, I knew that this would be the decision you would reach, it's the only decision I knew you would arrive at, and somehow we will manage. Give the solicitor a ring and ask her to get the ball rolling"

That afternoon I nervously rang our solicitor and asked her to start proceedings. I also rang the social worker and informed him that we were in fact going to go ahead with making an application for a residence order on Angharad in our favour. His response was to say that he had reservations as to how it would affect mine and Kevin's relationship. My curt reply was to remind him that the only two people that really understood mine and Kevin's relationship, its strengths and its weaknesses was in fact Kevin and I, He most certainly was not an expert in that field, he had known us for just over a year Kevin and I had known each other for over twelve years, we had been to hell and back on more than one occasion, and he certainly had underestimated the strength of our relationship. He had also underestimated the strength of this woman and I was determined that I was going to do this. Any reservations I may have had, completely disappeared in the instance that he had thoughtlessly expressed his opinion.

The next day was Saturday, I had been unable to get hold of Bo on the Friday night, but early on Saturday morning the phone rang and it was Bo.

"Hi are you alright" I asked her.

"Mammy please don't be angry with me"

There it was again, she had reverted back to her childhood name for me.

"What have you been and done now?" I asked her, fearing the worst, I was not prepared for what she told me next.

"I'm pregnant"

My stomach churned and my heart began pounding so fast that I was gasping; the girls were tugging at my skirt as they wanted a biscuit, and all I could hear over and over again was what Bo had just said to me.

"Oh Christ Bo, you have to be joking, please tell me that you are"

"No I'm not"

I can't tell you how much I wanted to put that phone down on her, and how much I wanted to run away from all of this.

"You bloody fool, how the hell could you let this happen, what in God's name are you thinking about"

She was not expecting my angry outburst, until then she had not heard so much as a raised voice form me, but my God I wasn't angry, I was bloody livid. My head was swimming. Jesus Christ Almighty hasn't she done enough, hasn't she been through enough was screaming through my head.

She hung up on me, and I just sat down buried my head in my hands and sobbed my heart out over her yet again. I had to talk to someone. I couldn't sit here with this on my own, I rang my Mam, by now we were all back on speaking terms. Telling my Mam was really hard, I was crying so much that I had difficulty getting out what I was trying to tell her, and then I just blurted it out

"Bo's pregnant again Mam"

My Mam greeted the news more or less as I had done minus the swear words, perhaps it's a mistake she said, maybe she has got it all wrong.

"There's no mistake, believe me this is happening, I have had a feeling for weeks that something was amiss, but she kept on telling me I was wrong"

Mam asked me what I was going to do, well what could I do, it was nothing to do with me, and I was just the one who cleaned up her mess after she had made it.

"I don't know Mam, I really don't know"

Kevin came in that night for his tea to find that I had done very little, he knew by the way I was standing that I had been crying,

"What's the matter Cariad?"

When I told him he too was livid,

"Well so much for her and her partner being separated then" he said,

And of course he was right, she had become pregnant during the time that she had told everyone including social services that she was separated form her partner, it turned out that on one of the occasions my Mam had babysat Angharad for her to go into town to attend a meeting, the meeting had in fact been with him, it was that day that she had fallen for the baby. She was playing straight into social services hands, and I knew that any chance she may have still had to getting Angharad back was now gone. Now she had another baby on the way, Christ what a total mess.

Over that weekend I spent a lot of time walking with the girls in their pushchair, I needed to be away from the house and the phone. I don't know where I was expecting to be able to escape from what was tearing at my insides, as no matter where I went it also came with me too, no matter what I tried to stir in my heart, this was a great sorrow that nothing could balance. No matter where I went or what I did to try and focus on something else I couldn't.

I was still on that bloody rollercoaster; yet again life had found another way to put me on it to ride it one more time. And with each ride it got more and more scary, each time the ride got rougher, each time the brakes needed more strength to get them to hold. This time the rollercoaster slowed down and long enough for a catapult to pick me up in its spoon and hold me there.

# ME, TURMOIL AND THE
## SECRET GARDEN

The most recent news of Bo's pregnancy had devastated me, I had spent most of Saturday and Sunday living through what I could only describe as the beginning of my worst nightmare, and it wouldn't abate either, it just constantly drove at me with a force so fierce that it made even the normal functions of my day really difficult. I had to get away on my own and think. Somehow I managed to stumble my way through the day, most of the things I needed to do like feed and change the girls had pretty well been done on autopilot. I had not even prepared an evening meal for Kevin and I, feeding myself was not even something I had thought of all day, I didn't want to eat. My head had pounded with a migraine since I had got out of bed in the early hours of the morning - and was now peaking as I hadn't eaten all day, the old familiar nauseous feeling I suffered when I got a full blown migraine was slowly biting at me and I knew I was in for a rough time. I gave in and took some tablets, soon the nausea went away, and the headache fell off to the cotton wool head stage.

The phone had rung several times throughout the day, it had rung unanswered, I did not want to speak to anyone, the world and his dog could just wait. I needed some time, and I needed it now.

As the afternoon gave way to the evening I think the girls must have picked up on my need for some peace as they began to yawn, so I helped them both up the stairs and ran a bath for them as they played with Oliver in his room, the happy, cheerful sounds as they played with him went somewhere over the top of my head. The bath was ready and soon the girls were splashing about in the warm lavender fragranced water, the lavender was having a calming effect on me too. As usual we sang nursery rhymes and played with their bath toys. After drying them and getting them ready for bed I gave them their milk, which they lay on my bed and drank as I told them a story. They were really sleepy, so I put them both to bed, as soon as their little heads touched the sheets of their cots they were drifting off to sleepy land, how I wished I could go too, but I had some serious thinking to do.

I decided to go outside into our front garden. We had a huge pear tree in our front garden that was overgrown with ivy, over the years the ivy continued to grow covering the tree and invading the hedge that ran alongside the house, it had created a perfect natural archway which led into a hideaway which we called our secret garden. Here you could escape the world around you as nobody would ever know you were in there. The children all thought that the fairies used to live in there, it was kind of magical and to them I guess a wonderful place for fairies to live, so I would feed their imagination with stories about the fairies that used to come out at night and play in my garden. I remember when Abigail was small I told her that if she left her Christmas wish list there for Santa that the fairies would come and take it for her and deliver it to Santa. She asked me how I would know they had been and I told her that they always left behind them some glitter scattered on the grass. That night Abigail and I tied her letter for Santa to the tree and sure enough in the morning when she went to look her letter had gone and there was glitter all around the tree

We had put a table and two chairs in there and often during the summer months after the girls had gone to bed Kevin and I would escape to our hideaway, and drink our way through a bottle of good wine whilst listening to some relaxing music. Only this time I escaped to our secret place alone, it was not quite as warm as it may have been but I did not notice, there was no wine and no music, just me and the peace and quiet. Silently I cried (I did not want anyone to hear me and be able to find me) I cried until all of me ached, my head was throbbing and felt as if it was going to burst, my stomach muscles ached and I felt sick, and there was a new pain so acute in my heart that it scared me. There were so many questions running riot around my head and I felt as if I was drowning, I couldn't see a way forward. I sat there in the peace and quiet that I had at last found and as the tears stopped - I don't think I could have physically cried anymore, I began to think about Oliver, Hope, Morganna, and Angharad, but now too I was also thinking about the unborn baby. It was all too much, but slowly the fog of confusion began to lift and I thought of all the things that were going to be affected by what was now happening. As I allowed myself to think more clearly I began to realise one other very daunting thing, and that was that if we were to continue to fight for a residence order on Angharad, then we would have to look to taking the unborn baby as well. I was for the first time looking at the wider picture. For the first time my head was having its say, my heart had to listen. Deep down inside of me I knew that I couldn't go on like this, I also knew my limitations, I may be proud and stubborn, but I also know when I am beat, and I am not afraid to admit it. This was now bigger than I could see myself ever becoming.

"No go away, I can do this, I will do this" said my heart which was now fighting with my head,

I was wrestling with myself and I was in turmoil. The more I let my head tell me I couldn't carry on picking up Bo's shattered life, the more my heart chanted at me

"Yes you can, you know you can, you can do it, and yes you can".

I was being steamrolled by my heart and it was travelling as fast as an express train.

"Well what about the practical side, you will have four babies under three to care for, have you thought about that"? My head was screaming.

Once again my heads thoughts were steamrolled by my heart.

"You can do it you know you can"

Every time my head threw a question at me, my already overburdened heart would scream back its answer. I wanted to start running, but I couldn't run I had Oliver and the girls, and I knew this was not the answer. I knew that somehow I had to be strong and reach whatever decision I made without my head fighting against my heart. It had to be a united decision

Closing my eyes I started to sing, it has always been what has grounded me in times of turmoil in my life. I closed my eyes on the world and for a short time completely lost myself in my singing, if anyone had heard me they would probably thought I had at last flipped. I don't know what I sang, but I knew it was peaceful, I imagined myself sat on top of the cliff tops of ST JUSTIANS,

I could smell the fresh sea air, I could taste the salt on my lips and hear the crashing sound of sea as it washed over the rocks below. It took me to a place inside myself that I felt safe in. I had been in this safe place a hundred times before, but with one big difference, I had always driven myself there in my car and walked to those wonderfully uplifting cliff tops and sat there, this time I had felt a force so powerful inside of me that I had been able to shut my mind off to the thoughts that were crashing into it and as I did so the rhythm of the sea calmed the erratic pattern of my heartbeat and it gently guided it back to a peaceful place. Now I could think clearly, even if it was so torturous that I still wanted to leave it all so far behind me that it wouldn't be able to catch up with me again. There was no way that I could ever achieve that, and I knew that whatever decision I eventually would reach would effect my life for the rest of my time on this earth. I was in a catch 22, I had landed between a rock and a hard place, there was to be no soft landing here.

I thought of all the things that would and could happen, they made my decision no easier, and it eventually came down to what was good for the children, I had to do what was right for them and not even consider what I wanted to happen, after all I don't have the elusive magic wand to wave and make the world a better place in my hands do I?

I was freezing cold by the time that I left that secret part of our garden, I was shivering from both the cold and of what I had just gone through, and strangely I could still taste the salt on my lips, probably from the tears that I had cried, but I think the mind is a powerful thing and somehow for the first time in my life I had allowed my mind to take me to my "safe place" and it felt both powerful and comforting, now I had a clearer image in my head and I knew I had to deal with this one step at a time, and so I decided that I must talk to social services before I went any further, I had to discover what their response was going to be to this latest development.

To this day I don't know where I found that power in me to find such peace for that short time, for although it was only brief, it was long enough to enable me to get some kind of grip on what was happening, I still didn't understand it at all, I couldn't then and in some ways I still don't today. I have never been able to understand the one thing that holds such a power over my daughter that she has chosen to turn away from her girls and continue to live in her strange world, but then I have come to understand that the only one's who do in some way understand this strange dark world she lives in is its other inhabitants. Before I had experienced that powerful event in my life that early Sunday evening I had for the first time in years not been able to look ahead. When Bo's world started falling apart, taking mine and Kevin's world with it, somehow I had always been able to see a future and I still felt in part in control of my life. Over the past eighteen months I had been at home looking after the girls, for me that was a huge life change, I was no longer this carefree person who went shopping if she wanted too, now I had to plan even a simple thing like that, and it sometimes became just like organising a military operation, trying to juggle everyone's needs was exhausting. I had always been in control, but now I was being controlled by what was going on in our life and by the other people who were now in it, I didn't have the energy to stand up and retake control. After spending that time alone in the secret garden I felt as if someone was actually giving me permission to try and start to be me again, I knew that what was to follow in the coming months would be difficult, but now I was looking at it in a different way. My heart was being told to leave me be and to let my head have its say, the two were no longer at loggerheads- oh believe me they still fought against each other, and I still had a long way to ride on this emotional rollercoaster. The one big thing that I was given that evening was an understanding within myself that I could think also about what I actually wanted to do.

I had to speak to the social worker before I could think anymore; I had to discover what their response was going to be to this latest development. I had to wait until the morning to do that so I tried desperately to leave it rest until then, but it didn't rest, it had other ideas and it intruded my thoughts and my dreams. That night I dreamt that I was the old woman who lived in a shoe, and woke up giggling as I had reached a part in my dream where the social worker was actually driving down the M4, and on the trailer behind him was a bright shiny new shoe much bigger than the one I was living in, this new shoe was complete with curtains and a blue painted front door!!

Monday morning came all too soon and as the clock ticked away, the hours passed. I sat the girls into their high chairs and gave them their breakfast, then Oliver got up and once he had his breakfast, he was off to school leaving me and the girls. Kevin came in for his breakfast just as the clock was approaching 9 o clock. I left Kevin with the girls and went to ring the social worker.

Thankfully he was there and I spoke to him about everything and anything, desperately trying to avoid the one thing I had rung him up to talk to him about. When I did tell him he was flabbergasted.

"Are you sure" he said to me

"Yes quite sure, what I need to know is what will social services do?"

"It's going to be difficult, but given the way things are progressing I don't hold out much hope, let me see what I can find out here and ring you back later"

When the social worker and I spoke again, he confirmed my worse fears, he informed me that social services would take the baby straight into care and place him or her with a foster mother, unless Bo pulled a miracle out of the bag, which both he and I knew was not going to happen, as miracles are rare in her world..

Replacing the phone onto its cradle, I sat on the floor with the girls and held them tight to me, I soaked them with my tears, the poor little things must have been frightened, but they must also have known something was wrong because they both cuddled into me. I needed them so much at that moment, together with Oliver they pulled me through the following few days as once again my head was in overdrive, as I thought more about how taking in Angharad and the new baby, would effect Oliver and the girls lives, how would we all cope. And for once I allowed myself to think about how I would cope, I was worried as to whether or not I could actually spread myself so thin.

I think the word desperate does little to explain just how I felt at that time. I had all sorts of unanswered questions rushing around inside my head. I tried to see into the future. I knew then that if I made the decision to continue with our plan to have Angharad with us, and then also the new baby, I would end up with four children under three years of age, I would be on my knees, any woman would, but I would also have all the emotional crap as well. I knew I couldn't do it; I had to find another way.

God was there another way?

I rang our solicitor and spoke to her about the latest development; as usual she was very supportive. After talking to her I sat and made the most agonising decision of my life. I was numb, I felt sick and very, very scared.

Oh God, if I go ahead with what I am thinking will the girls ever forgive me, would I ever be able to forgive myself?

Keri Swain

Kevin came in from work that night to find me very quiet, I couldn't speak, I didn't want to speak, because speaking would mean sharing my thoughts and my decision with him, and then with everyone else, I was so worried that people would hate me. Unable to hold it in any longer, I began to blurt it all out.

"Please don't say anything, don't interrupt me, just let me say what I have to say." I was shaking, I felt sick and I was scared, taking a deep breath I began to tell him what I had decided.

"I have decided not to go ahead with the residence order on Angharad. I have spoken to social services and have asked them if they will look for prospective adoptive parents for Angharad who will also adopt the new baby; this will mean that they both stay together, just as Hope and Morganna have. They have agreed to my request so that is what they will do. There I can't say anything else now; we can talk about it later"

Kevin just looked at me in total surprise,

"Are you sure?"

I nodded and ran upstairs to get the girls pyjamas; I went into the bathroom and was as sick as a dog. I had failed miserably with any routine I had tried to keep to that day with the girls which meant they were now late going to bed. Kevin helped me and once the girls were settled together we got our evening meal cooked. After Oliver went to bed the house was quiet, and instead of switching on the TV, we sat and talked. I told Kevin that I didn't know whether this would be the right decision, I didn't know if I would be able to live with myself afterwards, or if I could ever forgive myself, but I knew that the decision I had made would mean that I could give the best of myself to Oliver and the girls, and that Angharad and the new baby would get the best from an adoptive family, it was with the children's interests at heart that I had made this heartbreaking decision.

The following afternoon Oliver and I took the girls for a walk along the farm track, it was a beautiful place to walk, peaceful, and still, there was no traffic, just us walking and the nature all around us.

"Sweetheart, I have to talk to you"

Oliver stopped walking, and stood still.

206

"What's up Mum?"

Kevin and I had not told Oliver about Bo's new pregnancy, I had hoped to keep it from him for a while yet, but now I had to talk to him. I gently told him the latest news, and then I went on to tell him about my decision not to go for a Residence order on Angharad.

"Why Mum, why?"

I told him through my tears that it wouldn't be fair on any of us, that I had enough to do with looking after him and the girls, that I wanted to try and make a good job of doing that and that if I had Angharad as well, then I would have to take the new baby.

When I saw the crushed look on my brave sons face that day I hated my daughter. I wanted her to see the pain she was causing her wonderful little brother, to see the maturity he was showing everyday, to see how fast he had been made to grow up, and to see what he had so easily and unreservedly given up or shared already and still he wanted to give more.

"I can help Mum, we can manage together, I can give up youth club and stay in after school with you and help, we can do that can't we Mum?"

The tears were streaming down his face. If I could have stood my daughter in front of him that day I would have done. I was watching my son hurting because of her and that hurt me beyond anything I had until then felt, she could hurt me over and over again, but not my son, not my brave and wonderful son.

"I am sorry darling, it has to be this way, and I have to concentrate on what we have now"

We held hands for the rest of that walk, pushing Hope and Morganna in their double pushchair, both of us bravely trying to point out the birds and flowers to them, both of us trying to wrap ourselves up in the moment and not let the pain we were both feeling inside. He is such an incredibly gentle and strong young man.

Over the following few days I managed to find the strength to talk to Oliver's teachers about the decisions we had made, they had been terribly supportive all the was through our journey. I had told them straight from the beginning what was happening in our lives, I felt that if Oliver needed a friend or just someone to listen, or if he was not performing in school as he should be, that if they knew what was going on at home his teachers would be able understand and to support him. Oliver was also struggling to come to terms with his own problems, he had recently been tested at school and diagnosed as having Dyslexia, he was given extra support in school, and his SENCO along with his day to day helpers were a brilliant support to him, both with his school work and his home life.

I had reached this most heartbreaking and soul destroying decision. I had watched as it hurt those who I hold most dear in my life. I worried that people would think badly of me, that they would not understand. I worried about how Hope and Morganna would feel in the years that followed as they came to understand the true magnitude of what had happened all those years before, and whether or not I had been able to bring them up to understand and forgive all those who together made these difficult decisions about these four beautiful sisters. I thought too of Angharad and Rhiannon and how they will feel when they eventually discovered that their older twin sisters had been brought up by their maternal grandparents, would they ever understand and forgive me?

But most of all I worried that I might never be able to forgive myself, I knew that this pain was going to stay with me for the rest of my life.

# WE MAKE ANOTHER LIFE
# CHANGING DECISION.

What happened to me back on that day in October had also frightened Kevin and he became a little better at shouldering some of the responsibility, he also tried to be a little easier to live with. He began to talk to me more about the pressures he was experiencing in work and I in return was able to support him more, I also realised why he had become difficult, he was grieving and I had not even considered that he may have been, I had been so wrapped up in my own problems that I had completely missed the signs in him that he was struggling to come to terms with the death of his mother and the fact that as hard as he had tried he had not made it back to Pembrokeshire to see her just before she had died, he felt so let down by the farm and the agency area manager that was in charge of his contract. We were unable to see where our future would take us and this was something we had to be in control of now more than at any other time in our life together, we had to show that we could provide Hope and Morganna with a secure home. Originally the farmer had asked Kevin to stay with the farm until the herd was sold and then look for a new job somewhere else, of course he had offered to compensate us, but I had sat churning this over in my mind, I was the one with the most time to do this and I talked to Kevin pointing out that the only person who was to gain from us agreeing to do this was the farmer, we had the children to think about, this was important to both of us. Another thing that was standing out like a sore thumb was that we had no quality time together as a family. Now that we had made a long term commitment to raising Hope and Morganna, we had to rethink, we had to put things in order of priority and we had to plan ahead, could we actually continue to work like this with so much pressure in his job that it was affecting our home lives, the answer was no, it was not what either of us wanted.

As the days were rolling on the news of Bo's pregnancy was circulating around my family. I found it so hard to bear. I felt so ashamed, so helpless and so totally alone. I had always shared all my dreams and fears with Kevin, but now I felt that he had enough of his own pressures to cope with, so I just stopped talking about it all with him, in a way I think I was trying to protect him from any further pressures. In doing this I was actually isolating myself, I also stopped discussing what was happening with the rest of my family. I spoke to no one about how I was feeling, what could anyone say that could make it feel any better? It was beginning to have a huge impact on me and I knew I was looking both ill and tired.

In our personal life Kevin and I had become like ships that passed in the night, whilst he was out earning the money to keep us all, I was running the home and everything else, we had always done both together, now it was split and I felt as if I was shouldering more than him, Kevin's working day was from 4.30am - 7pm maybe later, we never saw each other, and the children hardly saw anything of him, his breakfast and lunch breaks were more often than not interrupted by sales reps, and it was becoming impossible, what little time we did have was taken up writing our statements for the court, seeing to the girls and Oliver, talking about what was happening in Bo's life as daily I was receiving news of one thing or the other, which involved her. I was coping with the actual phone calls with her, Kevin was putting me back together again after each call, once the children were in bed and settled, we both would fall asleep in front of the TV at night.

Kevin and I were beginning to drift apart, and this was something that was driving me insane, but I did not have the energy to do anything about it. I was so absorbed in what was going on around me that my personal life came so far down the scale of priorities that it didn't stand a chance. I loved this man for so many reasons, but most of all I loved him, he was the other half of me, and without him I had nothing. We all have faults, I more than most, but Kevin's faults are simple ones, he is lazy when it comes to relationships, I have always been the driving force, now this driving force was overburdened and worn out yet again something had to give, only this time it was something I treasured so very much it was my relationship.

The girls had been with us for over twelve months now. I had been on this rollercoaster ride for so long and it was taking its toll on me. I knew I looked tired, God I was tired, who wouldn't have been, but knowing that any mother of twins felt at the least sometimes exhausted was of no comfort to me. Sleep deprivation was part of my everyday life and the girls were also now getting very active, they were into everything and if it wasn't tied down they would move it. They were also great climbers, I was convinced at one point that they would go on to conquer Everest one day, they used to scare me to death as they scaled up the back of the chairs in the conservatory and somehow would manage to balance precariously on the window ledge that ran all the way around the walls, once up there they would walk along as if they were on a tightrope. I now needed 360 degree vision. I couldn't let them out of my sight. And as if the everyday pressures were not enough I also had to contend with Bo's ever increasing problems, not to mention what was going on in my own life.

I hadn't carried Hope and Morganna the ten long months of a pregnancy and so had not had the time to prepare and adjust to what was going to happen when they arrived, I was never given any practical help from anyone on how to raise twins, maybe they all thought I was coping really well, and the truth was that somehow I did, but it came at a cost to me and Kevin. Everything I did seemed like an uphill struggle, when at long last I would feel as if I was making some progress; something would happen that would send me reeling back to where I had started. I decided to tackle what I considered to be my problems one at a time and one of the things I had to take charge of again was how I looked, I had lost control over that and most days would see me running around in trousers and a fleece. I was very self conscious about the weight I had regained and rather cross with myself for allowing it to happen. I felt mumsie and unattractive, I knew I could do something about the way I looked, I had done so before and in 1999 I had lost over four stone, so once again I enrolled with a local slimming group, and once a week set off to jump on a set of scales, and be told what a good girl I was being! It worked for a while and I did loose over a stone, but then it stuck and no amount of dieting would shift it, but at least it was going the right way and I did feel in control of it which helped a little. Everyday I made an effort to dress a bit smarter, and to put on my makeup I slowly began to feel a little more like the old me again, my efforts soon began to have the desired effect and I began to like what looked back at me from my bedroom mirror, which I hasten to add was only a head and shoulders view, I still wasn't brave enough to stop at the top of the stairs and sneak a peak in the full length mirror in the archway as in it I would see the scary monster that would have greeted me in that one. I had often been tempted to either take it down from the hook in hung from or to cover it over with a cloth, but I never got the time to get around to doing that either, and besides Hope and Morganna were rather fond of making faces at themselves in that old mirror.

When I had lost this one miserly stone I was once again able to comfortably reach my toenails and so I painted them, much to the girls glee, they used to sit at my feet trying to pick off the pretty pink colour from my nails, now Hope will paint the toe nails on one of my feet as Morganna paints the other, which is fine until they both want to paint my nails with a different colour! Oh, and before you start thinking that I can no longer reach my toenails, yes I can, it's just that the girls like to paint my nails for me. They have also painted Kevin's toenails bright blue when one afternoon he fell asleep in the chair.

There was also another problem, Kevin and I had not been out for ages, actually the last time had been out together was when we renewed our wedding vows in June, we could not afford a babysitter. No one in my family offered to have the girls overnight which would have given Kevin and I time to be together as a couple, this would have been something that would have helped us greatly, perhaps everyone thought we were ok, how the hell could we be, the pressures we were under were enormous.

And so I just stopped trying, bed was for sleeping only and I felt every thing other than attractive or sexy. I felt like a mum who was overloaded, with other people's emotional crap.

This was make or break, neither Kevin or I wanted it to break, we were so much in love, we still are, but for me I needed that physical side of my relationship, I needed him to show me I was still the fantastic warm sexy woman he had married. I had lost my identity completely, who the hell was I? Where had I gone to?

I needed to find me and I needed to do so fast.

That was when we decided that Kevin was to look for another job, something that gave us more quality time together as a couple and as a family, we knew that come the following September Oliver was to go up to secondary education, we were unsure as to whether it was best to move now or leave it until Oliver was due to move into secondary school, would it be easier for him to go straight into secondary school without any of the friends he had made in his junior school, or would it be easier if we made a move now which would give him six months to make some new friends before he went up to secondary school, at least that way he would have some friends in his new secondary school. It was around about this time that I saw an advertisement that grabbed my attention. When Kevin first started with the agency, the first job he took was on a large dairy farm in Oxfordshire, he had enjoyed it there, and now it seemed as though there was a job going on that same farm, he rang the farmer and we went to the farm for an informal interview.

Kevin was offered the job and he accepted it. That Christmas period of 2003 saw us (mainly me) begin to pack up our home yet again, something I was quite expert at now, only this time with the hope that it was to be for the last time.

We told my family that we had decided to move again and that Kevin had got a new job. This move was to benefit all of us a little; it took an hour off our travelling time back and for to Pembrokeshire as we were now nearer to the M4, and it was to give us a fresh start.

October arrived and my birthday passed uneventfully again. On October 14the 2002, Hope and Morganna had an appointment at the JR hospital in Oxford to see the consultant paediatrician, this is for the results of the x-rays on their hips that were taken a while ago. Both the girls hips are fine there are no problems with either of them and after a thorough check over by the consultant who declares that she does not think either of the girls given their prematurely will have any long term problems, they are discharged from her care. This is fantastic news. I feel like celebrating. When I got home I rang Bo to give her the good news, which is something I always used to do, the news was greeted with indifference by her.

It was my Mam's birthday on October 28th and we had planned to go home to Pembrokeshire. We had told Bo that we were coming home and arranged to meet her and her partner in the TESCO'S in their town. I did not want to go as by now it was fairly certain that when Bo's baby was born it would be taken straight from her, I found watching her pregnancy grow difficult as I knew that in her tummy was my grandchild, one that I knew I was not going to watch growing up, I hated her inability to sort her life out at that moment.

Hope and Morganna were so excited to see Bo, they always were, we had always encouraged the relationship between them and Bo to be a happy one, and whatever else was going on between Bo and us, we never took those feelings into their time together, even where her partner was concerned we were always nothing other than pleasant to him. We sat in the café drinking tea and coffee, making small talk, whilst the girls and Oliver enjoyed a cake and a drink of juice. When it was time to leave Kevin went off to the toilet whilst I stayed with the children, Bo picked Morganna up out of the high chair she was sitting in, and as she did her partner picked Hope up out of hers, she froze and then looked at me and just screamed, the more he hung on to her the more she struggled, people were watching and a man sitting in a table next to us got up and came over asking if everything was alright

"Give her to me please, she's frightened, please give her back to me now"

By now the security guard had left his station and was coming over to us, and Kevin came out of the toilets, Oliver was in tears, and I was shaking, I wanted to give this man such a hiding, how dare he frighten Hope like that. He gave her back to me and she clung to me as if her life depended on it, as he had passed her back the smell of alcohol hit me, that is what had frightened her, it had taken her back to something she feared. Hope was trying to climb up my shoulder to get as far away from him as possible

Thanking the man who had come to help me I gathered up the bags and we walked with the girls towards the exit. Bo gave Morganna to Kevin and I told both her and her partner that we were  not prepared to put the girls thorough a repeat of what had just happened, explaining that up till now her partner had been conspicuous in his absence as regard to Hope and Morganna, he had failed to turn up at pre-arranged contact visits and that on the times that he had bothered to turn up both Kevin and I had felt that he was because she had encouraged him, and that on these occasions he would have much preferred to have been elsewhere, he stank of alcohol and both Hope and Morganna disliked this. If he wanted to see them again he would have to take us to court. Bo was angry with me, saying that we had no right to do this, but we pointed out to them both that we were in fact only thinking of the girls. Bo could in fact still see the girls whenever she chose to, if she wished to come over to us at anytime she knew she only had to let us know when she was arriving, we had even offered to pay her train fare over. She never did come over to visit them on her own. To this day she has never expressed a wish to do so.

Kevin took both of the girls and Oliver back towards our car, and as he did Bo in her next breath asked me to lend her some money. I was dumbstruck by her lack of scruples. Telling her that I only had a couple of pounds on me I gave her that, and walked away.

We also saw Angharad during that visit home to Pembrokeshire. I had already asked social services if we could have Angharad for the afternoon so that we could take the girls in to have their photograph taken at the local Boots store and they had agreed. Bo had meet us in town and we had picked Angharad up, the girls had a lovely time with their sister, and we have some treasured photographs of the visits when they were together for all too short a time.

When we got back to Oxfordshire, we knew that the next time we would go there would be Christmas time, so I began getting the Christmas shopping done so that we could take that back home with us when we went. I had bought Angharad some presents and made up a box of things for her, my heart was breaking as I bought those gifts. Each one was chosen with love.

Again the Christmas spirit fell onto our home, this year the girls were beginning to be aware that this was a special time, and we took them along to see Santa. I also took them to a Christmas party which HOMESTART had organised, Margaret came as well and the girls had so much fun. It was so far away from the pain I was feeling at the time as I knew that this would be our first and last Christmas with Angharad in our family, how do you try to put on a brave face when you are being crushed by an overwhelming pain so deep it tears at you. I put a huge effort into Christmas that year as if left to just how I was feeling Christmas would have passed just like any other day in our home.

Christmas arrived for the first time in Angharad's young life a week earlier than usual that year. We celebrated it with her in a pokey little room that social services had given us for two whole precious hours. There were no Christmas decorations just an old and sorry tree that had seen better days, it was such a miserable room, and it was a far cry from what Hope and Morganna were experiencing at home with us. Throughout that whole visit we had to put up with a lady who we had never met before being present who was there to supervise my daughter's contact. I felt as if it was me that was actually being supervised, I was annoyed that social services had not explained to this woman that there would be no need for her to stay in that room with us, as we could supervise the contact for Bo, but they had neglected to inform her, so she planted herself into a chair and stayed in the room, it ruined that two hours for us as we felt we could not spend quality time with Angharad, we were guarded as to what we said and did, none of us felt relaxed. We opened Jades presents with her, and then Hope and Morganna opened their presents from Angharad that Kevin and I had also bought, so that the girls wouldn't feel left out, I was trying so hard to think of everything. It was awful as this lady even though she did try to be inconspicuous, invaded our "special time" with Angharad. Given the choice I would have preferred to have taken Angharad out somewhere for a couple of hours.

After Christmas I did speak to social services and expressed my disappointment at what had happened that day, after which I was allowed to pick Angharad up from her foster mother myself and return her later in the day, this made it much nicer for us all and it also meant that we could take Angharad to my parents house so they too got to see her for a few precious visits before she was taken away. I know that those visits were so important to both my Mam and my Dad. In agreeing to this arrangement social services had also given me something very special, and that was quality time with Angharad on my own. I would drop Kevin and the children off at my parents home and then alone I would make the hour long journey to pick Angharad up form her foster mother, I would then make the hour long journey back to my parents house, and Angharad I would travel together, me singing away to her and her responding by chuckling away in glee, we would stop off on the way to pick Bo up from the bus station in Haverford west and then travel the rest of the way to my parents house. I value those hours with a love that knows no measure, we were alone and I talked to her about all kinds of things, I told her what my dreams were and how I would always be there when she came home to us. I would drive the car and tickle her toes, she would chuckle away, I would blow kisses at her and she would smile, she never once cried.

*Darling Angharad - I will always treasure those special hours. I miss you so much sweetheart. X*

All too soon the Christmas decorations from yet another Christmas were taken down and packed into their boxes. I was a little sad taking them down as I knew that this would be the last year they would be put up in the home we were leaving. Its funny isn't it how bare and plain everything looks when you take the Christmas decorations down, but weeks after the Christmas is packed away you somehow always manage to find at least one decoration that escaped the packing boxes! I was still tripping over the boxes that some of the girls toys had arrived in as they like most children preferred to play with the toys packaging than the toy itself. All of our rooms were lined with the removal companies packing boxes, which were stuffed to bulging with all our worldly goods, each box neatly labelled and clearly marked as to which room it should be put in at our new home.

For the past few months Christmas and the house move have pretty much occupied my mind. There had been a lot to do, one of the most important things was to look for a new school for Oliver, he had only 7 months remaining in junior education before going on up to secondary level, and fortunately we got a place for him easily. I too was entering another phase of my life with Hope and Morganna, - that of Pre school, and the very thought of it set my nerves on edge.

I began to build a protective barrier around myself; I didn't speak to my friends anymore about Angharad and Bo. I was so looking forward to moving and to the anonymity it would afford me. I knew that for a short time I could be simply "just a mum" No one would think anything of the new older mum with twins, who had just moved into the village.

Our last week in our old home was full of tearful goodbyes and farewells as we said goodbye to the friends we had made. Oliver's class mates were sad to se him leaving, and I was deeply touched by the handmade folder he had come home with which was crammed full of good luck wishes from each and every one of his classmates, they had all drawn a picture and written some truly meaningful words to him. Oliver had a really good friend in that school, they have remained good friends and often either Jack is here with us for the weekend or Oliver is at Jack's.

Hope and Morganna said goodbye to their small friends at toddler group, and I said a tearful goodbye to the Mum's, who had all accepted me, this older "mum" as a friend, I am so grateful to them for that. I still think about them a lot and wonder what they are doing. I recently found out that one of the mum's who I was fond of now runs a pub, so maybe I will take the girls along with me and go to visit her one day over the school summer holidays.

On Thursday 22nd January at the crack of dawn the removal Lorries turned up outside the house, and as quick as they arrived the men were out of the Lorries and in the house, it was like watching ants as they went backwards and forwards time and time again, their arms heavily laden with our worldly goods. Hope and Morganna had a whale of a time getting in the way and occasionally carrying something small out to the lorry. Late that afternoon, leaving us with beds and essential bits and pieces they drove off for the night saying they would be back early in the morning to pack up the remaining bits and pieces.

True to their word they arrived back at the house early and dismantled the beds and cots loaded them in to the lorry, and then went to empty the garden sheds. By midday the lorries were full to the brim and Kevin and I were packing things into our car. After a final brush up and wash down, it was time to leave. We put the girls in their car seats and leaving them in the car with Oliver, Kevin and I returned to the house to wish it goodbye. That house had seen more than its fair share of heartache over the few years that we lived there, and there was a big part of me that breathed a big sigh inside when I closed that door for the final time.

And off we went, Kevin the children and I, to our new home and hopefully to the start point of a journey that would see Kevin and I rediscovering each other again, and give us all the quality time we so desperately needed.

When we pulled up outside our new home the lorries were already being unpacked, our furniture was being placed in the rooms it was intended for and I sat in the car just looking at the 16$^{th}$ century cottage that was now turning slowly into our home. Once the girls found a box of their toys and spread the contents of that box throughout the house it certainly did feel like home!!

Kevin was not due to start his new job until the following week, this was a huge bonus for me as he had never been around before to help with the unpacking, this time he was and boy did I use that, he was soon putting up curtain tracks and putting furniture back together again, being helped by his young apprentices!

I remember the very first morning that I woke up in our new home, there was no noise, no traffic no nothing, just peace and quiet. It wasn't just the home that was peaceful and quiet, so was I, for the first time in so long that I couldn't remember the last time, I was feeling peaceful. The girls were still fast asleep, so I went downstairs and made Kevin coffee and a mug of tea for me and went back upstairs. Kevin and I lay there enjoying the peace, knowing that there was a mountain of boxes downstairs that we needed to unpack, but for that half hour they could wait.

The quality of life we were searching for soon began to transpire., as the routine of Kevin's new job soon started to mould our lives, and for the first ever when he came in for breakfast and lunch, that time on the whole stayed ours, and was not interrupted by either the phone ringing or a rep who was hell bent on getting him to buy something. When he came in from work at the end of the day, he was in before 6 o clock - something we had never enjoyed.

Kevin was now in early enough for both of us to sit with the children and have our evening meal, and we could get the girls ready for bed together. It made such a difference not only to me but also to him and the girls, they love having Daddy in every night to play with them as Mammy gets the evening meal finished off and dished up. Then after our meal we get the girls off to bed together, sometimes Kevin will bath them for me as I clear away the aftermath of the war that must have taken place in the kitchen and dining room. I bet most of you will have seen something resembling my kitchen and dining room after the children have eaten, well mine will have an assortment of tasty titbits strewn around the girl's seats, and all over the floor as they have missed their mouths with the spoon. If I had a dog it would be so fat that it I would probably have to clean the floor around it as it would be unable to get up and walk away! The same assortment of tasty titbits will be deposited in various other places between the dining room and the kitchen as the girls will have got down from their chairs with something in their hand that they are halfway through demolishing, only to loose interest in it again as they came across the toy they were playing with before their meal, and then leave the tasty titbit where they found their toy again. And of course there's the odd foodstuff that has somehow got stuck to the wall, Oh silly old me that wasn't the children, that was Mr Nobody, you see he too lives in this house and occasionally gets up to mischief - he is particularly fond of art, and has drawn some wonderful pictures on most of our walls, he is also has a liking for my make up bag and its diminishing contents, I have never seen this Mr Nobody, but he has been in my home a lot over the past 27 years. I had thought that he had at last gone when Oliver reached the age of about 7 years old, but needless to say he is once again back. He must look really funny as the last time he paid us a visit was yesterday, when he not only painted his toenails Barbie pink, but also used nearly the whole of the contents of my brand new blue eye shadow on his cheeks!!!!

After the girl's birthday in February, I took them along to visit the preschool in the village close to the farm where I live. It struck me how friendly everyone was and so I enrolled the girls onto the waiting list, they began preschool twice a week for two and a half hours each session, suddenly I had some time to myself, and it was great, I was also now making friends with the other Mums, who were not all young as I had imagined them to be, some of them were older like I was and that was a comfort to me. Hope and Morganna began to make their own friends which was nice and they began to have a social life, they were invited to birthday parties and now they get invited to their friend's homes to play after preschool sessions, and I have their friends over here as well, it is so nice to hear them all playing happily together. Hope and Morganna have a better social life than I have.

# ANGHARAD'S MEMORY BOX

Easter had been and gone, the mountain of chocolate eggs that were left hidden away in the cupboard under the stairs had been sacrificed I have broken them up and melted them down to go on top of a chocolate cake. I have no more excuses to fall back on, no more reasons why I shouldn't be tackling the one last thing I can do for Angharad.

I was very aware that I had been putting off lifting the lid of the beautiful box I had agonised over buying. I had searched everywhere in my local town for a box so special, so personal. But in God's name where was I ever to find a box that was big enough to hold my heart, my dreams, my soul and my prayers, had anyone created a box so special that it could hold within its heart all the things I have mentioned. Please tell me where I could find a box so strong that it could hold all these things safe for me for as long as it took for my precious Granddaughter to one day be given this box to look inside.

The box I had eventually found had been put into a cupboard; I had banished it from view because to have left it where I could see it would have robbed me of more time, hiding it away allowed me to forget about it. I knew that I would have to deal with it; I knew I was once again going to have to be strong because this box was not for me it was for Angharad.

Angharad's social worker had asked me one day if I would like to put together a "memory box" for Angharad. Once again I was to learn about something else I never thought would touch my life. The memory box would travel with Angharad to her new life with her adoptive parents, and then one day surrounded by the love of her adoptive family, Angharad would take the lid off this memory box and reveal its contents, she would hold in her hands all the things that I had so lovingly given. She would hold in her hands my soul, my love and every other part of me that I had tried to tell her about in that box. It would tell her about me and the rest of her birth family. I had a responsibility to put into this box things that were meaningful and precious.

Time is not on my side, I have ignored this box for too long and as the day is fast approaching that will see me say goodbye to my precious Angharad, I am aware that the memory box has to be ready to start her journey with her. On the day that my much loved Granddaughter leaves my world she has to take with her the parts of me that are in this box. I can't focus, I am torn in two.

We are now in our new home and only 4 weeks after moving in Hope and Morganna celebrated their 2nd birthday, they had a lovely time with a few friends coming over for tea. I have once again taken the memory box out from the cupboard. I am agonising over what to put in the memory box. Do I go out and buy lots of little things, do I fill it with things that are precious and meaningful - now where do I buy these things. What in God's name do I put in this box that will tell my Angharad how much I love her? Lifting the lid I look inside, my box is empty. I will never be able to fit into such a small space all that I need to put there.

Climbing the old oak spiral staircase, which has over the hundreds of years it has stood there had many thousands of feet climb it, I found myself wandering if this 16th century home of ours has carried such heavy laden and weary feet from its bottom up to its top that leads the way up to our bedroom. Stopping halfway up its spiral, I looked at the photographs that line the walls and those that rest on the windowsill; they are all photographs of my children, and my grandchildren. I picked up the one that has the three girls on it, Hope and Morganna are lovingly holding Angharad's hands, tears pricked at my eyelashes, and replacing the photograph back where it had stood, I stroked the faces in that picture, then climbed the last few remaining steps.

As always I went into the girl's bedroom to check on them, they were both fast asleep. Hope was lying on her side cuddled up tight to her teddy. Morganna was flat on her back, her adored Peter panda securely tucked in besides her, she loves Peter panda, he goes to bed with her every night, some days he is lucky enough to be taken to preschool with her. Whispering into their sleeping ears that I love them to the moon and back, I quietly left their room. Slipping into bed. I closed my eyes tight, but sleep evades me, so I lay awake staring at the old oak beam that runs through my bedroom.

"The box, that's it, that's what I need to put in the box"

I jumped out of bed and rushed around my home, and like a magpie collected the things I wanted Angharad to have. It broke my heart to pick out the things I did. Back down the stairs I went to once again fetch the box from its hiding place, only this time I would not put it back empty, this time the beginnings of my soul were to be left in that box.

I sat alone on the settee in my lounge and there in the dead of night and away from prying eyes I placed my hoard into the box. First to be placed into the box was the silver charm bracelet that I had been given when I was 18yrs old, it was so full of charms that there was no room for any more, I had taken down from above my inglenook fireplace the first love spoon I had ever been given that too was placed in the box, as was one of the three four leafed clovers my friend had found for me in his garden, and also one of the "fairy baskets" he had lovingly hand carved out of a peach stone - "Thank you David, those special things are now with someone very special to me - I hope they bring her luck and fantasy". I also placed in the box one of Hope's and Morganna' identity bracelets that had been on their tiny arms when they left hospital, a lock of Bo's hair form her 1st haircut, a flower from my wedding bouquet and one of the CD'S I had recorded for charity in 1997. I was sat there, just me and my box, when I realised that I was playing with the gold ring that Bo had bought me a few years before, it had not left my little finger, hesitatingly I turned it once more around my finger, I was forever doing that when I was upset or stressed, it had become a habit, sometimes when I was thinking about Bo I would find myself playing with it again, I removed it from my finger and tenderly placed it safe in the belly of the box with all my other gifts of love. Returning the lid onto the box I lovingly placed it back inside the cupboard.

Tears fell freely from my sore weary eyes throughout this heartbreaking journey of love that I travelled alone which saw the dead of night turn into the early hours of the morning. But I hadn't been alone, someone had watched over me, someone had guided me, I hadn't seen anyone or anything, but I had felt their presence. Before I closed the old oak door at the foot of our stairs, I whispered a silent goodnight into the heart of our lounge. Exhausted

I climbed the stairs once again, and curled up in bed just as the dawn was breaking over the farm.

Two days later I knew that the time had come to finish my box of love, so after the girls and Oliver had settled for the night, I began work once again on the most difficult of tasks. Kevin made me coffee as I sat on the floor in our lounge, in front of me was the pine blanket box that holds our family photographs. I selected photographs that I hoped would teach Angharad about us all, there were photo's of my parents, of me and my children, of Kevin, some of Bo throughout her childhood and some of the girls together. I cut each one to fit into the small album that I had bought Angharad, and on every page wrote something for her.

Then I cut some small tags and tied them with ribbon to everything that I had placed in the box, writing onto each one something about what it was joined too. On the charm bracelet I wrote that one day I would sit with her and tell her who had bought me each of the charms that were held securely in its links.

That all done I was left with the most arduous of tasks, I had to write Angharad a letter, once again my heart was ripped out as I agonised over each and every word that I wrote. Every word, every sentence, every paragraph, every page, from the very first stoke of my pen to its last, I cried. I am crying as I write this now, oblivious to the other people around me, I am writing this lying on the grass in a beautiful part of Abingdon called "Abbey Meadow" Kevin and the children are off playing in the park about 100 yards away and I am lying in the shelter of a line of lime trees, so tall that they look as if they are touching the sky. To the left of me is the River Thames which hosts an assortment of cruisers and narrow boats. I can hear the children playing and the birds calling, but none of it distracts form what I am doing.

*"Angharad and Rhiannon, wherever you are my beautiful girls, I hope that today you to are playing in the June sunshine having just as much fun as Hope and Morganna. I love all of you so very much"*

Most of the UK are indoors today, it is June 10th 2006; they will be watching England as they fight the first of their battles in the football. I am lying here in the glorious Oxfordshire sunshine, the narrow boats are floating on by on the River Thames, and I am surrounded by the music of life as the children fill the air with their funfilled screams of delight, but I feel totally alone, just me and my pen, and the tears that are falling onto the paper I am writing on are the only telltale signs that I too am fighting a battle, but this is my battle, and its much harder than any football match.

I will share with you just one of the things that I wrote in Angharad's letter -

"If I was given all the paper in the world, and the wisdom of the wisest men, I would run out of words and paper, my pen would run dry"

How true that was for even now I know that I left things unwritten.

*Dear Angharad,*

*"When you read your letter, please open your heart as I have done in the writing of it, feel the warmth that has been written into every word, the hope that hides in every sentence, the family in every paragraph, the memories on every page, but most of all Cariad, feel the love through the hand of its writer and the tug of the invisible thread that joins your heart to mine and which will one day lead you back home to me and into my arms"*

*Love Grandma x x x*

Over the few days that followed my finishing Angharad's memory box, I would lift its lid and once again go through the contents, holding each item tightly in my hand, almost as if I were trying to imprint more love into it then I did the time I had dared to open it before, I would kiss the envelope that protects Angharad's letter, and then before I replaced the lid onto the box I would whisper into its heart "I love you" quickly closing the lid down firmly so that I could capture my whispered words, where they would stay trapped until Angharad opens her box.

Kevin has now returned from the park and has found me with tears rolling down my face. Oliver Hope and Morganna are running through the water spouts that gush up out of the ground. Hope is stood in the middle of a circle of water spouts, she looks like a fairy captured inside a flower, Morganna is running through an arch of water, they are having a ball.

After I had finished Angharad's memory box it stood safe on the shelf in the old bread oven on the side of the inglenook in the lounge. Everyday I took it out and looked at it and every day I cried. Everyday I longed to awake from the nightmare that haunted my days, but it was no nightmare, I was not asleep, I felt every part of that pain - I still do.

On the 9th on May 2004, I tenderly lifted Angharad's memory box from its safekeeping place in the bread oven cupboard for the very last time, I placed it gently into another box to protect it, I was preparing to drive the box that contained a part of my heart and my soul, along the M4 that would take me home to Pembrokeshire, and see me say goodbye to my darling Angharad.

Later that night I had fretfully fallen asleep on the settee in the lounge, Kevin had also nodded off, but when he awoke he had seen something that he did not tell me about for weeks after it had happened.

As I had slept, he had woken up, behind me he had seen the face of a woman looking down on me, he rubbed his eyes thinking he was still asleep, but she was still there When he did tell me about her, he said that he was sure he had seen the face before in a photograph, but couldn't remember where or when, he also said that the face was more youthful that the one he had remembered seeing in the photograph.

"I would recognise her if I was to see the photo again" he had told me.

Well by the time Kevin had told me about what he had seen that night, I too had seen her.

# "HOW DO I SAY GOODBYE?"

We all have to say goodbye to someone we love during our lifetime. Nearly everyone of us will experience the sadness of saying goodbye to our grandparents and our parents as they die and pass on to another world, but bereavement is a normal and expected event in our lives, some of us will feel the grief as we say goodbye to the spouses, partners, and lovers that we have chosen to share not only our everyday lives with but also the most intermit parts of our lives too, we will be left behind, some of us will be unable to see a way forward, but eventually for most in time the moving forward process finds us. Some will feel the pain of loosing their siblings, or the friends they hold so dear in their lives.

Some of us will share the absolutely devastating pain of loosing a child, or a grandchild because they die as the result of accident or illness and are so cruelly taken from us too early in life. As parents we don't ever expect to outlive our children, it's supposed to happen the other way around, so the pain of burying a grandchild is immense.

As difficult as it is to cope and live through the effects a death can have on us, whether it is an expected death that follows old age or illness, or the untimely death that an accident or crime brings into our lives, most of us will work our way through the grieving process, some of us wont be able too and for those of us who find that we can not cope with the death of a loved one, there are specially trained counsellors who will work with us until eventually at our own pace we can learn to live with our memories and move on. Now maybe all this is possible because we have learnt throughout our lives that we all have two things in common, we will have been born and we all will die, death is as natural as birth, and whereas death brings immense sadness, birth brings with it a joy so profound that it enriches our lives.

But someone please tell me how the hell do I say goodbye to someone I hold so very, very dear in my life, and who brings into my world a love in me beyond all measure, someone I see sharing and enriching my life, a little person who is the future, my next generation, someone who I had hoped to live on through after my days on this earth have ended, a part of my most treasured family, someone who is to bring me so much joy, so much love, so much hope. This little person is going to be such a big part of my life because I am their Grandma, they are going to be such a part of me, both of us will enjoy teaching each other so much, they are part of my very soul and they hold such a special place in my heart from the very first time we met - until the day I die.

There was nobody who could tell me just how much being forced to say goodbye to my own flesh and blood was going to rip me apart. Nobody could understand why I felt so helpless, so overwhelmed with a grief that completely saturated me. Nobody could understand why I just wanted to curl up and die. At one point I did actually think that the only thing that would ever get this pain to release its grip on me was death itself. Once again my world clouded over and everything in it took on the tarnish of the blackest of days.

When I had gone through all the pain of fighting with every ounce of strength in me to keep Hope and Morganna safe with us, I came off that rollercoaster of emotions with a wealth of knowledge that surpassed my years, I had leant terminology that I would not have necessarily used in my everyday life, and would have required the help of a dictionary to help me understand some of the words that I came across, I came across people from all walks of life. These lessons stood me in good stead, and even if on times I felt that what was going on around and within me was bigger than I was, I coped, probably because I was driven with a passion so great that defeat was one word that I was not going to have in my life at that time.

But as I said goodbye to 2003 and welcomed in 2004, silently trying to wish myself a better year ahead of me than the one I had just said farewell too, just as I had done when saying goodbye to 2002 and hello to 2003, I knew that during 2004 I was going to be catapulted into something so painful, so soul destroying that not only did it rip my heart out, but it can't ever be put back together again, it has left me with a scar so deep that on times it splits open again and weeps.

"Please tell me how does a Grandparent say goodbye their Grandchild, or as in my case to my grandchildren. How can I tell these precious children that I love them, that I always will, how do I cram a life time of togetherness into the few miserly hours that if you are lucky social services allow you to have to be able to say goodbye. But I can't say goodbye, because I don't want to, but I have no choice"

I was to have to do just that not once, - but twice.

I can't grieve, I can't say goodbye. I feel the pain everyday of being bereft of my two beautiful granddaughters. I have no grave to visit, no special place to go and sit to remember them, for they have not died, what I am feeling isn't bereavement. There is no final resting place in my mind, no sequence or process that eventually brings me some kind of peace. I have a big empty space in my life and in my heart, it's a space that Angharad and Rhiannon should be filling, and it's empty because social services took them into care and they were adopted. Now believe me I know there was no option to this decision, it was what was best for Angharad and Rhiannon, but that does not make any of it any easier for me, if anything it makes it harder. I wanted the girls to be here, all four of them together. If only I had been given hindsight, if only I had dug in my heels, battened down the hatches, and not paid the heed to the social worker that I had afforded him two years ago, and if I had the knowledge that I now possess, at the very least I would have been more forceful in trying to get the results I wanted for all the girls before Angharad and Rhiannon's adoptions were finalised, even before the process of finding them a new family, what social services term as "twin tracking" had even begun.

As every day comes and goes I watch as Hope and Morganna meet the milestones in their little lives, and I cant help but wonder if Angharad and Rhiannon are meeting theirs. Who is it that is loving them - oh yes I know they are loved. I also know that their Mammy and Daddy are, like me, very lucky people because thanks to my daughter, we are all living each and every day watching these most precious of little girls growing up. But it also saddens me that social services, the courts and all those involved in adoption seem to think that it is best for the child if all ties with their birth families are severed. In some cases I must admit that this may well be the correct thing to do, but in my case I wonder how much thought was actually given to mine Hope and

Morganna's part in all of this, I think very little time was spared on the one request that I put to the adoptive parents via the social worker, indeed did it ever reach the ears and hearts of the adoptive parents? In truth I shall never know the answer to that, but I think if I had been asked to consider the future welfare of my girls I would have at least have given it much thought and not just made a decision based on my own feelings.

Now I know nothing about Angharad and Rhiannon's new Mammy and Daddy, their new Grandparents, their family, their friends and their lives. I don't know where they are, or even if they are well. I will not share any of their milestones in life. I miss them each and every day. It is the most horrible of pains.

Last year not long after I had said goodbye to Rhiannon, who was just one year old, her social worker said to me

"You have to move on, you have to let go"

Until she said that to me I had always considered that she had shared with me some of the deep sorrow I was feeling, she hadn't, she couldn't, for if she had she could never have made such a derogatory remark. It was said by someone who has never experienced this most devastating and soul destroying event. The truth is she didn't understand and the reality is that she in all probability never will. Those of us who have felt this awful, most unrelenting pain, will know that we don't have to say anything to each other; they like me will just want someone to hold us, to tell us it is all going to work out alright. We just want our grandchildren brought back to where they should be- with us.

We do move on, we have to as life goes on and you either move with it or you get left behind. I had some very good reasons to move on, I had Oliver Hope and Morganna, as well as my brilliant husband to look after, they all needed me in this world with them, I could not get left behind, so I did the best to dust myself off, paint on a brave face and a smile to greet the outside world, and face my audience, and they were my audience as I knew that not only were my family and friends watching me, but so was everyone I knew, they were all watching to see how I coped with this devastating part of my life. Did I cope? Well I don't truly know the answer to that, you would have to ask those around me who know me best, I know I buckled with the pressure of it on many occasions not knowing from where I was going to summon the strength and determination to pick myself back up again. The pain has and will never go away. Sometimes something in my everyday life will trigger in me a feeling of absolute longing.

I can remember the day that I brought my uncle to my home to meet his sisters for the first time, one of his sisters is my Mam. When David and my Mam met for the first time in over 55 years the look on their faces was pure magic-please God don't let my girls have to wait 55 years before they are reunited with each other. The feelings that I experienced that day made my stomach lurch, it was yet another of those occasions that was to make me regret that I did not have two years ago this wealth of knowledge I now have.

One thing my uncle David has taught me is that when you are adopted you spend a lot of time dwelling on who you really are and where you came from, who your birth family are. He told me that he never felt "complete" as if something in him was missing, he no longer feels like that, he knows who he is and where he came from and who his birth family are. It was because of what I was going through at the time that I had the determination and drive to find Mam's sister and brother, no social worker had given them any help. Now I know things were very different 55 years ago, but some things have remained unchanged.

# A CARPET OF PURPLE BLEUBELLS

Until the 10<sup>th</sup> May 2004 bluebell's only ever evoked in me the memories of a little girl dressed in a frock coat who was holding tightly onto the hand of a tall willowy man who wore a trilby on his head, they were walking hand in hand through a carpet on purple bluebells, all around them were tall green trees. The man was my Grandfather William Stowell, the little girl whose hand he tenderly held was mine. Crashing into that memory and totally swamping it is a huge wave of nauseating pain and sadness, that captures my thoughts and chases away the memories of my childhood, holding me tight it then it carries me along in its spewing froth until it finally leaves me high and dry engulfed in the memories of what happened to me on that damn awful day in May 2004.

It was 10 o clock in the morning and as prearranged with social services Bo and I had arrived at the "safe house" to meet Angharad and the lady who was going to supervise the "final contact" The final contact was to be for just two short hours, yet those two precious hours were to be the most painful hours in my entire life, hours which I was to relive time and again until the day I die. No pain will ever surpass it and no love will ever erase it, it is etched like an open sore in my heart and will never be healed completely,

It had only been 2 weeks since I last saw Angharad on her 1<sup>st</sup> birthday, that visit was the one and only time that the four sisters were ever to be together, Hope, Morganna, Angharad and Rhiannon were for a few hours able to share Angharad's 1<sup>st</sup> birthday, it was also the last time that Hope, Morganna, Oliver and Kevin as well as my parents were ever to see Angharad. It was agonising to watch the girls all together knowing that they would not see each other again until they were adults, if indeed they do see each other again.

I was more fortunate, as the week after Angharad's first birthday Bo had rung me to ask if I would go with her when she had her final contact with Angharad. In one way I felt honoured that after all we had been through she still felt that she could turn to me, but at the same time I also felt that I could have hung her out to dry, I was so angry that my child could be the cause of so much heartache. None of what was happening made any sense to me, it all seemed so surreal, this wasn't even one of those things that happen to other people, and I could never have imagined this ever happening to anyone at all.

Now here I was sat in the most impersonal of rooms. Clutching tightly to me the memory box that I had agonised over as I tried to put so much love into it for Angharad, holding it so protectively that you could have been forgiven if you had thought the box actually contained my heart. My heart was broken in two, what was in that box was me. In that room with me was my daughter, my granddaughter and the lady from social services who I shall call Karen. I had been catapulted into my worst nightmare and I was about to begin living it, I had absolutely no idea of the pain that lay ahead of me.

I have to say Karen was fantastic, she had supervised the major part of Bo's contact with Angharad, and also later with Rhiannon as well, she had always been nothing but understanding, she had also tried everything she could think of to try and get Bo to understand the enormity of what was happening.

The three of us sat in that god forsaken place watching Angharad as she played with the present I had brought her. Someone came to the door and walked in, it was the CAFCASS Guardian, I saw the look on Bo's face, and I asked him what he was doing interrupting that last special contact meeting. He did not get a chance to respond to my question. For the first time I saw Bo actually stand up for herself, she told him to go away and leave her alone. He asked Bo to go and see him later in the afternoon at the court; he turned to me and asked if I would still be around that afternoon as he felt that Bo would need someone with her. I had no idea what he meant, but Bo answered him by saying that she would call in later and for him to go. He did. I was annoyed at his interruption and so was Karen.

Once he had left we decided to go to a place called SCOLTON MANOR, it is a beautiful country park just outside Haverfordwest its grounds are lovely, and they are lined with the most magnificent rhododendron trees. I had suggested that we go out somewhere instead of staying in that awful room, I did not want Bo's last memories of Angharad to be of that room, I wanted her to have something special to think back on, to have felt free for those final hours.

When we arrived at Scolton Manor it was warm and sunny. Bo carried Angharad the whole time we were there; she didn't put her down once. At one point she was sat on a swing with Angharad and I took some photographs of her, I can remember thinking how slim Bo looked especially as Rhiannon had only been born less than a month before. Watching Bo with Angharad tore at my insides, I was watching a mother who so obviously loved her child - but it wasn't enough.

We walked into the woodland area of the park, where beneath the trees and for as far as the eye could see, nature had carpeted the ground with fragrant purple bluebells. I desperately tried to stop my hands from shaking as I held the camera to my eye and focused on the picture before me in the lens, if you had seen what I could see at that moment through my camera lens you would have cried with me. The scene was fabulous, there was my daughter kneeling on natures purple carpet, my beautiful grand daughter was sat on her knee and Bo was holding a bluebell up to Angharad's nose for her to smell - the most poignant of memories

I wonder if Angharad will ever remember anything about that day - will she like me, have a love of bluebells, will they stir in her a memory from so long ago, just as they do for me.

All too soon it was time to say goodbye, none of us wanted it to be over, we all wanted those few hours to last forever, well in my heart they will. I had expected Bo to go to pieces, but she didn't, she stayed calm, almost a step removed from reality. I just wanted to take Angharad into my arms and run forever. In silence the three of us made our way back to our cars. On the way we passed the Scolton Manor sign post with the Owl painted onto it, I got Bo to stand there with Angharad still in her arms and took one last photograph.

Handing Angharad over to Karen, Bo turned and walked away, Karen quickly fastened Angharad safely into her car seat, and without another word got into the drivers seat and drove away with my dreams in her car with her. I was left standing there watching my beautiful grand daughter disappear form view, my heart was broken, instead of holding Angharad in my arms Bo had somehow made her way into them, I held my daughter, I stroked her hair and spoke soothingly to her as a mother does to her child when she is hurting, but no one was holding me. My family were not even aware that I was in the county for I had told no one.

Bo and I went for a coffee, I couldn't drink mine, all I wanted to do was hurl that cup at the wall, I wanted to scream and cry, but I couldn't I had to stay strong for Bo. Leaving our coffees undrunk, we got back into the car and I drove through the town and up to the court offices where Bo had agreed to meet the CAFCASS Guardian. When I got there the enormity of what I was going to witness began to reveal itself. Until that afternoon I had thought that Bo had fought each court appearance regarding Angharad's adoption, but the CAFCASS Guardian had with him the paperwork for her to sign that gave her permission for the adoption to proceed. Numb I watched as my daughter signed away her own daughter. I did not think it was possible to hurt any more but it was, something inside me snapped and died in that office, I felt numb, yet still I offered my daughter support.

We both left that office in silence, got in the car and I drove to a quiet spot in the town where once I had parked the car we cried and cried. Eventually Bo said that she was going, she wanted to be with her partner. I watched her walking away and I knew that the love and comfort I had given her was the only support she was going to get, and once again I feared for her safety. That afternoon I sat alone in my car and I cried not just for Angharad, but for myself, for the girls and for my Bo, those tears stung my face, and left my sides aching form the racking I had done inside as they had fallen, I sat there for ages, I dried my tears, started up the car and drove off, where I ended up I didn't care, I just had to get away. Leaving the town behind me I found myself driving along the familiar roads that would lead me to my parents home, someone guided me there, for I had not made the decision to drive that way, I had thought of driving to ST JUSTINAINS, but I am glad I didn't.

I arrived at my parents home, parked the car outside their house got out and walked down the garden path that led to their back door, just as I had done thousands of times before over the years my family have lived in that house. But the footsteps that trod that path on that day were not the footsteps of a carefree girl, they were the footsteps of someone who walked as heavy and as wearily as the heart she was carrying, I opened the back door and saw my Mam and Dad sat at their kitchen table eating their tea, I didn't notice whether or not Mam and Dad's dogs barked as I entered, they always do usually after you are already in the house. I was vaguely aware of the familiar aroma of good home cooked food, but I wasn't hungry. I just felt sick, so sick that I thought my heart was breaking. Somehow I had delivered to the safety of my childhood home and into the arms of my parents their badly broken eldest daughter - me.

"Ker, what you doing here love" my Mam said

I just broke and I sobbed, Mam put her arms around me and held me close, as through my painful sobs I tried to tell my parents where I had been, Dad had got up and was busy making me a mug of steaming hot tea, into which he put copious spoonfuls of sugar. I remember thinking, "silly old thing, he knows how I hate sugar in my tea" but my Dad bless him was thinking of shock, it was going to take more than a few spoonfuls of sugar to help make this dose of life's medicine down.

Mam and Dad were mortified when I told them I was travelling back to Oxfordshire that night. Oh they protested, and jumped up and down, but I had to go as Kevin was working the following morning. Kissing them both goodbye I began that painful journey back home and into the arms of the man I loved. My Mam rang Kevin and told him I was on my way back home again, and between them they took it in turns to ring me until I was home safe. My parents were afraid for me, they did not want me travelling home alone, but I wasn't alone, my Guardian angel was with me the whole time. To this day I can't remember driving through Swindon with its many roundabouts. When I eventually reached the farm entrance that led to my home I began to shake, I parked the car in the garage and sat there in the peace and quiet, until somehow I managed to drag myself down the back garden path that led to my back door.

Kevin was waiting for me, he was sat on the sofa in the lounge, I went to him and he took me into his arms and held me, I lay on our sofa curled up tight in the foetal position and fell apart. Through racking sobs that tore at my insides I tried to share with him the most awful of pain that I was feeling, but I couldn't find the words that were strong enough to explain to him just how battered and heartbroken I felt inside, but I didn't need too, he knew me well, he knew that I was broken. My world had crashed down around me and at that moment in time I didn't even care if it never flew again. I was a total mess; I couldn't even begin to think about how I was going to put myself back together again. Kevin took me upstairs, lovingly undressed me and put me into our bed, then getting in besides me protectively took me into his arms and wrapped his body around the foetal position I had once again adopted and held me until exhausted I fell asleep. I was home, I was safe, but I was in pieces.

The following morning for the sake of the children, I had to try and act as if I was alright. I had woken before them so I quietly got out of bed and went to get dressed, it was then that I discovered the mirror in our bedroom was cracked, the morning after I had arrived home in Oxfordshire from Pembrokeshire; Kevin had already gone out to work when I woke up. In our bedroom hanging on the wall at the foot of our bed was a very old mirror that was enclosed in a solid wooden frame, apart from a few old marks on the mirror it was perfect - that was until that morning. When I looked into the mirror there was a crack down the whole length of the mirror, it was completely broken in two, just as my heart was. That morning there was something else in that old mirror. I saw the gentle face of a young lady, that lady was my maternal Grandmother,

On autopilot I dressed and went downstairs to get the breakfast ready. The children got up and were delighted to see me home, as usual the girls and I took Oliver to school. It was only just before 9am and yet I felt as if I had been up for hours when we went back home, I got the girls dressed and brushed their hair, which is always a battle of will with Morganna as she hates her hair being brushed and it always brings her to fits of frenzied screams, that morning however I did not notice her screams of protest as I brushed her long hair back into a ponytail. They grabbed their rucksacks from the door handle of the cupboard and skipped up the garden path out to the car. I didn't want to go anywhere that morning and taking the girls to preschool was a daunting task. The first person I saw was one of the other Mum's who had a little girl the same age as Angharad, it made me wobble for a moment, but I pulled myself together and entered the hall, as I did the girls key worker saw me and came towards me, as she got nearer I could see the tears in her eyes.

"Are you OK" she asked in her caring manner.

"No I am not, I cant talk now" I replied through tears that would no longer stay hidden behind the big grey/blue eyes that was so desperately trying to hide them, it was too much for me and I had to make a hasty retreat, leaving a bewildered Hope and Morganna with her, I lowered my head so that no one could see the river of tears I was crying, and out of the hall I went. Once

I had somehow managed to drive myself back to the sanctuary of my home I closed the door on the world, collapsed onto the sofa in the lounge. I was alone, no distractions, no anything, just me, my broken heart and a head full of swimming memories. I buried my head in a cushion and wept my heart out.

A few weeks later I got the photographs back from the developers that I had taken on that heart rendering day, and when I eventually found the strength to look through them it was the very last photograph that I had taken that broke me, and sitting there all alone with the photograph held tightly in my hand I cried my heart out yet again. The photograph was the last one I had taken of Bo and Angharad stood by the Scolton manor signpost, Angharad was reaching her hand out towards me and her eyes were saying

"Grandma, come and get me"

But it was too late, my precious, beautiful, darling had already gone.

A little while after that awful day in May Kevin and I were sat in the back garden late one night watching the stars flickering away whilst we listened to BBC Radio Two, when the DJ played a song by Beth Neilson Chapman, its title was "You touch my heart" I sat there with Kevin, I wanted to move, but I couldn't, I had to stay and listen to the whole track, by the time it had finished I was once again in pieces with my darling husband wrapped protectively around me. It made me cry then and when I hear it today its opening bars make me cry again. It could have been written for me, its poignant lyrics are from beginning to end the sentiments in my heart. When I do find the time to go and record an album, this track is just one of many that I wish to record

My broken mirror stayed on the bedroom wall for 18 months after that day, I wouldn't let Kevin take it down, and I couldn't bear it. Somehow I felt that if the mirror was removed so was Angharad.

My maternal Grandmother stayed with me as my guardian angel until September 2005. It was in September 2005 that I finally traced my own mothers Sister and brother who had been adopted as babies; I had also found the grave of her sister who had died whilst in care. My Mam's family were now back together after over 55 years apart. I had also said goodbye to Rhiannon in 2005. My Grandma had stayed with me and kept me safe as I said goodbye to my precious Grand daughters, and I had put her three children back together again.

You will recall that early in my story I told you that I had been a big sceptic when it came to anything unknown to me, well not anymore. Today I truly believe that our mind and hearts are our most powerful senses, they guide and protect us. If we open ourselves to the spiritual powers that surround us we may be rewarded by learning and knowing something as beautiful as love itself.

*"Goodbye Angharad and Rhiannon, wherever you are and what ever you are both doing, please know that I love you very much and that you are constantly in my thoughts"*

# *RHIANNON*

As the days began to slip away, I was still caught up in the unusual mixture of emotions that had become part of my life. In one heartbeat I would be engulfed in a deep and painful sadness as I thought about having to say goodbye to Angharad, and then with the next heartbeat I would find myself thinking about the impending birth of Bo's latest pregnancy. I worried about how Bo was going to cope with the painful time ahead of her, but in the months that I had been talking to her since Angharad had been placed with a foster mother, I had struggled with her ability to just get on with life as if nothing was wrong, true there had been days when she had cried, but the tears were short lived and her ability to "bounce back" was incredible, there were times in those darkest of days when I had wished I could have been afforded the luxury of that ability,

Rhiannon arrived into the world at 8.50am on April 18th 2004; she weighed a healthy 6lbs.

I was driving to the John Radcliff Hospital with Oliver when the news of Rhiannon's arrival finally reached me. Oliver had been ice skating with some friends the evening before and had taken a bad fall on the ice, he had been checked out by the staff at the ice rink and was told that he was just bruised and nothing was broken. When he was brought home by his friends mum, he could hardly walk, after giving him some painkillers Kevin and I got him to bed. When he woke the following morning he could not walk, he was in agony, so we got him into the car and I left Kevin with the girls whilst I drove Oliver to the hospital. I was just entering Oxford when my mobile rang, it was Kevin, and he had just received a phone call from Bo. He tried to pacify me by telling me that she would ring later, but I recognised that tone in his voice, it's the one where he tries so hard not to tell me something as he knows it is going to hurt me,

"Come on what's the matter" I prompted

"Nothing" came his reply

"Kevin just tell me, you know I won't be able to settle"

"I knew I shouldn't have rung, Bo's had the baby, and it's a girl"

"Ok, I will see you later" I tried to sound indifferent about the news, but he knew me as well as I knew him and he was aware that I was hurting.

Oliver and I waited in the waiting area to be seen, and as we did I tried to put all thoughts of Bo and the baby out of my mind, Oliver was in agony and I had to concentrate on him. Together we sat there and talked, I held his hand and cuddled my brave son, he had been so incredible lately, and even now he was thinking of me.

"Mum what's the matter?"

"Nothing sweetheart, I'm alright"

My 11year old son looked at me with eyes that were full of the physical pain he was suffering and asked me if it was something to do with the phone call I had just had from his Dad, he asked me if Bo was alright, he was worried that she had self harmed again, then he said to me that I hadn't kept anything from him or lied to him at all, so why was I doing so now. I had to tell him as there was no way that I could let him think his much loved sister was hurt again.

"Mum I'm sorry" he said

I cuddled my brave son who was yet again showing me wisdom and an understanding that was much older than his tender years; it was something that I would have failed to find in some adults. I am blessed with an incredibly caring and empathic son.

The Doctors and nurses who cared for Oliver that morning must have thought they were witnessing the anguish of an overprotective mother when they saw us together, there was no way they could have imagined what had caused the pain in me that had left my face tearstained.

Oliver had in fact bruised his kidneys and some ribs as well as badly bruising his spinal cord, he was to be in agony for weeks as he recovered, we were sent home with some strong painkillers and a cream that would give him some local pain relief. It took Oliver nearly a month to recover from that accident; today he will go nowhere near an ice rink.

When Oliver and I finally returned home from the hospital, Kevin and I sat down with a mug of coffee and I told him what the consultant in the hospital had said. He in turn told me of the telephone conversation that he had had with Bo. I rang the hospital and eventually spoke to Bo, she seemed alright, not at all how I imagined her to have been, I expected to hear tears of sadness, but there were none, the only tears I remembered were mine, she told me how the social worker at the hospital had taken Rhiannon from her and placed her in the SCABU unit for safety until the foster family could collect her. It was all so matter of fact, it was all so surreal. I asked Bo what she was going to do and she said she was returning home to her partner. Christ how I hated my daughter at that moment, how in Gods name could she just walk away from her child, but she had done this three times already.

I later discovered that my parents had been in to see Bo and Rhiannon shortly after her birth; they had not even rung me to tell me that Bo was in hospital, I was absolutely devastated. Why had they not told me? I rang them and asked why I wasn't at least told that my own daughter was in hospital, they told me that it was up to Bo to tell me. I felt betrayed and let down, and it hurt. A few days later I discovered that I was in fact one of the last to know.

Bo left the hospital alone and went back to her partner.

Rhiannon left that hospital, without her Mammy, and was placed with a foster family. I struggled with knowing that Rhiannon was alone, I knew she was safe and well, but she should have been here, just as Angharad should have been, but I had no control over what was happening, I was just their Grandmother, I had no automatic rights. I cant find the words to tell you just how strongly I felt about what was happening to us all, I cant find the words that could ever express how painful it all was and still is, but it hurts like no pain I have ever felt in my life.

Again Bo was given contact with Rhiannon, and on some of these contacts Bo had Angharad and Rhiannon together, but Hope and Morganna had yet to see their new baby sister.

Angharad had her first birthday on April 25th 2004, and I had managed to arranged that Bo could have Angharad and Rhiannon together at my parents home when we went home to Pembrokeshire, it was the one and only time that all four girls were to ever be together, it broke my heart, Hope and Morganna lovingly cuddled their sisters, I watched and my heart ached, I tried so hard for the tears to stay hidden, I had to fight them away, I had to stay strong for the girls, this was about them, not me. But deep inside I felt as if my whole world was there in my parent's house that day, and as Hope and Morganna helped Angharad to blow out the candle on the birthday cake we had bought for her, as they blew out that flame, so a flame died inside me. In the kitchen of my parents home that day as we all sang "Happy Birthday" to Angharad we all knew that it would be the one and only time, we all ached, we all cried, we all felt that pain, because that day was also the last day that we were to ever see Angharad.

The taxi that had delivered Rhiannon to my parents home that day arrived to take her back to her foster family again, Bo travelled with her. We all kissed Rhiannon goodbye, and I walked out to the taxi with my daughter, carrying my grand daughter in my arms, I placed her into the car, turned away quickly to hide my tears and walked back into my parents house. When the time came for Angharad to go back to her foster mother, I was to take her. My parents kissed her goodbye, Kevin and Oliver hugged and kissed her goodbye. I gathered Hope Morganna and Angharad together and tried to explain to my precious girls that they would not see Angharad again for a long long time. They didn't understand what I was trying to tell them, how could they, after all they were so used to going back to Pembrokeshire to see their little sister, they talked of her all the time when we were in our own home, they would kiss one the many photographs we have placed around our home of her, photos are all they have left now, there are no more trips back to Pembrokeshire to see their little Angharad.

I left my parents home that afternoon to make the journey back to Angharad's foster mother who at the time lived in St David's. As I drove through Newgale I pulled into the car park on the seafront, taking Angharad out of her car seat, I carried her in my arms across the pebble bank and down onto the beach, I walked the length of the golden sands on that beach, oblivious to anyone else that may have been there, and as I walked with my precious Granddaughter held tightly in my arms, I talked to her, I sang to her, I told her over and over again that I loved her. I buried my nose into the softness of her neck and drew in the scent of her, she smelt of birthday cake, all sweet and sickly, and beneath that aroma was the smell I had come to know so well, it was her, I can close my eyes and smell her now. We weren't on the beach for long maybe an hour, but it was a lifetime that I shared with her in that hour, it was my lifetime.

When I took Angharad into her foster mother, she smiled as I gave her to her the lady who had looked after her for the past months, she was happy there I could see that, and after chatting to Angharad's foster mother for a while I left to return with empty arms and an aching heart to my parents home.

No one knew that I was to see Angharad for just two more precious few hours. I had told no one except Kevin, and my friends Heather and Raul.

In June we saw Rhiannon again, and every month after that we went back to Pembrokeshire once a month to see her. The visits were arranged so that we could have Rhiannon with Bo and go out somewhere for a few hours, they were difficult visits. I had to watch as Bo cuddled Rhiannon and I would try to make some kind of sense of it all, but there was none. Hope and Morganna were restless after these visits and they couldn't understand why Bo didn't do much with them. They also asked after Angharad a lot and got cross when their questions were ignored by Bo, I guess she didn't know what to say to them, maybe she hadn't thought that they would expect to see Angharad as well, but when I got home with the girls I would get the questions, we would be asked over and over again when we were in Pembrokeshire when was Angharad coming.

It was so difficult to watch Bo with Rhiannon so close to having said goodbye to Angharad, often I wondered what was going through her mind as she cradled Rhiannon in her arms. Bo also had fresh cuts on her forearms, so she was self harming again, her way of coping with the pain. I had no way of coping with my pain.

# CHRISTENING DAY

Kevin and I had been giving a lot of thought to how we both felt about having Hope and Morganna christened, we both felt it was right for them and for us, we had christened all the other children, and for me it was important, it seemed like the only thing that Kevin and I had not done for the girls. We discussed it with Bo and she was in agreement so we went on to discussing with her who we felt ought to be asked to be Godparents. Kevin and I had already discussed who we would like to ask to be Godparents to the girls, Bo agreed with who we had chosen. All we had to do now was to talk to our local Vicar and see if he would agree to christen the girls.

We explained to him what had happened to us all over the previous few years and how important it was for us that the girls "belonged" somewhere, he was fantastic and agreed to the christening. For us christening the girls was also a way of celebrating their arrival with us, a way of drawing a line beneath it all and trying to move on, and a way of the whole family getting together and sharing some joy.

"What about august the 22nd" the vicar said.

"Brilliant, Kevin is off on annual leave then as well I said"

And that was that we had a christening to organise.

I spoke to Social Services, and asked if it was possible for Rhiannon to come over and share the celebration of her older sister's christening. They agreed that as long as Bo and Rhiannon travelled up and back again with my parents who were attending the christening, and that I took responsibility for Rhiannon whilst she was here, then yes she could come. I was on cloud nine, I had not even dared to imagine that Rhiannon would be able to spend a night under our roof, just as Angharad had, but she was going to, and for 24 hours there was a peace in me.

We asked our chosen loved ones if they would do the honour of becoming Hope and Morganna's Godparents, and they were delighted. The invitations were sent out and everything fell into place all we had to do now was wait. We bought a couple of marques to put up in the garden, hired a bouncy castle for the children and the bigger kids in us, bought some good food and champagne and all was set. I can still remember my Dad pulling up in front of the cottage with Bo and Rhiannon in his car along with my Mam. I was overjoyed, but I was also sad that Angharad was not with us.

Everyone was ready to go to church, Hope and Morganna were like princesses in the dresses I had made them, and with the off cuts of fabric I had made a dress for Rhiannon as well, they looked great. The table was spread with food and everything was ready, so off for church we set. Kevin and I had asked the vicar to remember Bo, Angharad and Rhiannon in his prayers and he did, it was a lovely service and when the time came for us to take the girls up to the font, we took Bo with us, she stood there alongside us as the Vicar christened Hope and Morganna.

After the service we spent a fabulous few hours amongst our family and friends celebrating the girl's birth and the fact that they were safe her with us.

The night before the christenening I had stood and watched Rhiannon as she slept soundly in Hope and Morganna's travel cot, she was such a contented baby. Hope and Morganna fussed over her like mother hens, trying to feed her and change her, it was so comical to watch. Those 24 hours were so important for the girls, it was also the one and only time that Bo was to sleep under the same roof as Rhiannon. As I watched Rhiannon that night I couldn't help but think about the life she was going to have, I hoped it would not be too long before she was placed with her older sister, as I didn't want her to be in care for long. Rhiannon was to turn 1 years of age before she was placed at long last with her sister.

In the evening after the christening our family and friends slowly began to depart, it was bad enough saying goodbye to them, I always get tearful when I say goodbye, my parents had hung on until last to leave and as they walked away up the garden path with Bo following I carried my tiny granddaughter to my Dad's car. I hugged my Mam and Bo and gave Rhiannon a kiss - I had already cuddled her before I had put her into her car seat, Dad got in the car after giving me a hug and then they too were off up the farm lane, when my parents left taking Bo and Rhiannon with them, yet another part of me slipped away.

It had been a lovely day my family and friends all celebrating two special little girls still being within our family, safe and well.

# _AUTUMN AND WINTER 2004_

In October of 2004, we arranged to take Rhiannon and the girls along to a local photographer in Pembrokeshire to have some photographs taken of the three girls together, that was the last contact visit that we had with Bo being present, after that we had Rhiannon on our own as we felt it was better for Hope, Morganna and Angharad. By this time it had also become evident to us that Bo was not attending her contact visits that had been arranged for her to see Rhiannon, and I was finding this so hard to bear, she would come to a contact visit if we were there and a part of me felt that she was in some way using us, I was struggling to try and hold any kind of relationship with Bo. I really did understand now that I loved my daughter dearly, but I did not like her.

I took Hope Morganna and Oliver Christmas shopping in November as we were all travelling back to Pembrokeshire to see Rhiannon before Christmas. Together we chose some gifts and when we got home we wrapped them carefully in pretty paper, then I painted the girls hands with paint and got them to place their hands on the cards they had chosen for their baby sister, they were too young to write their names, but they could stick their handprints onto the cards, we did the same on the cards that we were sending to Angharad via the letterbox contact that we had been given on her adoption.

We travelled back to Pembrokeshire yet again. Social services had given us just two short hours to spend with Rhiannon. I had no idea where I was going to take her, I had asked my Mam if we could go to their home, but she was unsure as she said it would upset my Dad as he would be home. So we met with Rhiannon's foster mother in the car park and she handed Rhiannon over to me, it was cold and miserable and Rhiannon would soon need feeding. I put her into her car seat in the back of our MPV and with Hope and Morganna sat one on either side of her and she beamed at them both. I am convinced she knew who they were; she must also have felt safe as she just seemed so happy with us. After the foster mother drove off Kevin asked me where I wanted to go.

"I don't know" I replied, there is nowhere, it was too cold to just hang around the town for a couple of hours and besides which Rhiannon would need a feed soon. I had nowhere to take her, and all I wanted was to have somewhere to take all three of the girls so that they could spend those two hours together. It was a blasted awful thing to be going through on top of everything else I was feeling at the time.

Tearfully I rang my Mam, I really didn't want to as I was by now getting truly fed up with the way that everyone was seemingly choosing to ignore Rhiannon's existence, with the exception of my Mam who had given me a Christmas gift for Rhiannon, and my brother Michael and his wife Nita, no one else in my family sent her a Christmas card or gift on her one and only Christmas with us, I was hurt that nobody else bothered as I knew that in the years to come Rhiannon will read her life story book, and it will have written in it who had sent her a card and gift on that one and only Christmas she had with us before going to her new family, and also what she had received on her first birthday, It will make for grim reading. I know that the probability was that maybe no one else thought they could send her a gift or a card, but they didn't ask us either. Rhiannon was and still is a part of our family unit, she hadn't died, and she just wasn't living with her mother. I know it has been hard for all of my family, but it has been by far hardest for me.

We did take Rhiannon to my parent's home that day, just for an hour the girls were together for just one hour before we had to take Rhiannon back to her foster mother. Meeting up with the foster mother I handed over the Christmas gifts for Rhiannon and the small gifts that Kevin and I had bought for the foster families own children, after all they too were looking after Rhiannon, and they were sharing with her their Mammy and Daddy.

"Have a lovely Christmas cariad" I whispered to Rhiannon as I handed her over to her foster mother. The foster mother placed her into her car seat and then came over to me and we hugged each other. Rhiannon's foster mother and I became quite close over the year that she was caring for Rhiannon. I owe her and her family a great debt of gratitude. They were a wonderful family.

We went straight back to Oxfordshire later that day I needed to be in my own home, to close the door on the world, to be alone.

Just a couple of miles from our home in Oxfordshire is a wonderful garden centre. At Christmas time it is crammed full with the most beautiful decorations you can imagine. I went there one day a week before Christmas I wanted a candle to put in the window, a special scented candle to light on Christmas day for Angharad, you see Christmas 2004 was the first Christmas that she would not be with us and I had to somehow do something that was just for her. On the day that I had taken Angharad back to her foster mothers after we had celebrated her first birthday, I had gone into a church and lit a candle for her. I found a candle in the garden centre, tearfully I carried back to the car and I cried all the way back home, by the time I pulled the car into our garage I was sobbing so much that I had to ring Kevin and ask him to come to me. I did light my candle for Angharad on Christmas Eve and on Christmas day, Hope Morganna and I did it together, and into the starry night I whispered her merry Christmas.

After that awful Christmas experience I found it very difficult to talk to my family about Rhiannon again. When we went to visit her again we went with out saying anything.

Once again the New Year came and went, and as it did I once again knew that the year that lay ahead of me was to be as painful as the one I had wished farewell. Once again there was a knowledge in me that my heart was to break again, again I knew that the months that lay ahead were to be as devastating for me as the ones that had gone.

On February 18th 2005, there was a preliminary hearing held on Rhiannon, then on March the 8th 2005, the panel sat to decide were Rhiannon was to be placed, they decided to place her with her sister. I was heartbroken that she was going to be adopted, but I was relieved to know that she was to be placed with her sister; at least they would be together. Knowing this also made me aware that time was coming to an end for us all. I knew that the time was approaching when we would have to say goodbye to Rhiannon as well.

# *GOODBYE MY DARLING RHIANNON*

I thought that after saying goodbye to Angharad that I would know how to say goodbye to Rhiannon and that I would know what to expect. Ignorance was now replaced with a naivety in me that allowed me to believe that this time I would know to react and how to cope after all I had already gone through this once.

I sat and thought long and hard over how I wanted it to be so different this time. Hope and Morganna were 12 months older, they could now understand simple things, and I felt that I owed it to all three of the girls and to Oliver to try and make this final day together something we could look back on and somehow know it was alright to smile as we remembered those final hours. Once again my telephone line was hot as I spoke to the social worker and put forward my request.

"I would like to have Rhiannon for the day if possible, it would be nice if the girls could spend a happy day together" I nervously said to her.

"OK I will see what I can do" she replied.

Fortunately Social Services agreed with my request, so I was given a date of the 16th April to say goodbye to Rhiannon, it was just one day after her 1st birthday.

I told none of my family what truly lay behind our visit to Pembrokeshire that week. I invited them all to come over for tea to the cottage we were renting, we had a great time and I tried to be as jolly as I could, I must have been pretty convincing because no one suspected a thing. When at last everyone had gone I had no distraction to pour myself into and I began to fret about what lay before us the next morning. Most of my pain was for me, it was a deep and endless ache, but I also hurt for the girls. Over the washing up I cried as I thought of the disruption in all their little lives. It was more than most adults would have ever encountered in their whole life. Sleep evaded me again that night, I turned all the events that had happened over the years since Hope and Morganna had been born over and over again in my mind, it was torturous. The morning light was just peaking through the night sky when I drifted off to sleep. I woke as fretful as I had gone to sleep.

On Saturday 16th April, we met with the Social worker at Scolton Manor - the same place that just one year before I had said goodbye to Angharad. It was the first time since that heartbreaking day that I had returned to this beautiful place. I was nervous, my insides shook and again that familiar feeling of nausea swept over me, my stomach lurched, my hands were sweating and my head swirled. As we drove into the grounds of the Manor we had to drive past the signpost that Bo had stood by with Angharad in her arms less than 12 months before, for a fleeting moment I thought I saw them stood there again, and then the moment was gone.

This day was to be different; this was a day for Hope and Morganna to remember, a fun day, a precious day. The sun shone and even though the air still had an early spring chill to it, none of us really noticed. As Kevin turned into the parking bays the social workers car came into view, she was there already. We greeted each other and she got Rhiannon out from her car seat and passed her over to me

"There you are go to Grandma" she said with her cheerful smile.

Rhiannon didn't hesitate she happily came to into my outstretched arms and I held her close, the tears slipped unguarded down my cheeks, I was never to hear that again, no one was ever going to refer to me as Rhiannon's Grandma. My goodbye's had already begun.

I could hear the tears in her voice as the social worker told me that the foster mother would meet us there later on in the day, she returned to her car and drove away, leaving us to enjoy our time with Rhiannon.

We all sat at one of the tables and Hope and Morganna helped Rhiannon to open the birthday presents we had brought her, we also had a picnic with some birthday cake, and then we walked around the grounds, just having fun, the girls played happily together, whist I carried Rhiannon around holding her tight to me. Those final hours will stay with me forever, Rhiannon didn't cry once that day, I wonder if she knew in some small way just how special that day was for me, perhaps she was so contented because she sensed she was safe, or maybe she had picked up on the serenity that was in me as soon as she was placed into my arms. I remember thinking how heavy she was, she weighed much more than Hope did, she was a solid baby, with thick chunky thighs and was still making no attempt to get up and walk. The girls loved having her with us that day, strangely I had expected Hope to be jealous of me carrying Rhiannon around as she hated me carrying someone else's baby, but she made no fuss at all. As the girls played together we managed to get some lovely photographs of them together, we also took an amazing photograph of Oliver with Rhiannon, and the sadness in his eyes as he cuddled her was enough to make anyone cry.

I was determined that Rhiannon and I would have some time on our own that day, she was getting sleepy so I cradled her in my arms and as Kevin played with Hope and Morganna in the park I walked around the grounds of the manor with Rhiannon in my arms. As she snuggled into me I began to quietly sing to her, it came so easy to me as I have done it to every baby I have held in my arms. I was singing "Somewhere over the rainbow" to her as her eyes finally shut and sleep took her. I can't sing that song now without thinking of Rhiannon; it became our special song that day.

It was such a contrast to the day when I had said goodbye to Angharad. I was happy and as the day went on this happiness stayed with me, somewhere deep inside I was breaking, but I didn't break that day, oh yes I was tearful as the foster mother placed my Rhiannon into her MPV, but I knew she loved her, I knew that soon Rhiannon was to be with Angharad, that the two girls would be together, just as Hope and Morganna were, and in a strange way that comforted me a little. I had told Rhiannon to let Angharad know that I was thinking of her and to tell her I loved her more than words could ever say.

We travelled back to the cottage in silence, I felt numb I just wanted to crawl into a corner and be left alone. Kevin and I had invited Heather and Raul over to the cottage for a meal that night, it gave me something to focus on, something pleasant, they are both such good friends of ours. They have been incredibly supportive, and I knew that if I had sat there that night and cried my heart out, they would not have minded at all. Instead we sat there around the table and talked about everything and anything. We had a lovely evening; it was good to be with such good friends. We travelled back to Oxfordshire the following day.

It was two days later that I fell apart. I was in my local town shopping. I was in a shop just about to pay for something, when a wave of great sadness came over me, it crushed me and I fell apart, I wept and wept. Placing the basket of things I had wanted to buy on the floor I walked out of the shop and returned to my car in the multi-storey car park. I sat in the car and cried racking great sobs of endless tears. I drove home knowing that it was going to take me a long time to recover and come back from the hell I was in. but just as I had done after Angharad had gone I tried to hold it all together for the sake of the children, I fought back my tears and saved them for when I was alone and they became lonely tears, I cried on my own, and I got very good at it too, I didn't even share them with Kevin - I couldn't.

Something else hit me hard during the days that followed me saying goodbye to Rhiannon. Angharad celebrated her second birthday, its passing marked for me the first of many birthdays I would not be able to actually see my girls, I would not be able to share their special days, to watch them blow out the candles on their birthday cakes and to share the joy and happiness that these special celebrations bring, and it hurt. I had sent Angharad's birthday cards through the post to the letterbox contact centre. It all seemed so cold and calculating, so impersonal and worse of all for me was the knowledge that even although the cards I had sent were for my Granddaughter, they would first be vetted by somebody before they were sent on to Angharad's adoptive parents, who would keep them safe until they felt it was time to share them with her.

I also knew all too well that the beautiful boxes of love that I had prepared for Angharad and for Rhiannon would go through other people's hands, minds and hearts before the girls ever got to see them. For me that was extremely difficult to tolerate, these memory boxes were about the girls and me not about anyone else. I truly trust that whoever has been fortunate enough to be able to look into those boxes is left with a marked memory in their hearts and knowledge that one day God forbid they too may have to do what I had done.

For nearly three weeks I did not answer my telephone when it rang, I went through the motions of everyday life like taking the children to school, pretending to be alright, I carried on doing the shopping and other household chores, desperately trying to fill every available minute of my day so that I didn't have time to dwell on it all. I didn't speak to Bo. I couldn't, by now I had reached the point of no return with her, I knew that I needed to put some time between the two of us otherwise I would say something that later I would regret. God it was so hard not to tell her exactly how I felt.

I locked my emotions away from the world and kept them to myself. If I didn't try to share them with anyone, I knew that I could not be hurt further when I was greeted by a total lack of understanding, or the odd uncaring thoughtless sentence that would slip out totally unguarded.

No one truly understood my hell. How the hell could they, for they had never been in this God forsaken place that was at that moment my world. I hurt and I hurt so bad that when I looked around me I could see no one strong enough to rebuild this shattered me. No one could pick up this broken heart and put it back together again, it had broken so many times.

God how many times can one person's heart break?

# RHIANNON'S MEMORY BOX

I had made a very conscious decision not to prepare and have Rhiannon's memory box ready to hand over to the social worker when we met with her in April. It would have seemed to final to me, I just couldn't do it. So when we returned to Oxfordshire, knowing that Rhiannon would still be with her foster family for six weeks, I began to get her special box of love together. I had already bought her box; I had had it for a while tucked away safe until the dreaded day that would see me filling it with love and memories.

I sat and thought about what I had put into Angharad's memory box. I had to ensure that Rhiannon's box was filled with the same amount of thought and love and me. I had to treat both the girls the same, I had had dreams where I had seen the two of them comparing their boxes when they were old enough to be given them, just as Hope and Morganna compare gifts they are given. Oh God how do I fill them with the same amount of love and thought, and still make them individual?

Somehow I had to try and find things to go into Rhiannon's box that held for me the same amount of sentimental value. The first few things that I placed in that special box were easy to find, Rhiannon too was given one of the hospital bracelets that Hope and Morganna had worn, I still had a four leafed clover left after giving one to Angharad, now Rhiannon has one as well. I took form my little finger the ring that Kevin had bought me years before, I had always worn it, you will recall that I gave Angharad the small Celtic ring that Bo had given to me, well Rhiannon has the one that Kevin gave me, I no longer wear a ring on either of my little fingers, no one has replaced them for me, I doubt that anyone could. My rings are with my girls. Piece by heartbreaking piece the box began to fill; everything that I placed into it was hugged with so much love. I tried to find photographs of the family that were different from the ones I had given Angharad. We had gone to LONGLEAT in June and I had bought Rhiannon a small box which contained 3 guardian angels, I do hope they are looking out for both of my girls.

I also bought a wind chime to go by my back door, when the breeze blows through it; it reminds me of Angharad and Rhiannon, It gently tinkles away chiming sweetly in the background.

When it came to writing Rhiannon's letter, I agonised not only over doing it, but also over what I wished to say to her, each line had to hold as much love, each sentence had to be as long as Angharad's had been. It had to hold as much of me as the one I had already written for Angharad. I couldn't do it, try as I might, I just couldn't bring myself to write that letter. My eyes were full of tears of frustration as for the umpteenth time I threw my pen onto the table, pushed my chair away from beneath me got up and walked away. Writing Rhiannon's letter had beaten me.

Days later I was sat in our dining room with a mug of coffee, and as on so many times before I sat there dreaming, when without a thought I found myself writing on the back of a piece of paper that Hope had been drawing on before I had taken the girls to pre-school.

In no time at all I had written Rhiannon verse after verse of the beginning of a poem that depicted everything I had in my heart that I wanted to say to her, but days before couldn't find the words. Over the following days I added more verse's to her poem, one day I was in the middle of cooking our tea when an idea popped into my head and I sat down and wrote her a verse about fireworks. The poem covers many stages that she will go through in her life, they are all the things I wanted to share with both her and Angharad. This is just two of the verse's I wrote for her.

"I wanted to give you the moon, the stars and the sun all wrapped up as one

We would listen to the morning song of the birds, and the evening one as it's sung

The morning dew as it rests on the leaves, the smell of the April rain

The sun as it shines down on the land, and dries up all the flowers again

The beautiful arch of a rainbow, its said at its end a pot of gold can be found

We would watch the seasons as they change, and crunch the leaves in autumn as they fall to the ground

We could leave our footprints in the sand where we had walked, and the sea could wash them away

Then watch the seagulls chasing each other, soaring up high, and then diving into the bay"

I hand wrote each verse into an album and added photographs and other appropriate things that related to each verse. Alongside the verse about what it feels like to have your own baby, I stuck a photograph of Bo when she was just a few hours old. When it was finished, and believe me I cried over every word and over every photograph I stuck into that album, I knew that what I had done was to create a beautiful and meaningful piece of individual work that was full of love, pride and sadness, but again it was full of me.

*"Darling Rhiannon*

*I wanted you to have something as individual as Angharad's letter was for her. I wanted to be able to give you both so much love, care and time, to be able to tell you who you really are and where you really came from, but most of all I needed you to know that I love you more than I could ever write on a piece of paper. Our time together was too short; it was supposed to be a lifetime of time together. Your poem is all about the things I would have liked to have shared with you, read it well Cariad, it was written for you and sent to you with immense love*

*Until we meat again my precious darling - know always that I love you*

*Grandma x*

Days later after I had added that beautiful and poignant piece of work to Rhiannon's memory box, I sat and wept as I took everything out once more and this time tied the tiny labels I had made to each item just as I had done for Angharad. When it was all finished I added my endless love to the box and replacing its lid I tenderly and carefully placed Rhiannon's box into the bread oven cupboard in the exact same spot that just 13 short months before Angharad's memory box had also sat. it wasn't the last time I took the box down from that shelf because just as I had done with Angharad's box over the following days I took that box out everyday, and every time I tenderly took out it's secret contents and replaced them with an immeasurable amount of love, care and tenderness. I treated that box as a mother would treat her newborn baby. every time I took that box out of that cupboard I knew as I replaced it that one more day had passed, it was one day closer to when I would have to hand my gift of love over to the social worker, and trust that it would be given to Rhiannon's new Mammy and Daddy, who would hopefully recognise it for what it was - a heartfelt and agonised gift of love for their daughter, who will always and forever remain my beautiful Granddaughter.

I had needed no help in finding the precious things I had placed in Rhiannon's box, my guardian angel did not need to guide me, or maybe she did, maybe it was her that put my hand to paper that day when I wrote Rhiannon's poem, maybe it was her that sat alongside me and comforted me, maybe it was her that held me up when I fell and felt that I had no one to turn to.

# *SOMETHING KIND OF WONDERFUL*

The postman who calls on us often delivers little packages for the girls, the girls love him to bits and when they see his van pull up outside our front gate they race around to the garden gate at the side of the house to collect the mail from him. Today he was late and the girls were just on their way out the door with Kevin who was taking them off to go to pre-school. I took the letters off the postman and signed for the small parcel he had in his hand. Unusually it was addressed to me and I did not recognise the writing. I carefully placed it on the kitchen worktop, and hurried the girls off into the car with Kevin. I had planned to have a nice long soak in the bath once Kevin had taken the girls off to pre-school, its not very often I get an uninterrupted bath or shower these days as one or other, or if I'm really unlucky both the girls will barge into the bathroom under the pretence of "we need to clean our teeth". All thoughts of that blissful uninterrupted hour vanished from my head as now the small brown parcel was intriguing me, "to heck with it the bath could wait a few minutes". I made myself a mug of coffee and with the parcel in one hand and my coffee in the other; I climbed the old oak stairs up to our bedroom. I placed the parcel and my coffee down on my bedside table went to the window and drew back the curtains. I returned to the bed turned the radio on and sat down to drink my coffee.

Picking up the small brown parcel I nervously opened it. Inside was a pretty Winnie-the Pooh box. I gently removed the lid from the box. The contents of that box made me cry buckets. It was the most lovely and thoughtful thing that anyone could have done for me. The box had been put together by Rhiannon's foster mother, it contained some photo's of Rhiannon, some small gifts for Hope and Morganna from Rhiannon, as well as four gold charms which I will keep here safe in the box until one day I can put one on each of the bracelets myself, there was also two letters, one for me and one for us all. That wonderful foster mother had taken the time and trouble to put together something that I will keep safe for the girls. I cant put into words just how much that kind and thoughtful jester means to me, the letter she had written to me were warm and heartfelt, she too was going to miss Rhiannon, she had been caring for her for over 12 months, Rhiannon had been a part of their family.

I read and re-read those letters. When Kevin came back from the school run he found me sat on our bed sobbing.

"What's up sweetheart?"

Through my tears I tried to tell him of the precious gift I had just received, he took the box from me and gently looked at what was inside. Taking the letters into his hand he looked at me and said

"Can I"

I nodded and as he read quietly to himself I started to cry again, he took me in his arms and rocked me tenderly until I was all cried out.

The gift of that box knocked me sideways for days, everyday I read the letters, stroked the face of my lovely granddaughter on the photographs and looked at the gifts that the box held for the girls. I know that one day they will be so grateful for what the foster mother had done for them on Rhiannon's behalf.

One day in the future I shall sit with Hope and Morganna and we will open the box together, it will mean so much to them.

Until then the box will live safely tucked away in the bread oven cupboard at the side of our inglenook fireplace in the exact spot that both Angharad and Rhiannon's memory box had stood for the short time that they were here before I handed them over to social services for the girls.

When I have a bleak day I take the box out of its secret hiding place and go through its precious contents again, I take the photographs of Rhiannon in my hands and find myself wandering how much she will have changed, I try to imagine what both Angharad and Rhiannon look like now, but I cant, in my heart and my mind they remain the small little girls when I last saw them. I try hard to envisage if they look like Hope or Morganna, or a mixture of both of them.

# *PARTING GIFTS*

With Rhiannon's memory box all tucked away safe I turned my thoughts to how I could further give to my girls something that will stay with them forever, I came up with three ideas. The first one was to ask the social worker to seek permission from the adoptive parents to allow me to buy a gift for the girls that I could add to each Christmas, this gift was to be a gold charm bracelet, every year we would add another charm to each one, Hope and Morganna's bracelet Kevin and I would add to, and every Christmas in their Christmas cards we would send the same charm to Angharad and Rhiannon, so that their adoptive parents could add them to the bracelets on our behalf. This would mean that over the years that followed each of the four girls would have a bracelet that was identical - a common link, something that all four of them would have.

The other thing I did was to name a star after the girls. My girls star will be up there shining down on them for longer than my lifetime. When I bought the star, it came with a certificate and a map telling where in the galaxy their star can be located at various times in the year. I had the certificate copied at local printers, and keeping the original for Hope and Morganna, I wrapped the copy up to hand on to the social worker for Angharad and Rhiannon.

I also bought four identical teddy bears, Hope and Morganna's teddy's sit at the head of their beds, they are always there, and sometimes both the girls will take them into bed with them, but most often than not they are sat on the side of their pillows. I wonder where Angharad and Rhiannon's teddy's are?

Of course in putting these parting gifts together what I was actually trying to do was to in some way bind the four girls together, to give them something that formed a link, something they would recognise. The star served this purpose well, it will always be there. The charm bracelet is from me, it gives me something positive to focus on at Christmas time, and it is the only was I can give Angharad and Rhiannon something special; so much love went into choosing the gold teddy bears that were sent to the girls last Christmas. I had asked Hope and Morganna what they would like to send to their younger sisters and they told me they would like to send a teddy bear. The day I went out looking for their charms last year was truly a day of mixed feelings for me, in one breath I felt elated that I could at least do this small thing, but that feeling disappeared in the next breath as I felt totally bereft of my Grandparental role with Angharad and Rhiannon. If the lady who assisted me that day in the jewellers shop reads my book, she will now understand why I stood before her that day agonising over what charms to choose with tears so freely falling from my tired eyes.

Now of course the girls have this book, when they are old enough they will be able to read it for themselves and hopefully hear my voice as they read the words I have written, that is why it was so important to me that this book was published as I had written it. It's a legacy that I have left for them.

The social worker rang me one day in June to tell me that Rhiannon would be leaving her foster family in July. The news was like a kick in the stomach, I knew it would be happening, I had tried to prepare myself for it, but I had failed, again I found that I was often in floods of tears, trying too get a grip on something that was completely out of my control. Once again I was aching deep inside. I felt so alone.

The social worker and I arranged to meet in her local town in Pembrokeshire on the 10th July 2005 so that I could hand over to her Rhiannon's memory box and the other parting gifts we had collected for my precious girls. My brother and his wife came to our home and baby sat the girls and Oliver for us and on Saturday 9th July Kevin and I went off together for the first time, and the last without the children. It was really strange not to have the girls around me all the time as they had constantly been at my side.

In 2004 I reopened my search for my Mam's sister and brother who had been adopted. I traced her sister really quickly, and on that weekend in July Kevin and I travelled to Pembrokeshire via Cardiff - the city of my birth, we went there to do some searching in a street where I had discovered my Mam's brother had lived as a small boy, we spent the afternoon there and then went on to Pembrokeshire. We spent the night with Heather and Raul, leaving them after breakfast on the Sunday morning to meet with the social worker. I rang her to say we were on our way, she wasn't answering her mobile. Kevin and I sat in the car park for nearly two hours during which time I tried and retried to get hold of her. I was besides myself, I knew that Rhiannon was due to leave her foster family on the 14th July, I also knew that the adoptive parents were in the county slowly getting to know Rhiannon and to prepare her for her final journey to her new home on the 14th.

"What shall we do Kevin we have to somehow get the parting gifts to Rhiannon; they have to leave with her"

We decided that the only thing we could do was to contact the foster family, I didn't want to do it as it felt as if I was intruding on their time with Rhiannon and her new Mammy and Daddy, but this was important to me and I saw no other way. The foster father answered the telephone and said not to worry they would meet me and take the gifts for Rhiannon. I felt a huge amount of relief, and that was how it was done. Instead of handing over the parting gifts and the memory box to the social worker, I entrusted my special cargo to the two people who had already done so much for Rhiannon. I shall be indebted to them forever - Thank you both so much, for all the love and care you showed my beautiful Granddaughter, and for the friendship you both gave to me, it made such an awful time in my life a little easier.

As Kevin drove away from that car park once again I was in pieces I felt as if my heart had been torn from me, I cried nearly the whole journey home; this truly was the last farewell.

# MOVING ON

In August 2005 my sister gave birth to a little girl which yet again set off a cascade of questions from my girls. Hope told me one day that Aunty Debbie only had one baby growing in her tummy, but I had had two growing in my heart, she told me I must have a big heart. In September my brother got married, and a few days later I received my first letter from the adoptive parents which the court ruled that I was to get in June every year telling me how Angharad was progressing, my letter arrived in September, nearly three months late. The letter was basic and could have been written about any child, I felt really hurt that they hadn't put more effort and warmth into that letter. I know that for them it must be difficult to have to write it at all, but it can never be as difficult as what I am living through every day. I, along with Hope and Morganna are very much the victims in all of this. I hope that this year when the letter arrives that they have thought more about what they put into it and that I receive something that I can draw comfort from. I am also sent a photograph, last year I couldn't get over how much Angharad had grown, I cant wait to see how much both her and Rhiannon have changed in the last 12 months, as now I shall also receive a letter from them about Rhiannon as well. At the time of writing this chapter (July) I have still to receive my letter about Angharad which should have been here in June, Rhiannon's letter is due to arrive in July.

As I wait for my annual letters, so does Bo, she also receives these letters, only waiting for her is intolerable, she can't cope with the waiting. I had to contact the letterbox contact officer, as Bo had self harmed badly because she had not received her letter, waiting is bad enough for me, but for her it must be hell.

My rollercoaster ride for now seems to have slowed down and stopped, I have managed to apply the brakes and they are holding, I still have my bad days, I know that it is only natural that I do, I expect them and cope with them. There are times when I cry, this too is only natural, but I know why I am crying, I can identify the pain and cope with it, sometimes it creeps up on my and swamps me and on those occasions, it will be something that one of the children say or do that grounds me again. Losing Angharad and Rhiannon has left me with a big empty hole in my heart; it's the not knowing that hurts so much. The other day someone very close to me said to me that at least I knew they were alright and that they were loved. Well this is one of those things that although well meant is most hurtful, because any Grandparent who is living through what I am will understand that we neither know if they are alright or if they are loved, the most we can do is trust that they are, but that comes nowhere close to actually sharing your life with your Grandchildren. It is far worse than bereavement, it is a living hell. I for one will only ever know my precious Granddaughters are alright when they themselves can tell me.

When I man the advice line for the GRANDPARENTS ASSOSIACTION I am amazed by how many people call that line and say to me "You can't understand what I am going through"

When I tell them that I do they are amazed to discover that so many other Grandparents are going through what they are experiencing. I know what it feels like to experience what happens when your own scn separates form your grandchildren's mother, the mother moves on and eventually into a new relationship and does not want any more to do with her ex-partners family, this makes contact with your grandchildren at best difficult, at worst impossible. Then I know the experiences I have shared with you here in this "my story" I feel and know the deep and unrelenting pain it causes, I know how it can change you and how it can so easily swamp a person until they feel they are drowning in that pain. I understand the pain, confusion and heartache it causes to have to stand back and watch your own daughter self destruct, I live everyday with the fear that the day I am waking in may be the day that brings me the news any parent dreads so much. I also know the pain and confusion it causes within oneself as you wrestle with your own feelings about your child when things go so badly wrong, I have lived through that most awful of times when you finally come to understand and accept that it is alright to love your own child but at the same time as loving them you do not have to like them. And I also know the most soul destroying and unrelenting of pains ever imaginable, and that is the pain that lives within you when you have to say goodbye to your own grandchild.

But I also know forgiveness; I also know hope and I also know a love so strong that I know that as long as I have that I can accomplish anything.

When I began out on this rollercoaster of emotions, someone had to help me, it was just a small glimmer of hope, but it was enough to start a fire within me that drove me forward each time I faltered, somehow in my darkest of nights and my very bleakest of days something pulled me through, I somehow, God knows how managed to survive and to be here to tell my story, there were times when I thought it was all bigger than me, but I wouldn't let it beat me, I couldn't I had some very good reasons to get through it all.

Some of you reading this will be saying to yourselves that it is an incredible thing to do and that the girls are so lucky to have me, I hear this most days from someone.

Well

I am the lucky one for as painful as my journey has been, for as much as it has cost me emotionally and physically I am rewarded every day when I wake up and on either side of me tucked up and fast asleep are my beautiful girls, they wake each night and creep into our bed, snuggling back down again and sleeping until the morning light breaks through our bedroom window. I am exhausted most evenings, but I would rather feel that than them not be here. Financially on times we struggle, materialistically we are not rich, but what I have nothing could ever buy, no wealth could ever replace. I have my girls and Oliver, without them I would have nothing.

The changes to my life over the past 5 years have been immense. I have gone from career girl to stay at home Mum, I have re-educated myself, not just in education, but also in rediscovering who I am, and I really love me, I like this caring, nurturing, loving, dependable me. I miss parts of the old me like the carefree me I used to be. And on times I do wish that Kevin and I had some time to ourselves, after all I think we are owed at least that. I have learnt some very important lessons over the past 5 years, I have learnt that nothing is forever, and that just as dreams are made so they can be taken away from you or shattered altogether. I have also learnt that nothing is impossible.

This story I know is a remarkable one, it has been difficult to write and on times so hard not to apportion blame in one direction or another. What has happened to me happens to other Grandparents, I listen to them on the helpline, every one of our stories differs in some way, they are unique to the person who is living it, but we all have one thing in common, we are all Grandparents, we are all hurting because we are being deprived of our grandchildren or we feel that we are being deprived of our right to be a Grandparent.

Throughout the past 5 years I have endeavoured to hold as much of my family as I could together. In taking on Hope and Morganna I became a "mother" again, I so wanted to be a Grandmother, I feel cheated of that role, and I grieve the loss of it.

Some days when I have a really bad day with the girls I do find myself resenting my daughter, but as a "Woman Stress Practitioner" I know this resentment is to be expected, I would worry if I didn't feel it at all. I have never once felt regretted the decision to have Hope and Morganna with us, and if I had been told of all the heartache I would experience I would still have chosen to do what I have done.

My heart bleeds for my Bo, she has lost so much and for what? I don't know if she will ever really understand exactly what she has put us all through. She has told me that she fears the girls will hate her when they are older and understand what has happened, but I try to reassure her, I tell her that we are bringing the girls up to love not to hate, that they are being thought that forgiveness and understanding are much better words than hatred or ignorance. One day after she had attempted to end her life I sat and talked to her for a long time. I told her that I had brought her up to love, I asked her if ever on any occasion did I tell her that her father was anything other than good, had I ever spoke badly of him to her, she admitted that I had never said anything derogatory about him. I had not influenced her feelings towards her father at all. There was no way I would intentionally influence Hope and Morganna's feelings towards Bo in anything other than how to love her.

There are many areas of Bo's life that even though I try hard to fathom out, understanding still eludes me, and try as I might I can not work out why or even how some of the events and issues she has gone through have even occurred. Sometimes I will manage to convince myself that she has just been unlucky and been in the wrong place at the wrong time, but are there truly so many wrong places and wrong times - I think not. I can not keep on

269

placing the blame wholly on her partner, because on times there has been no escaping her instigation of a situation or event. Her life choices are difficult to understand, and sometimes I question why it is that I am still there to catch her when she falls especially when whatever I am catching her from is going to break my heart. Surely the answer has to be that I am her mum, and I have never lost sight of the little girl I held to my breast and fed, I have never been pushed so far by her that I have lost sight of the beautiful girl she once was. Perhaps that is what they mean when they say love is blind, but I know love has not blinded me, for love is the one thing that has seen me through all of this.

For me I feel that my unconditional love for my child no matter who or what she is to become is so strong that it enables me to eventually see past her problematic life and to remember who she was, and coupled with my belief in hope I hang on in there to catch her when she one day falls from that God forsaken world of hers and comes back to ours. I just pray that if and when that day should come I am still here to catch her and save her, for I truly fear that when it happens it will be then as she realises the enormity of what she has lost, that she will take her own life.

I am trying to bring Hope and Morganna up to love Bo, they truly do love her and I am delighted that they do. Some of you may find that strange, but this is how I see it---

If I bring Hope and Morganna up to love Bo, then they will know and love the person she is, one day they will understand that she is actually their birth mother and because they love her they hopefully will find feeling anything other than love for her difficult. She is a beautiful person; she is just "lost"

I just pray that she will still be here with us when Hope and Morganna begin to understand our story.

There have been times in the past when I have worried that Bo will try to reverse the Residence Order, but those fears have now gone, she has told me many times that she will never try to remove the girls from us, she says she knows they are loved and well cared for. In one way Bo is very fortunate, if Kevin and I had not fought to the bitter end to keep the girls, they too would have been put into care and adopted, and there was the possibility that they would have been separated. They are still here and she knows she can see them whenever she wishes, but the reality is that she has made no attempt of her own to visit the girls in our home since August 2004, the only time she sees them is when we all go home to Pembrokeshire. The last time she saw them was before Christmas 2005.

# WELCOME TO
## MY WORLD OF GLITTERGLUE
### AND TANTRUMS!

My story will have been as hard to read as it was to write, like me you too will have shed a tear or two. My life today is neither sad nor negative, oh it has its moments when I feel both sad and negative, but these moments are overridden with new emotions, those of happiness peace and elation. I didn't want to leave you on a sad or negative note. I promised at the beginning to share some of the laughter and the sheer joy with you. It felt right to tell you how we are today and just how far we have all come. I hope that what you read in this chapter will show you that there is fun, there is joy, and there are rewards beyond all measure.

*Welcome to my world of glitter glue and tantrums!*

Well life still holds its hectic pace, the girls don't let me slow down at all they really do keep me on me toes, and there is never a dull moment in this house. Most days will see me at some stage reaching the point where I am meeting myself coming backwards as I wrestle with the seemingly endless pile of washing, drying and ironing that my family produce, along with the other everyday chores that I have to do. I have become extremely adept at finding quick ways in which to get my house looking ship shape and lived in, and just as quickly Hope and Morganna have found ways to completely wreck all my good intentions. I try really hard to finish everything I start in one day, but inevitably I will go to bed at night thinking "now did I remember to" last week for the first time ever I simply forgot to take Hope to the eye clinic, the appointment that I had been given 6 months previously, and I hasten to add had actually written onto the calendar, had completely gone unnoticed on the day I should have taken her, between you and me I think that day just never happened, I think that week didn't have a Friday, or is it possible that I am only human!

I have some lovely drawings of smiley faces on the lounge walls done by that wonderful artist MR NOBODY, although strangely he seems to be hell bent on trying to get Hope into trouble these past few weeks as he now autographs each drawing with her name! And I have learnt the hard way that if I forget to lock my makeup bag away from their busy hands, its contents will end up transforming both the girls angelic faces into that of Coco the Clown!

They love baking cakes for Daddy, we often pull their chairs to the worktop in the kitchen so that they can help to weigh out the ingredients and get the eggs from the rack that Oliver's chickens have laid, and then they help mix the cake. I try not to watch as I know all to well from past times just how it will end up, as they spoon the mixture in great big heaps towards the cake tin, sometimes they don't quite get it to the tin before it falls of, and all I can hear is the roar of laughter and "OOOPS" being declared. When we make Kevin's favourite cake - cherry, I have to watch the cherry's otherwise MR NOBODY eats them and poor old Daddy gets a cake with one surprise cherry in it! One day we made two cakes, a cherry one and a chocolate one, later in the afternoon I had gone upstairs and on my return I found Morganna sitting cross legged on the worktop with the chocolate cake between her knees and lumps of crust off the top of the cake in her hands. She looked up at me with her cheeks full to bursting.

"Well madam, what are you doing" I had asked her.

When her mouth was at last empty of all the evidence, she casually said "Nice cake Mammy" and smiled at me

What could I say. The best part of baking a cake with the girls has to be watching them with the bowl as they run their fingers around it to collect the left over mixture to eat. God didn't I do just the same with my own mother; it was the reward for helping to bake the cakes. Hope and Morganna love licking out the mixture bowl, and so does Oliver so sometimes all three of them are running their fingers around the inside of the bowl.

Trying to have a telephone conversation is a nightmare with both the girls demanding to speak to whoever is on the other end of the line, the other day I was roaring with laughter as I hadn't heard the phone ring and when I came downstairs Hope was sat cross legged on the kitchen floor deep in conversation with someone, I asked her who it was and she told me it was a man, so I took the phone from her only to discover that it was a man from a call centre trying to sell me plastic windows, he told me that she had been talking to him for about 5 minutes and he had listened and chatted to her as she had told him that her twin sister was fetching me, Morganna was actually sat in the lounge with Peggy and had no intention of coming to find me - I call that pure justice, the poor chap was as confused as anything, I felt like giving Hope back the phone and letting her talk to him for even longer.

Last year I hung a line along the wall in my kitchen - no it wasn't to hang washing on, what I have so proudly pegged onto the line with pretty pegs are the wonderful masterpieces that Hope and Morganna have brought us home from pre-school, dotted in amongst these masterpieces is a ever growing collection of birthday invitations that the girls have received to friends birthday parties which are due to fall over the next month or so. It really does warm my heart to look at those masterpieces, each one tells a story, and as the girls have grown so has their ability to draw and colour. Hope in the past month has started to draw bodies, arms and legs on her smiley faces, her drawings of faces always have smiles, they are never sad faces. Morganna has a flare for colours and will spend ages choosing colours that work together. Lately we have been adding another dimension to the masterpiece line and that is the growing number of lovingly drawn and coloured pictures that the girls get given from their small friends, it is an absolute delight to stand there and look at them. I am so proud of My line of masterpieces.

Occasionally the girls will present me with a painting or a picture that they have done and they will say it's for Grandma, Bo or some other lucky person, and I have to mail it off for them. They sometimes give their artwork to their friends at pre-school.

Although my whole life centres on Oliver and the girls I do get rewarded with some wonderful experiences. On times I reflect back on what life was like before the girls arrived and it was so very different to life as I know it now, before the girls came to us I would enjoy an afternoon with my friends drinking coffee whilst we set the world to rights, now I have afternoon coffee with other mums and we revel in the pure joy of watching as our children play so happily together, it goes without saying that whilst I do on times long for my carefree days (or at least in some of the freedom it afforded me) I would never wish to change it back again.

Hope used to have a cuddly beanie baby crocodile which was given to her by Oliver, it went everywhere with her, one day Croc was nowhere to be found and Hope had to get used to being without her loyal friend, it was around Christmas time last year that Croc disappeared. Last week Kevin and I were emptying the last few remaining boxes form the attic room as in August a new a new roof is going onto the house. Some of these boxes contained our Christmas decorations; I went through the boxes and came across a small red and gold box that I use as decoration around the base of our Christmas tree. On opening the box I discovered something lying inside, it was Croc, Hope must have put him in there at Christmas time and forgotten, I had then in turn packed the box away and he had spent the next 6 months in the attic room.

We were eating breakfast outside the following morning, and after we had finished eating I asked Morganna to give the box to Hope and to tell her to look inside, her face was an absolute picture, Morganna was a little upset that she hadn't been given a box to open so I asked Hope to give Croc to Morganna to hold. As she held Hope's much loved Croc I explained to the girls that Croc was very tired and that he had been very lonely in the box and had used up all of the love that Hope had cuddled into him before he had got lost. Hope complained that he had got smaller, which of course he hadn't, she just remembered him bigger, so I told her that he was smaller because he needed to be hugged again so that the love would fill him out. I went on to tell her that Morganna could fill Croc up with some of her love if she was allowed to cuddle him for a few minutes.

"Well cuddle him then" she said to her sister in the manner that usually means do as you are told, Hope can be very bossy with Morganna

Morganna tenderly cuddled Croc and gave it back to Hope who then passed it to me and to Kevin to do the same. Hope is ecstatic to have her much loved Croc back, but bedtimes are a nightmare, she takes all her loyal friends with her to bed. She has "Spotty the dog, Pinkie the rat (bright pink of course), her pink monkey who gets given different names everyday, and now she has Croc the much loved friend. every night we have to go through the same ritual as she lies on her back, gets herself comfortable, and then proceeds to lay each of her friends across her chest, once this is accomplished (no easy task) she covers all of them including herself with the duvet, then the fidgeting begins as she breathes and one or another of her friends falls off her chest, which is when the whole blasted performance begins again. In the meantime Morganna will have selected one of her precious Panda's tucked it in alongside her and be fast asleep. When the girls come into our bed for a cuddle each morning it will be Morganna who arrives first all fresh and wide awake, she will be followed a little later by her sleepy sister, who no matter how sleepy she is will have somehow managed to gather all her friends up into her arms, and appear around our bedroom door, her hair all over the place and her eyes half closed, with her precious cargo of friends in her arms, she will clamber onto our bed and then throw all her friends over the side of the bed, and that done she will snuggle down into the crook of my arm and fall back asleep. Hope loves her bed.

The girls have spent a fabulous two and half years at their pre-school, they have always enjoyed going and hate it when they are on school holidays as it means that they cant go to pre-school. They have been loved to pieces by all the staff there who made it so easy for me to just slip in to pre-school life, they have become my friends and I too have enjoyed being a part of the pre-school. Hope and Morganna have been well liked by the other children, and have made some really good friends.

We wanted to thank the pre-school and all our friends there for playing such an important part in the girl's lives, so a week before the pre-school broke up for the summer holidays we held a Teddy Bears Picnic here, we hired two bouncy castles and the children had a great time. It was a lovely day, Kevin and I watched as all the children played together, it was a delight to watch as they all looked out for each other. We took them to see the baby calves on the farm and they loved it as the calves tried to suck their fingers. I shall miss everyone at the pre-school, and I am sure that I shall stay in touch with them.

As the summer holidays began to approach I was beginning to feel the blossoming of a new challenge, how on earth was I going to amuse four year old twin girls and a teenage lad as well for six whole weeks, I decided that this challenge was going to prove tough, and I guess that as I try to make the best of it I will inevitably fail in some part to please all three of them. Then came the realisation that as the summer holidays pass I will meet a new phrase in mine and the girl's lives. In September the girls will start school, at first they will attend mornings only, and then hopefully after Christmas they will be going full time. They have already been on an induction day at school, as well as attending for a morning and an afternoon. When Kevin picked them up from the first induction visit, they came home with a picture that some of the children had made for them, written on the picture was " I hope you enjoyed your first day at school, you are both very small" which of course they are. I knew when I saw the picture that Kevin and I had made the right decision to send them to the small school that is associated with the pre-school they attend. It is such a happy school, I have never seen any of the children unhappy there and that says such a lot for the way that the head teacher and her staff run the school. Hope and Morganna can't wait for September to come. We have also decided that the girls will attend the pre-school twice a week in the afternoon for extra visits; this will prepare them for full time school hopefully in January 2007.

But the girls starting school also makes me feel very sad. It will mark the time that they begin take their first steps towards independence; I will be trusting someone else with my precious little girls. This phase also marks how far we have come. Although it has been a long four and a half years, suddenly it seems as if it has passed in the blink of an eye. I feel incredibly sad that it is me and not my daughter that is experiencing yet another milestone in the girl's lives. I know that on the first day at school I shall not be the only Mum at those school gates who sheds a tear or two, so I decided to ask the other mums if they would like to get together for coffee straight after we drop off our precious children, and this is what we will be doing, I hope it will mean that some of us will not go home to an empty home and cry alone.

We haven't been on a proper holiday for the past four years as we could not afford to do so, but this year we have bought ourselves a huge trailer tent, (I call it our holiday in a box!) next week the MPV is off to the garage to have a tow bar fitted and then on Kevin's weekends off we shall hitch up the holiday in a box and join the band of other campers in search of a nice pitch besides the seaside. I was thinking back to my own childhood the other day, we used to have so much fun in that old camper van of Dad's, I hope that the children will also have some fond memories of their holidays in the trailer tent, it should at least provide them with some amusing tales of Kevin and I wrestling with the trailer trying to erect the tent before bedtime!! Kevin and I have yet to attempt erecting our holiday in a box, I told him that when we do go on holiday with it, if it should be raining and blowing a howling gale when we arrive at our destination then I shall stay in the car with the children and hold the instruction manual up in the back window in the car so that he can read it!!

Over the last weekend I travelled back to Pembrokeshire in Margarita (the new car) I was accompanied by one of my best friends Lynn, who is also one of the girls Godmothers, we left Oxfordshire behind for a blissful two days. We felt like Thelma and Rhiannon as we set off early on the Saturday morning. It was the first time in over 5 years that I had actually done something without the children that was not in some way connected to helping others, and I really enjoyed it. It is a long time since I laughed like I did on that weekend. We stayed at a pub I have known for more years than I care to disclose, when we checked in we were taken to our room - which was up three flights of stairs, I needed a lie down by the time I reached the top. After we closed the door on the young girl who had shown us up to our room we preceded to investigate what we had. There was a single bed and a double, I got the double, and well I am bigger than Lynn. The room was comfortable but could have done with a good clean, if there's one thing worse than a critical bed and breakfast guest, its an ex landlady. Lynn decided to see if the bedside lights worked, well mine did, but hers didn't. it wasn't plugged in and there was no socket near enough for the plug to reach, she got up off her bed and went to her bag, and out of it produced an extension lead - now who on earth would think of carrying an extension lead!, she plugged in the lamp and passed the extension lead plug to me to plug into the socket by my bed, that all done she tried the lamp again, no it wasn't working, so I told her to check the bulb, there wasn't one!, we rolled about like schoolgirls roaring with laughter.

The reason I had gone back to Pembrokeshire was to sing in a concert/ picnic in the park, that Raul had organised. I haven't sung in public since the girls came to live with us, I have been emotionally wiped out, but there is a flicker of a flame inside me that has rekindled a fire in my belly to sing. I found it so hard to stand there and sing, but I did manage to get through two of my favourite tracks, something else happened that day and it took me aback a bit, until fifteen years ago I used to play a twelve string acoustic guitar, an injury to my right hand prevented me from playing as I have lost the finer movements in that hand so strumming, plucking etc was impossible, but I have this need in me to try again. So after fifteen years of being hung on the wall my twelve string guitar is going on a journey of its own, I am having it restrung and I am going to try and play it again. I doubt I shall ever be as good as I was back then, but who knows. I also want to start singing again - maybe I have moved on further than I thought I had.

That weekend was all part of this progressive plan of self - rediscovery. I am enjoying the challenge. And I like who I am.

But boy did I pay for my small break when I got home. On the Monday morning the girls did nothing but fight and Morganna threw her cat into the paddling pool as she thought it might like to swim - all this happened before 9 o clock!! I was well and truly grounded again Welcome home Mammy!

Both Hope and Morganna are showing signs being musical and I revel in it, I can imagine Hope playing a Welsh harp, something I always wished I could have done. Oliver is progressing very quickly with his drum lessons, and is enjoying playing them. Morganna is always singing, she sings to Peggy all the time. My home is always full of the sound of music, I play anything from classical to rock, and the girls have picked up on my diverse taste in music.

I have laughed a lot over the past year as the girls have begun to develop their quirky little ways. One day I had a right go at Kevin as I had been asking him to put some bigger screws into the knobs of my welsh dresser, everyday I would be on my hands and knees trying to retrieve them from under the dresser, and of course I can never catch MR NOBODY twisting them off again. So one evening after I had retrieved them once too often, my nagging paid off as Kevin took on board that I wasn't going to shut up this time and promptly went out to his workshop and screwed and glued the knobs back on. MR NOBODY was sure going to have his work cut out removing them now. A few days later I had forgotten about these knobs as now they were staying on the doors, when Hope, hands on hips said to me

"What's wrong with the knobs on the dresser Mammy?"

"Why sweet pea, what's wrong with them" I asked her

"Well I have been trying all morning to get them off and they wont come off they are stuck, and it's spoiling my fun"

Kevin and I roared laughing; it seems we have found our MR NOBODY!

When my Mam came to stay with us for a few days last summer, she saw first hand just how adept Morganna is at catching bugs. Morganna likes nothing more than to have some creepy crawly or another climbing all over her. Both the girls have taken great delight in taking various creepy crawlies into pre-school for all the other children to look at during show and tell time.

One afternoon Morganna brought me a tiny frog which she had caught in the back garden, now I know my Mam dislikes frogs intensely, so I told her to go and show it to Granny. Mam was in my kitchen when she found her

"Look Granny, look what I have found"

As soon as she saw what was in the little hand she rewarded Morganna with a display of behaviour that sent us all into fits of laughter and made Morganna even more determined that Granny must have a closer look, by which time the sight of the frog had made Granny climb onto the kitchen worktop from where she was shouting hysterically at Morganna to take her new found pet away, and of course the more she shouted the more determined Morganna became.

Recently Hope has developed a fear of spiders, much to Morganna's delight who now goes around the house to look for a spider, she does not have to look far in this house, and some of them are great big hairy things, expertly, she will then catch it and spend ages chasing her sister around the house who screams on top of her voice, which only serves to encourage Morganna to do it al the more.

Morganna is the clown of the two of them, she is always messing around at something, and it is her who will come into the house and tell me that she has either hidden Daddies shoes or put something into them. When I ask the girls to go and get dressed Morganna will come downstairs saying she is dressed and I will find her in the lounge with her trousers on her head and her legs through the arms of her tee shirt.

Hope should win an Oscar for her acting ability, she will adapt whatever role she deems necessary to get the most impact from a situation. She can throw you a look that leaves you in no doubt that she is not amused and can often be heard taking on the "big sister role" over Morganna and with all the effort she can muster will begin to tell her off over something, much to Morganna's amusement. One day Kevin was cuddling Hope who had been sulking over something, he said to her

"Well there's only one thing for it then Daddy is going to have to tickle you until you laugh"

Hope by now had adopted a limp posture in his arms, and as he began to tickle her he thought she would begin to wriggle and laugh, there was no way that Hope was going to give in, so in true actress fashion she just continued to lay there as limp as anything.

Both the girls are also dreadful climbers, they always have been, they do not see danger at all. We were down on the beach at New gale a few weeks ago, I was laying in the sun suffering from a tummy bug as Kevin and my Mam amused the children, I looked up to see Morganna halfway up the cliff face, Kevin had to climb up and get her down again, she not only has the ability to scale most heights she is also very fast.

Each of them is developing their own traits and it is so wonderful to watch. They also change character traits and just as we get used to one of them being moody and the other one being cheerful, they will swap around and we have to start all over again.

The most intriguing part of bringing up the girls is the common link they share, they have the ability to just look at each other and will just start giggling which quickly turns into the most contagious laughter and will have Kevin Oliver and I joining in as well, the only two who will know what they are laughing at is the girls! They also know instinctively if and why their twin sister is sad and will comfort her, if they are hurt, it is the other one who will tell us what happened and where their sister Is hurt.

What a joy, what an honour.

No wonder I am shattered.

# WHAT'S NEXT

WHAT NEXT? I hear you cry - Well apart from trying to discover the ultimate cure for the wrinkles that life is beginning to draw on my face, and to invent automatic ear defenders that prevent all nagging from Hope and Morganna penetrating my brain as soon as it leaves their mouths - that is a very good question and I don't know if I have the answer. I am looking forward to having some "me" time, I am also thinking of returning to work, but who knows, maybe I shall take some time out just for a while and watch the world go by - HUH, somehow I think not. I now have a Diploma's in Beauty care, one in Counselling and another in Woman's stress. Whether I decide to go on and practice as a counsellor I don't know yet, but it is something that I would like to do. Whatever I do it is really important to me that it fits in around the needs of Kevin and the children. What I have learnt over the past five years is just how important they are to me, they are my life and that will never change. I would also like to talk to young girls about the effects drug and alcohol abuse, and self harming can have on not only there lives but also on that of their families, if just one heard me and listened long enough to make a difference then it will have been worth it.

There is one thing I know and believe in without a doubt, and that is that I can't imagine for one minute that I could have suffered all this pain and heartache for nothing. There has to be a purpose to it all, it has to have a positive ending. So far in my life I have managed to turn all my negative experiences into a positive ones, and in all my negative feelings have been able to find a positive, I now have the ability to find a positive in the most difficult of negative situations - that is just something else that these past five years

282

have taught me. I really do wish that I had in some other way learnt about the pain and frustrations that I have experienced in the past five years, but there is no text book that can ever teach you, it is something you have to have been through and to continue to survive to understand exactly what it does to you and to others. I must not waste this knowledge I have to put it to good use.

I have inside me a passion for wanting to reach out and hold any Grandparent who is suffering, to let them know they are not alone as believe me, they will feel so alone just as I did, they will feel desperate and will try anything to hold onto their adored grandchildren, just as I did.

I count the day's everyday, it's like wishing my life away. And I have so much living that I want to do yet, I have so much more to learn, so much more to give, and yet with each day that passes I am a day nearer to when my girls will come home again, this remains the painful, heartbroken me, its still there and will always be a real part of me, it's a longing that I wake up with and go to bed with. When I close my eyes I can see and smell Angharad and Rhiannon but there's something really surreal in my world, if I watch Hope and Morganna in whatever they do I can imagine Angharad and Rhiannon doing the same, maybe because the girls are so close in age. It's a bitter-sweet thing and it can make me smile or make me cry.

I guess that this part of my "what next" is very much up to them. Will they come home? God I truly hope so, I hold onto that like it is the invisible thread that links them to me. If they ever have any doubts as to whether I or their older twin sisters would want them to come home to us the answer is in every line of their letter and poem.

*"Come home girls, neither my story nor my heart will ever be complete until you are home again"*

Today is July 21ˢᵗ, we have decided to go home to Pembrokeshire, I have a need in me to see my family and friends, I cant believe that it was only last weekend that I was there with Lynn, I cant make up my mind whether I am home sick or friend sick, whichever I am giving in to it and going home. The MPV has been in for a major service and when we got it back Kevin noticed it had been overfilled with oil, so he took it back to the garage in the morning and they drained the oil and refilled it to its correct level. So with the car all packed up with enough bags to last us a week, we eventually leave for Pembrokeshire. We got no further than 2 miles down the road when thick black smoke began to belch from the exhaust and our faithful, no trouble

MPV began to die. It was twenty five past five on a Friday afternoon, the children were making a mighty fuss and I rang the garage that had done the service on the car. We slowly nursed it back to the garage, where she was inspected and after a lot of head scratching it was decided that it must be a faulty fuel filter. Promising to get one in for the morning Kevin and I got back into the car and began the 2 mile drive back home again, the children were screaming their protests, and neither Kevin nor I were amused. We were just in sight of the farm when once again thick clouds of obnoxious black smoke belched out of the exhaust pipe, peppering the windscreen of the car behind us which made a hasty retreat back to a safe distance!

Somehow we had to pacify the children as by now they were giving us hell.

"I know let's put up the trailer tent and sleep in that tonight"

So at 7.30pm after a fraught day, for the first time we took the manual in our hands and with a determination that was scary Kevin and I began to unload all the parts of the tent. Surprisingly it went up without too much shouting and cursing and at gone midnight we desperately tried to get our two very tired little girls to settle down and sleep, in the end Kevin and I had to give in and he cuddled up to Morganna as I snuggled Hope into me and we all drifted off to sleep.

Crash, bang, flash. I woke with a start, it was just after 3am, and we were in the middle of an almighty thunder storm, I lay awake for hours listening to the thunder roar across the sky and watching the canvas light up as the lightening lit the sky, it was a spectacular thunder storm, and then the heavens opened and the torrential rain began to beat down on the tent. I lay there watching the tent looking to see if I could see any rain falling inside, no, it was fine no rain inside the tent. The mugginess of the air that we had all suffered from for days had lifted and despite the lashing rain, it felt light and airy. Ollie woke and was followed quickly by the girls we all lay there watching the lightening and listening as the thunder roared and the rain lashed. Eventually later that morning Kevin got some sense form the garage, who said that they couldn't get the part for the car until Monday, but there was a courtesy car we could have, the children were still whinging about not going to see Granny, so we decided that as we couldn't all fit into one car we would take both, Kevin could then come home on Sunday evening and I could extend my short break and the children and I could stay on at my sisters. Well now if I was going to be in Pembrokeshire for a few extra days I began to wonder if I could book some time at John's recording studio in Cardigan. The idea of beginning the next album filled me with excitement, so I rang and yes he could fit me in on Tuesday, I rang Heather and Raul to see if Raul would like to come with me and that was that, it was all arranged.

Kevin and I forced as much stuff into the boot of my much loved sports car, got the girls into their car seats and off we set to make the journey back home. As we got into Swindon the rain began to lash down so badly that for the first time in my 30 years of driving I was frightened of the weather conditions, it was terrible, as we drove out of Swindon on the horizon we could see the sun. That's it keep shining I willed the sun, and it did.

On Sunday afternoon we went to Scolton Manor for a picnic, I was dreading it as it was to be the first time I had been there since I had said goodbye to my precious little girls. As I drove in through the gates I drove past the signpost which has the owl painted onto it, for the fleetest of heartbreaking moments I was transported back to those painful days, and once again I clearly saw Bo stood there with Angharad in her arms, shaking the vivid memory from my head I looked over towards the park, Kevin was already there with James my son who had brought his girlfriend and her baby with him. I was thrilled; I had only briefly met her the weekend before, so having a chance to meet her again was great. Cailyn is beautiful, and it seems that I have a new Granddaughter I am thrilled. I watched James and Clare that afternoon, it was so lovely to watch two young people in the first throes of love, and I pray that the two of them remain focused on each other and Cailyn, as I couldn't bear to loose them now. Perhaps my guardian angel is still watching over me and turning my life around at long last. I was really sad that night as Kevin and I said goodbye to each other, it was going to be difficult for me over the next couple of days as I suspected the children would run rings around me - and they did!

On Monday morning we saw Bo for an hour, I had tried all morning to get hold of her and failed she was not answering her mobile. Then as we were all getting ready to go down to Tenby my mobile rang,

"Damn it's Bo" I said to my sister, answering the phone I asked Bo if she would like to see the girls and we arranged to meet at her local branch of Tesco's, she asked if her partner could come as well. I tried to explain that I was not happy about it and in the end I had to just spell it out for her. She agreed to meet us alone. I told her that if he turned up with her then I would just drive off again and she wouldn't see the girls.

I arranged to meet my sister and my Mam at Tenby and then set off with Ollie and the girls to meet Bo, thankfully she was alone and we went into Tesco to have a coffee and for the children to have some lunch. Bo looked dreadful, she appeared sad and lost, her arms carry a map of new and old wounds that she has inflicted on herself, it broke my heart when later Hope asked me what Bo had done to her arms, I found myself lying to my darling girls and telling them that she had been scratched by her cat, was I lying or was I in some way trying to protect them from the hurtful truth that even I don't understand. It surprised me to see how the girls interacted with Bo that day, neither of them was a bit interested, they were if anything a bit removed from her, oh they love her, but there was a distance between them that even Oliver had picked up on.

Saying goodbye to Bo I loaded the girls back into the car and we set off for Tenby.

# SAND, SEA AND WET TOWELS!

The sun was blazing in the sky when we arrived at Tenby, I got the towels etc out of the car and we caught the park and ride bus down to the beach from the car park. The girls were as excited as they caught their first glimpse of the seaside, they couldn't wait to get out of the bus. It is years since I have been to Tenby and not a thing has changed, we walked down the winding slope to the beach and once we were on the sand we removed our shoes to make it easier to walk on the golden sand, which was so hot that you had to keep walking. We found a nice spot not too close to the waters edge, which was by now coming back in, laying claim to the sand it washed over. By the time I had erected the sun tent, and got the bags into it to stop it blowing away, the girls had disappeared with Oliver, Abigail and Adam, together all 5 of them were exploring the rock pools and with their bare hands catching shrimp and small crabs, which they then placed into their buckets. Carrying buckets so full that water was spilling out over the top of them, the girls came waddling up the sand to show Deb and I what they had caught, their faces a picture of delight as they proudly showed us what they had so bravely caught.

They built sandcastles in the sand digging away with spades and hands creating a castle fit for any mermaid to splash around in. this was a new part of the world for Hope and Morganna, as up until now they had only ever played in the sand on the beach and dipped their toes teasingly into the icy cold waters of a beach in Pembrokeshire during the winter months, only to retreat again as it was far too cold. After a while they all got up and ran into the sea, they splashed and jumped around in their dare - devil way, laughing and just simply having fun, they loved it, they didn't have a care in the world,

287

and they were purely enjoying nature's free gifts. I even went into the water and had a splash around with them, we roared with laughter as we jumped over the small waves that lapped the shore. I felt free and elated I was at last allowing myself to enjoy the girls, I was not so wrapped up in trying to protect them, and I was just having fun. All too soon it was time to get ready to go home, I took the girls down to the sea and washed away the sand that clung to their bodies, dried them and popped their beach towels over their heads, by the time I had got Hope ready, Morganna was once again in the sea, only this time she had gone in complete with towel! As I turned around I just caught the tail end of Hope as she ran down the beach and into the water to be with her sister.

Two wet towels and a lot of shouting later we reluctantly made our way back to our car; the girls were wearing the only dry thing they had left, their knickers!

I had sat on the beach earlier watching as the girls played so happily, and I couldn't help thinking about just how different a world they could have been growing up in, the thoughts made my spine shiver and set my nerve endings on edge, their little lives would have been so very different, I felt an immense sadness as I thought of how Bo would have enjoyed this afternoon of freedom, her idea of having fun was to sit around with her friends and drink the day away. In that moment I knew that all the heartache and pain, all the tears and all the dark days I have been through was worth it, - even if it was just to see what I had seen and enjoyed that afternoon.

Hope and Morganna didn't want to leave the beach, they wanted to stay there and play. But they were also hungry, so I offered to stop off in Haverfordwest and buy us all a chip supper, it rounded off a perfect day. We had enjoyed the beach and now we were eating fish and chips, what more could a girl want?

Later that night after the girls had settled into bed and gone to sleep, I went outside to clean my car. I must have hovered half a ton of Tenby sand out off my car that night, it was everywhere. I went to bed that night feeling both excited and nervous about my day in the recording studio. I had chosen the songs I wanted to do. I slept like a baby that night, and when I woke in the morning I woke with a clear head and a clear chest, something that I haven't had for months as every morning for the past few months I have woken up in my home with a thick head and a thick throat as well as constant itching.

# SOMEWHERE OVER THE RAINBOW

It was a mad panic to get ready to go to the recording studio on that Tuesday morning, I had to be in Cardigan at 11am, and I had to pick up Raul from Solva first. It was impossible, I dropped the girls off at my Mam's as she had agreed to look after them, and I reached Solva just after 10.30am. Thankfully Raul was ready and we were able to set off as soon as I had said "Hello and Goodbye" to Heather.

I know I was very quiet on that journey up to Cardigan, I had a lot going on in my head, this was the first time I had actually done something for just me, this was the first time I had sung in a studio for nearly 10years, I was afraid of my own emotions, as for far too long I have not paid any heed to my own emotions as I have been so wrapped up in looking out for the other people in my life that there was no time to sit and ponder over how I was feeling, now I was being given some "me" time and I was scared to death of how I was feeling. I felt like a fish out of water, Hope and Morganna have been my life for four and a half years, I looked into the rear view mirror of my car expecting to see the girls safely sitting in their car seats, but their car seats were not in the car, they were at my Mams's. I had hidden somewhere amongst the girls for far too long, I didn't have my crutch with me, they had been my crutch, with them around me I was never lost for anything to say, after all don't all us Mum's talk endlessly of our children, forgetting to ever talk about ourselves. Suddenly I was aware that I would have to talk to Raul sooner or later, but not about the girls or Oliver or even Kevin, but about me. I had chosen a good companion that day for Raul was more than happy to fiddle around with the buttons of my car's CD player, inserting different CD'S and taking great joy in flicking through the tracks until he could find something in my diverse collection of music that he liked - and there was not much of it. I have a lot of what I call my mood music, my latest addiction in music is SHAYNE WARD what a voice that guy has and I have just discovered a female singer called LIZZ WRIGHT she has the most amazingly rich and seductive voice, I love her track "WITHOUT YOU"

By the time we reached Cardigan the whole of my CD collection had travelled in and out of the slot in the CD player, to various noises from Raul ranging from a tutts to him declaring "this ones not too bad" I'm sure he finds my music frustrating.

The hours that I spent in the recording studio with John were the best; he is so easy to work with. I had deliberately left one track until last. I knew I was going to find it difficult to do. "Somewhere over the rainbow" is one of many songs I have sung to all the girls, but there is one occasion that is fixed foremost in my mind. On the last visit we had with Rhiannon at Scolton manor, I had taken her for a walk alone; it was just her and I, a final bonding time, a time for me to hold her and without anyone else imposing on that time. I walked with her in my arms, she was so heavy, and as I walked I snuggled into her and held her close and sang quietly to her "SOMEWHERE OVER THE RAINBOW"

As I sung it that day in the studio, I could see images of us walking alone. I was choked as I sung the words, I have listened to it time and time again since I got back home and the emotion in it is real.

After I had taken Raul home I travelled the few short miles to St David's and briefly called on David and Sandra. I gave David a copy of the tracks I had laid down that day, and a promise that I will finish it. I can't wait to get back into the studio again.

So this is me moving on, this is where I am at, and it feels good. The girls and I have done the school uniform shopping and we are having fun enjoying the summer holidays. Just as I get some days that pick me up and keep me up, so do I get days when life isn't so good, today is one of those days where I am reminded that sadness does still belong in my life. I had rung Bo to ask if she had received the photographs I had sent her of the girls. Bo told me that she had done something stupid, this sentence always fills me with dread, she had self harmed again, only this time she had cut herself really badly, this time she had run the razor down her arm, not across it, she had cut herself down to the muscle, she had refused to go to hospital. When Bo tells me of these events, I am so sad, so alone as I can't talk about it to anyone, but I am also afraid as I know that one day she will cut too deep or hit a vein, or get an infection that will claim her life and take her away from me forever. But for today and hopefully many more today's my beautiful Bo is still with us. When I see her I still see the little girl she used to be hiding behind the lost woman she has become. I still feel the overwhelming love for her that I felt when she was placed in my arms for the very first time by the midwife who had delivered her. I miss my Bo.

# _FOR MY GIRLS_

My darlings

Oh if only life had been different, if only us adults had not had to try and do what we thought was best for all of you, but that is what we have endeavoured to do. I pray that we have got it right. I pray that as you read this "Our story" you can see past the pain and try to understand why we all did what we did.

Hope and Morganna - having you both here with me everyday is the best thing that could have happened to me. It has been a hard and heartbreaking journey, but so worth every painful part of the process. I have enjoyed giving myself to you, you both made it so easy for me to do. You have rewarded me time and time again for the dedication and commitment that I have given to you. For the love that I have bestowed upon you, you have returned it to me a thousand times over. I bless everyday, no matter how much you have tested me, because I know all too well the heartache I would have felt if you were not here. I feel that heartache each and everyday, and even though it will never go away the both of you help to ease its passage. In the both of you I have a hope for the future, and I have my dreams.

As you grow we will tell you why the things that happened did, and how hard we have tried to install in you both a passion and a love for life and for all those in your lives. I shall endeavour to always be there for you, to always be the one you turn to when you need someone to be there.

My one regret is that Angharad and Rhiannon were not able to share their lives with you, I tried so hard, but it beat me, please try to understand. One day you will all be together again, when you are don't let anything or anyone ever try to separate you again.

I love you both so very; very much I can not imagine my life without you both filling it.

I am looking forward to the rest of our lives together

Mammy x (Grandma)

Angharad and Rhiannon

It has been a lifetime, and I have greeted each day with the great sadness of not knowing how you both are. Everyday I feel the pain and relentless heartache of being bereft of you, of your laughter, your tears, your joys and your pains, I have missed each and every one of your first's, I have been unable to share your lives, but always know that even though we could not be together, you have been in my life each and everyday. I have never for the fleetest of moments forgotten you. One day we shall meet and I will look at you both and the young ladies you will have become and I wont be able to see anything other than the little girls you were when I last saw you. I am sitting here writing this and crying, I am already trying to imagine how I will feel when you come home.

I want you both to know that when you want to come home the door is always open, my home is your home, and my heart is your heart. I will try and keep Hope and Morganna safe for you, I promise that I will keep you alive for them, they will never forget you.

I know that as you turn 18 years of age you will be able to come and look for Hope and Morganna, as well as me; this is where you can find us.

Angharad -

On APRIL 25TH 2021 you will turn 18 years of age.

At 10 o clock on the 10th May 2021 I will be with Hope and Morganna, we will be at SCOLTON MANOR. We will wait for you by in the front of the manor house that overlooks the whole park. I truly hope that you come to meet us.

Rhiannon - you will turn 18 years of age the following April, I am hoping that you will come along with Angharad on her birthday.

Until then my precious Cariad's my love and my heart flies alongside you. God keep you safe for me. I miss and love you both so much.

Grandma x x

OLIVER - what can I say other than thank you for sharing me and Daddy with the girls, thank you for making all of this so easy for us, for never complaining, and for always being there. One day you will get your reward, the girls worship you, and you have got and always will have a very special relationship with Hope and Morganna. I know that you too have missed Angharad and Rhiannon, they will come home darling, I promise. Remember always that even though I may not have told you as often as maybe I should have done so that, I am so immensely proud of you. Carry on being the adorable young man you are who is loved by everyone who knows you.

I love you Oliver

Love Mammy x

MY BO - I can still remember as if it were yesterday how I felt the first time I held you. I am so heartbroken that you are lost, but I hang on everyday, hoping that that day I am living in may be the day that the devil releases you from his grip and let's you come home again. For as long as there is still breath in your body I have hope, I shall wait, I will be here. But if you are taken from me then I promise you I shall always for as long as my heart beats look after the girls. You have given the world four beautiful girls; you have given me so much joy in them, but also so much heartache. Try to stay strong, try to stay with us. I know that you too get your dark days, you too hurt, and I am here to catch you every time you fall. I love you Princess,

Mam x

To all my family, my friends, those who have touched my life over the past 5 years and those of you who I have yet to meet. I wish that I had a magic wand; I wish that none of us had to go through any of this heartache, but most of all I wish I had arms so long that I could hold you all in them forever. But you are here in my heart; you are all parts that have gone into making me who and what I am today.

To all of us Grandparents who are bringing up their Grandchildren, what stars you are, continue to shine.

To all of us who live each and everyday with bereavement so forceful it can stop us dead in our tracks, I hope my story helps to bring you a peace and a comfort in knowing you are not alone, someone else can and does feel your pain.

To all of us parents who are struggling to try and understand the life choices our children have made, please do as I do, don't ever give up on them, carry on telling them that you love them, even when you think they are not listening, because one day they might just hear your voice and turn there lives around, always be there for them, always hang on to my favourite word HOPE.

Kevin -

When I had forgotten who I was, someone took me in their arms and loved the broken person this rollercoaster had made me, he held me, he taught me to love, to laugh, to cry in strong arms, and to feel safe when I was afraid, he taught me how to trust and how to believe in myself, to follow my instincts and my heart. But he also gave me something else, he believed in me and he encouraged me to write this for my girls, our girls. Every time he has come in and found me crying over what I was writing he has held me with warmth a truth and a devotion that not many of us are so fortunate to have in somebody else. Without my rock I would never have been able to get through any of this. This story may be about me and my girls but it also has its unsung hero - I love you so much Kevin

# THE GRANDPARENTS ASSOCIATION

The Grandparents Association was founded in 1987 as a response to the problem of grandparents losing their grandchildren to adoption. Nearly 20 years on the organisation still fulfils this role and more besides.

Every year 10,000 grandparents and professionals call the only national advice line for grandparents working both in public and private law and on issues involving contact, residence and childcare. We estimate that some 1 million grandparents are denied contact with their grandchildren because of relationships, family feud, bereavement and many others issues. It is thought that up to 250,000 children live permanently with their grandparents.

The charity provides advice, information, publications and services such as support groups, grandparent and toddler groups, mediation and welfare benefits advice. Many of our services are supported by volunteers like Keri and we could not operate without them.

If you read Keri's book and want further help please contact our advice line on 0845 434 9585 weekdays between 10.30 and 3.30, or if you are moved by Keri's story and would like to become a volunteer then please contact us on 01279 428040

Lynn Chesterman
Chief Executive.

When I asked Lynn if The Grandparents Association would like to put something in my book I did not expect what she gave me to have such an impact on me, I think it did as I have never really given much thought or time to the statistics that surround the issues of grandparents and their grandchildren, probably due to the fact that when I was going through my story I felt as if I was the only person in the world to be suffering the way I was. The statistics have really hit home with me.

Hope and Morganna are just 2 of the 250,000 children who are living with their grandparents, that in itself creates a great number of blessed grandparents, I say blessed because each and every day I feel so truly blessed that Hope and Morganna are with me, but I can also relate to the heartache that an estimated 1 million grandparents feel each and everyday as I too live with that pain as part of my life, it is deep and unrelenting and inside it tears us grandparents apart, and just as we carry in our hearts the memory and love we have for the grandchild or grandchildren that we no longer see, so to do we carry that pain and longing.

In 2006 I was invited by Lynn to give a talk at The Grandparents Association annual conference which took place at The Middle Temple in London. There was a vast range of people attending that conference, and some excellent speakers, some who shared with us the wealth of knowledge that they have learnt from their professional dealings with grandparents issues, and some who like me shared with the others their stories, their experiences. At times there were not many dry eyes to be seen amongst those listening to the speakers as it stirred in us emotions that we all try to keep in check for appearances sake.

When it came to my turn to share my experiences with my listeners I was very nervous, I was also very emotional and for an extremely good reason. The date of the conference fell on the exact date that four years before had seen me picking up Hope and Morganna from Withybush Hospital in Pembrokeshire and bringing to mine and Kevin's Oxfordshire home, it was the date on which my life, our lives changed forever.

Six years ago I would not have in a million years given any thought to the fact that I may one day be stood shaking and sometimes tearful in front of such a group of fantastic people retelling them of my rollercoaster life event, they all in their own way could identify with my story, they too cried the same tears that I did, they too could feel and share my pain. I came away from that conference knowing several things.

I now know that there are some great people out there striving to do all they can for us grandparents, but they need help, they are not able do this alone, they need us grandparents. Together we have to raise the profile of grandparent issues and to do that we need two very important things. We need a voice and we need someone to hear us.

We also need to reach more grandparents, to let them know that they are not alone and that help is there.

Without The Grandparents Association there would be no advice line, there would be nothing for us grandparents, I volunteer and help the Association because I can and it is something I feel passionate about, after all it was their advice line that gave me the first piece of good advice that I was to be given, I acted upon that advice and look what I gained, I have Hope and Morganna, but when I lost Anharad and Rhiannon, the Grandparents Association were also by my side and shared with me my pain, they still do. At first I had names in the Association, then one day as I attended various training courses with them the names became faces as I was introduced to them, those faces are now my friends. Every week I listen too and share experiences with other grandparents - most of whom have just been thrown onto the emotional rollercoaster, and do not know where to turn or who to turn too, somehow they find us and together we begin to work through it all. The advice line is unique and when a grandparent rings that number they will know that on the other end of the phone is someone that has an empathy with their situation. If you are able to help why put it off, go on ring the Grandparents Association, we really do need you.

# About the author:

I was born in Cardiff in 1959, at the age of three my family relocated to Pembrokeshire where I grew up with my 2 younger brothers and younger sister. All my life I have had two things that have driven me, my tireless love and devotion for my family and friends, and my love of music - singing has always been my emotional outlet.

I have four children and six grand children.

11 years ago I left my beloved Pembrokeshire and relocated to East Sussex. Today I live in Oxfordshire with my husband Kevin, our son Oliver, and the girls - Hope and Morganna. Home is a beautiful 16th century cottage, on a dairy farm. Life is now peaceful, but it hasn't always been that way. I have lived through much turmoil and heartache especially over the past 5 years which has seen me fight with every breath in me to keep Hope and Morganna within my family.

This is my first book, when I started writing it I had no way of predicting the importance it would hold, that is not until when on August 27th 2006, just 2 days after submitting my final manuscript to AuthorHouse I suffered from a double brain haemorrhage, which reinforced in me my books importance and gave me even more determination to see it completed. I am currently working on my latest book "Promise Me" which tells of my battle to survive my brain haemorrhage and of how this life changing event has affected me.

Once again someone was watching over me. On August 30th at the Heath Hospital in Cardiff I underwent a process called Embolisation, some extremely gifted people put me back together again. I am now back at home in Oxfordshire and well on my way to making a full recovery. I am so grateful for each and every day that I wake to the sound of my children playing.

Printed in the United States
66453LVS00003B/56

9 781425 966553